BORN IN THE GDR

BORN
IN THE GDR

LIVING IN THE SHADOW
OF THE WALL

Hester Vaizey

OXFORD
UNIVERSITY PRESS

OXFORD
UNIVERSITY PRESS

Great Clarendon Street, Oxford, OX2 6DP,
United Kingdom

Oxford University Press is a department of the University of Oxford.
It furthers the University's objective of excellence in research, scholarship,
and education by publishing worldwide. Oxford is a registered trade mark of
Oxford University Press in the UK and in certain other countries

First Edition published in 2014

Impression: 1

Published in the United States of America by Oxford University Press
198 Madison Avenue, New York, NY 10016, United States of America

British Library Cataloguing in Publication Data

Data available

Library of Congress Control Number: 2014933817

ISBN 978-0-19-871873-4

Printed in Great Britain by
Clays Ltd, St Ives plc

Acknowledgements

I would like to thank the people who have helped me to write this book. The East Germans I interviewed were extremely generous with their time and their stories. Without them, this book would not have been possible. William Cavert, Mark Fenemore, Jan Hennings, Catherine Ormc, Matthew Stibbe, and David Tinnion read early drafts of the manuscript and provided insightful feedback. Angela Abmeier gave me a roof over my head in Berlin while I was conducting my research. Clare College, Cambridge, provided funding for this project. My agent, Peter Robinson, was instrumental in helping this book to see the light of day. And Matthew Cotton and Luciana O'Flaherty at Oxford University Press were most helpful in the final stages of getting the manuscript ready. My family, Margaret, Russell, and George Vaizey, gave me their unstinting support as ever. Above all, though, it is my husband, David Tinnion, who has lived and breathed this book with me every step of the way. This book is dedicated to him.

Contents

List of Illustrations

Glossary

DTA	*Deutsches Tagebucharchiv* (German Diary Archive)
FDJ	*Freie Deutsche Jugend* (Free German Youth Organization)
FRG	Federal Republic of Germany (West Germany)
GDR	German Democratic Republic (East Germany)
Ostalgie	Nostalgia for the former East Germany
PDS	*Partei des Demokratischen Sozialismus* (Party of Democratic Socialism)
SED	*Sozialistische Einheitspartei Deutschlands* (German Socialist Unity Party), the East German the Communist Party in the GDR
SPD	*Sozialdemokratische Partei Deutschlands* (Social Democratic Party)
Staatsbürgekunde	Citizenship lessons
Wende	This literally means 'change', and is a term used to describe the period of transition following the fall of the Berlin Wall

Preface

In Germany, 9th November is referred to as a *'Schicksalstag'* or 'Destiny Day'. It was on this day in 1918 that Kaiser Wilhelm II abdicated; it was on this day in 1923 that Hitler first tried to seize power in Munich in the so-called 'Beer Hall Putsch'; it was on this day in 1938 that the Nazis vandalized and looted Jewish synagogues; and, of course, it was on this day in 1989 that the Berlin Wall fell.

To this day, the legacy of Germany's divided past remains evident to all visitors crossing between the Eastern and Western parts of the city. Hordes of tourists continue to visit the remaining preserved section of the Berlin Wall for a reason. For twenty eight years the Wall divided Germany into two countries, and was the most powerful symbol of ongoing Cold War divisions.

East Germans born after the Berlin Wall was built in 1961 knew no other reality. But while life under Communism felt normal to some young people, others felt severely constrained by the travel restrictions, the Stasi surveillance, and the penalties for voicing views different from the Communist leadership. In the twenty-eight years that the Berlin Wall remained up, over 5,000 dissatisfied East Germans successfully escaped across the border. One man hired an American Army Officer's uniform from a dressing-up shop and walked across the border, another man smuggled his girlfriend out curled up in the boot of his car.

That left approximately 17 million East Germans living behind the Iron Curtain. This book is interested in those people. How did they experience the transition to a united Germany? How had they been affected by immersion in the Communist culture? And now, twenty-five years on, when enough time has passed to allow for genuine reflection on the impact of the change, how do they feel their lives are marked by the country's divided past? These are the questions that this book explores. By offering answers to these questions, the book hopes to help readers to imagine what it was like to live through this momentous phase in German history.

Born in the GDR details the individual experiences of eight East Germans, forming a framework to understand the variety of views of the GDR and its demise, looking back from the perspective of a unified Germany. These eight stories are complemented by accounts from many others, to give a broader context. They explore a range of themes relating to life in the GDR, such as religion, the environment, sexuality, travel, and education.

Experiences of this time were far from uniform as the conversations reveal. Through conversations with many East Germans, this book reveals the many and varied ways in which people think about about and make sense of this momentous phase of German history of this time. How people responded to living under Communism undoubtedly informed how they subsequently adjusted to reunion with Capitalist West Germany. Although all of the people featured in this book were born into what is often called 'Germany's second dictatorship' of the twentieth century, they nonetheless remained individuals, each of whom had to live their life and was presented with a set of choices. This book offers eight different perspectives on the transition from East Germany to a united Germany. Each of the stories that follow is about survival, as well as adjusting and adapting to life in the newly established habitat of reunited Germany.

Introduction

When the Berlin Wall fell on 9 November 1989, the physical division of East and West Germany came to an end. Huge changes followed this pivotal moment. The two countries were officially stitched back together a year later, and—on paper at least—German unity was achieved. Though the Wall had been knocked down and the debris tidied away, getting to the point at which Germany is one country again has been a much more protracted process. For East Germans, whose communist-run country was amalgamated into capitalist West Germany through the reunification process, the changes were particularly dramatic. The whole fabric of their daily lives changed, from the way they voted, to the brand of butter they bought, to the newspapers they read.[1] And yet in spite of these external changes, East Germans understandably continued to think and act in ways that were informed by their socialist past. Different mentalities continued to divide East and West Germans to the point that Germans on both sides could be said to be still living with *Die Mauer im Kopf* (the Wall in their heads) years after reunification.[2]

New divides have also emerged among East Germans about how they remember their old lives in the German Democratic Republic (GDR).[3] For some, it is the restrictions of living in a dictatorship that loom large in their recollections: the lack of free elections, the absence of freedom of speech, and the inability to travel freely.[4] Others, by contrast, look back fondly to an era in which a paternalistic state provided for all. Views of the GDR therefore range from being a 'Stasiland'[5] at one extreme to a benevolent welfare state on the other. These polarized depictions of life in the GDR have been reinforced by two popular films: *Goodbye, Lenin!* (2003) and *The Lives of Others* (2006). *Goodbye, Lenin!* is nostalgic for the best elements of life in the GDR, which is shown as a protective yet benign (and at times ridiculous) state looking after its citizens, in contrast to the relentless and often difficult reality of reunification. *The Lives of Others* suggests that East Germany was a Stasi-state, since two of the main characters, a couple, feel constantly vulnerable and afraid. Crucially, although the GDR is often characterized in terms of this dichotomy, many East Germans' experiences lie somewhere between. *Born in the GDR* offers a more variegated picture and aims to deepen our understanding of how the transition from communism to capitalism affected the daily lives of 'ordinary people'—individuals who would otherwise remain anonymous in the historical record.[6] This in turn will help to explain the longer-term legacies of the GDR.

Let us briefly consider the backstory. How was it that Germany came to be separated into two countries, divided by a Wall and then reunited? At the end of the Second World War Germany was defeated and physically occupied by the four Allied powers: the US, Britain, France, and the Soviet Union. Each of the four was in charge of a zone of Germany, as well as a sector of Berlin, which was situated within the Soviet zone. However, even as the post-war peace settlements were being decided at the Yalta and Potsdam conferences in 1945, relations were already becoming strained between the Soviet Union and the other Allied powers. Relations broke down irretrievably from June 1948, when the Soviets blocked access to Berlin by road and rail, allegedly for 'construction purposes'—an action which the Western Allies called the Berlin Blockade. In response the Western Allies flew in key supplies for the Berliners in their sectors in what became known as the Berlin Airlift. The Berlin Blockade was lifted eleven months after it began, in May 1949, when it became clear that the Western Allies were able to convey more supplies by air than they had delivered by land, but nonetheless the blockade paved the way for the formation of two separate German states later that year: West Germany officially became the Federal Republic of Germany (FRG) with Bonn as its capital on 23 May 1949 and East Germany officially became the German Democratic Republic (GDR) with East Berlin as its capital on 7 October 1949. Berlin, in particular, had a special position in these developments. Although located deep in the GDR, it remained divided into a Western sector and an Eastern sector. Those living in West Berlin were officially citizens of the FRG but stayed under occupation by the Western Allies until 1990. When this territorial division was completed, East Germany occupied less than one-third of German soil and was home to around a quarter of the population of post-war Germany.[7]

Over the next twelve years, the equivalent of a town's worth of people per year moved from living in East Germany, which was rapidly transformed into a socialist society and state, to West Germany, where capitalism was being restored, because the living standards and job opportunities were seen to be better.[8] This was a problem for the GDR authorities, but it was not just the number of people leaving that was a cause for concern. Those leaving included some of the brightest and best from East Germany, in particular highly qualified young people whose education had been paid for by the East German state. In the competitive Cold War climate between East and West this state of affairs troubled the communist leaders: East Germans were voting with their feet and if they continued to leave at the same rate, soon there would be no one left in the East. Their solution was a wall.

On Saturday 12 August Berliners went to bed being able to move freely between the eastern and western parts of the city. When they woke up this was no longer possible, because overnight the GDR authorities had erected a temporary security fence guarded by border police to prevent people from crossing into West Berlin. In

FIGURE I Divided Germany, 1949–1989.

fact, the little boy (on the book's cover) who became separated from
his family on 13 August due to the ever-expanding barbed wire
border was only reunited with them when an East German border
guard disobeyed strict orders not to let anyone pass, and helped the
child to cross back to the East. Over time, however, this fence became permanent. In many ways, the Berlin Wall appeared to be
the nail in the coffin for any prospect of German unity, but in
reality Germany had been divided since 1949, and from 1952 the
tightening of the border between East and West Germany had
made it almost impossible to cross by that route.[9] Nonetheless, for

the twenty-eight years following the Wall's appearance, Germans living in East Berlin or the wider GDR were literally walled in and were only allowed to travel to other communist countries within the Eastern bloc such as Poland, Czechoslovakia, and Hungary.[10] GDR citizens could apply for short-term visas to visit relatives in the West, but whether these would be granted was entirely at the whim of the authorities. Those who asked to leave the GDR for good were marked down as politically unreliable, subject to career blocks, and often put under surveillance by the Stasi, the East German secret police.

All this ended in November 1989. Just over forty years after the GDR had been founded in 1949 and thirty-seven after Germany had been physically divided in 1952, the Berlin Wall was torn down in a dramatic turn of events. A combination of longer-and shorter-term factors played their part, including the thawing of relations between East and West Germany, which was instigated by the fourth West German Chancellor Willy Brandt in the 1970s. In that era of so-called *Ostpolitik*, Germans on both sides of the Wall were allowed a greater number of visits across the border (though it was much easier for West Germans to travel to the GDR than the other way around). These visits underlined to East Germans just how poor the quality of their consumer goods was in comparison to that of their Western neighbours.

Even for those who had not stepped outside the Eastern bloc, it was at this time that the cracks in the economic policies of the socialist countries became particularly apparent. In the GDR and elsewhere in the Eastern bloc food was heavily subsidized and basic necessities were sold at very low prices. In fact bread reputedly cost so little that people fed it to their pigs. People with allotments were forced to sell a share of their crops to the government in order to ensure a minimal supply of fruit and vegetables throughout the GDR. This sometimes had ludicrous consequences, for example a man selling the cherries he had produced to the state, only to buy them back again at a lower price than the one he had sold them for.[11] It was this fundamental disconnect in the GDR's economic policy that became increasingly apparent in the mid-1980s. The country was going bankrupt, as its overall earnings did not cover the cost of the extensive subsidies, and ordinary people found it increasingly difficult to get hold of basic household items.[12] This fundamentally challenged the unspoken social contract between GDR citizens and their government, whereby the government delivered security and welfare in exchange for conformity to the regime's dictates, and it ultimately contributed to the instability of the regime in the autumn of 1989.[13]

Added to this sense of dissatisfaction with the East German government (run by the *Sozialistische Einheitspartei Deutschlands*, SED, the Socialist Unity Party) was the advent of a new reforming General Secretary of the Communist Party in the Soviet Union, Mikhail Gorbachev. Taking power on 11 March 1985, he appeared to offer radical reform and the relaxation of strict ideology, especially with his policies of *glasnost*, which referred to openness and transparency in government institutions, and *perestroika*, which referred to the easing and restructuring of socialist rule. Gorbachev changed Soviet policy, based on suggestions from a new team of experts who had been studying Soviet–East European relations for some time. They told Gorbachev that Eastern Europe was no longer a strategic necessity for Soviet security and was in fact an expensive drain on resources. Gorbachev's new policies meant that the Soviet Union was not committed to preserving the status quo as it had been in the past. This made it difficult for communist leaders in the Eastern bloc to continue to block reform, as they could no longer rely on the pretext of Soviet disapproval to justify their actions.[14] Gorbachev's policies promised a more relaxed style of communist rule in the Soviet Union, and this in turn gave hope to ordinary people in the Eastern bloc that there would be improvements to their own daily lives. His new policy of non-interference in the Soviet satellite states also effectively freed reformers within the ruling parties in countries like Poland and Hungary to begin the struggle to change their own political institutions, without fear of Soviet intervention.[15] And all of this significantly widened the potential for change in the region.

In Poland, opposition to the regime had been brewing amongst workers since the start of the 1980s, with the establishment of Solidarity as a national organization of opposition headed by electrician Lech Wałęsa. Though Solidarity operated underground for most of the decade, it attracted more and more support in its mission to reform communist rule in Poland.[16] And with further industrial unrest breaking out in August 1988, the government finally agreed to open negotiations with the opposition. Between February and April 1989, round-table discussions took place between them. One of the outcomes of this discussion was that Solidarity was legalized. The biggest decision, though, was to allow non-communist parties to stand in the next election. Ultimately, this led to free elections in June 1989, when Solidarity won a landslide victory and the communists were ousted from power. These developments in the Soviet Union and in Poland certainly encouraged unrest elsewhere.[17]

In Hungary, too, popular acceptance of the communist regime waned dramatically in the 1980s. When the Communist Party leader János Kádár responded to the intensifying economic crisis by introducing harsh austerity measures rather than a change in course, opposition to the regime became more vocal as the notion that the state was protecting workers' interests became increasingly undermined.[18] Under mounting pressure, Kádár was removed as leader after nearly thirty-two years in May 1988. In a climate of radical reformism, the half-hearted efforts of Kádár's replacement, Károly Grósz, were soon dismissed as inadequate.

Leading the reformist wing in the Hungarian Communist Party was Imre Pozsgay, who argued that the Party's future could only be assured by working with sections of the cultural and technical intelligentsia. Under his influence, and in response to mounting external pressure, the Hungarian Communist Party agreed to join in round-table discussions with the opposition. Inspired by the

Polish model, these talks lasted until September 1989, and it was agreed that Hungary would become a multi-party political system operated through free elections which were set up for spring 1990.[19]

From May 1989, the reforms in Hungary had a knock-on effect in East Germany, when a group of Hungarian soldiers, at the direction of both the Hungarian and Austrian governments, began to remove the barbed wire which had previously closed the border between Hungary and Austria as part of the Iron Curtain. This led to an exodus of 130,000 East Germans, who used this border crossing to flee to West Germany between May and November. The sheer scale of departures served to erode the GDR's authority substantially.[20]

Buoyed by developments in the Soviet Union, Poland, and Hungary, thousands of GDR citizens took to the streets campaigning for reform. The so-called Monday Demonstrations in Leipzig in September 1989 drew more and more supporters campaigning for freedom of speech, a relaxation of the travel restrictions, better care of the environment, and peace. In Dresden, Jena, and East Berlin, demonstrators met in the shelter of churches and discussed their demands for reform. Gorbachev's visit to East Berlin to celebrate the forty-year anniversary of the GDR on 3 October added further momentum to proceedings. He was greeted like a pop star by large crowds which chanted 'Gorbi! Gorbi!' and 'Help us!' In a speech that day Gorbachev gave demonstrators further hope, declaring that 'life punishes those who come too late'—a clear message to the East German government that it should implement reforms or risk the consequences.[21] At this stage, the desire for change among ordinary East Germans was clear. It was not until 9 November, however, that matters really came to a head. On that day, just before a press conference, Günter Schabowski, a spokesperson for the SED Politburo, was handed a note saying that East Germans would be able to cross the border with proper permission. Since the note had no further details, Schabowski had to improvise when answering questions. When he was unable to give specific details about the new travel arrangements, East Berliners were filled with optimism and flocked in huge numbers to the border crossing points across the city, where confused guards allowed them to pass through. Soon after, the entire Iron Curtain collapsed.[22] Few, if any, of the East German protesters had bargained for the reunification of Germany, but that is what transpired over the following year.

The opening of the Wall was met with euphoria across both Germanys. West Berliners greeted East Berliners with glasses of champagne as they crossed the border, most of them for the first time in their lives. In the excitement, strangers embraced, overwhelmed by the enormity of what they were witnessing. The party atmosphere continued all night in downtown Berlin. In other parts of the city, Germans awoke the following morning to hear the news on the radio or from neighbours rapping on the door, eager to tell them what had happened. At this stage, the collapse of the GDR was in no way inevitable and many East Germans expected the border to be resealed. However in the months that followed, with more and more Easterners flocking westwards, it became clear that there was no going back.

In stark contrast to the other countries in the Eastern bloc, the GDR—the so-called 'jewel in the USSR's Eastern European Empire'[23]—had a prosperous Western counterpart, which had the wherewithal to subsidize East Germany's transition into an operational democratic system.[24] In March 1990, there were free elections in East Germany for the first time since 1933. Rather than voting based on Party allegiances, East Germans voted to choose their preferred vision and timetable for reunification. Helmut Kohl's party, the Christian Democratic Union (CDU) offered reunification as quickly as possible, the idea being that the GDR would be divided into states (*Länder*) that could then apply to join the West German Federation of States (*Bundesländer*). The Social Democratic Party (*Sozialdemokratische Partei Deutschlands* or SPD) argued for a slower process with more protracted discussions about how to create a new Germany. Other parties, such as Alliance '90/The Greens (*Bündis 90/Die Grünen*), which represented East German dissident movements, and the Party of Democratic Socialism (*Partei des Demokratischen Sozialismus* or PDS), which was the successor to the SED Party, were more sceptical about reunification and offered alternative programmes instead. In March 1990, East Germans voted overwhelmingly in favour of the quickest available option. Though the decision to unite was clear from the election results, putting reunification into practice was far from straightforward. Each country had its own flag, its own national anthem, its own armed forces, and critically its own military allegiances, with the GDR committed to the Warsaw Pact and the FRG to NATO. There were other problematic differences too, such as a different legal code, a different educational system, a different approach to health care, and a different method of taxation. Deciding how to deal with this was logistically very difficult.[25]

Replacement, it seems, was the theme of the *Wende* (the name given to the political changes prompted by the fall of the Wall). Whatever one might think about whether an alternative approach was feasible, in many respects reunification ended up being a wholesale takeover by the West, much to the disappointment of many of the dissidents who had first taken to the streets of East Germany in 1989. Once the protests became a mass movement the original protestors, who had sought a more democratic form of socialism through reform from within, were drowned out by growing calls for the end of the GDR per se.[26] This, perhaps, accounts for why the celebrations of reunification in October 1990 were far more muted than the festivities in November 1989.

After forty years of division, East and West Germany had evolved into very distinct societies. That the differences were so marked surprised Germans from both sides, and presented enormous challenges to feeling a genuine sense of unification as one nation. In 1980, for example, only 6 per cent of West Germans lived in communities of fewer than 2,000 inhabitants in contrast to nearly 25 per cent of East Germans.[27] The GDR was grounded in the ideology of Marxism-Leninism, and therefore committed to eradicating class differences, while the West was a capitalist consumer society. The overall standard of living was higher in the West, but so too was the difference between rich and poor. All of this meant that at the moment the Wall was torn down, East and West Germans looked, thought, and behaved very differently.[28] Perhaps even more challenging than adapting to new systems for employment and welfare, was the apparent need for East Germans to shed a set of behaviours that had been developed subconsciously by living in a socialist state.[29] As many East Germans found, including those who were keen to blend in with West Germans as quickly as possible, it simply was not that easy to erase the experiences of forty years and start from scratch.[30]

When the structures, organizations, leisure activities, shops, and customs of the GDR effectively disappeared and were replaced by West German ways over the course of the transition, many East Germans experienced a loss of their sense of self, of their sense of identity.[31] Identity can be shaped by a variety of factors including ideology, belief, or allegiance, but it is also rooted in everyday behaviour: the newspapers people read, the food they eat, the buildings that surround them, the travel choices that are available. A sense of identity relates to where a person is from and this certainly colours where that person is going. It is also linked to expectations.[32] Decades of living under the GDR undoubtedly informed the attitudes and mindsets of ordinary East Germans. The vast majority of citizens there participated in the communist system and through that involvement they were themselves changed. The extent to which they had internalized the values of the system was far greater than many had thought. The fall of the Wall and comparison with their Western compatriots brought into stark relief how much they had been part of that system.[33] And with rapid reunification, suddenly East Germans were confronted with the fact that many of their habits, the practices of daily life that they had developed unconsciously, were at odds with the way West Germans behaved. West Germans were foreigners to East Germans, they just happened to speak the same language. And in this context East Germans could not simply shrug off their past or the fact that they were, in many senses, products of the circumstances they had been living in.[34]

'I didn't move a metre but I suddenly lived in a new world', observed one East German.[35] How acutely individuals felt the loss of their old GDR world was undoubtedly related to how successful a transition they made into living in the new reunited Germany. East Germans could simultaneously feel both freer and frustrated.[36] Those former East Germans who continue to buy familiar Eastern products may well simply be seeking out the comfort of the familiar from their old lives as GDR citizens. Overall, their feelings of disorientation were captured by the East German journalist and writer Andreas Lehmann, who wrote in 1993 that 'they [politicians leading the reunification process] are asking us for a complete renunciation of the old and a cheerful subordination to the culture of the West, which above all does not translate into the surrender of some "ideals" (political or otherwise), but, worse, into a total loss of one's own biography'.[37]

Essentially, after the end of the GDR, East Germans continued to exist as East Germans but in an environment that had seen fundamental changes. The stories that follow look at how, despite the end of a state and the failure of an ideology, the values and mindsets that these produced, in both conformist and oppositional variants, lived on. All of this helps to explain why in the initial period of transition, and indeed in the years that followed, 'Germany was no longer two nations, but it certainly was not yet one'.[38]

The changes wrought by German reunification reached far into the daily lives of all East Germans.[39] Yet the different ages and stages of life which people were at when the Wall fell meant that East Germans were affected unevenly by the changes. Adults nearing retirement age were often forced to stop working early since it was not obvious to Western employers how their skills could be put to good use in rapidly modernizing and labour-saving industries. Some, decades into building a career, had to retrain to fit in with the modern, capital-intensive modes of production, often taking a pay cut and a drop in professional standing to do so. Others, of course, were successful, building new businesses in the wake of reunification. But whether successful or otherwise, reunification brought huge changes to the day-to-day. And many had to cope with this transition while also caring and providing for a family in a markedly more expensive world.[40] In this context, it would be easy to assume that young people, who had spent the least time building their lives under socialist rule, would adapt much more easily to the new state of affairs than their older counterparts. The world was already changing and getting bigger for adolescents anyway, so in many respects the *Wende* was just another layer of change.[41] Certainly this group, who had most or all of their adult lives ahead of them, was best placed to profit from the new educational freedoms which allowed individuals far greater choice about what they studied and pursued as a career—choices that were based on ability and interests rather than political conformity. At the same time, however, these children and young people had been born into the GDR, and had no experience of another system. And just as they were about to launch themselves into the real world as adults, the rules of the game changed drastically. Older East Germans certainly struggled to adjust to life in unified Germany, with all of the attendant changes to daily life. But younger people, who had been subject to SED propaganda their entire lives, also had a lot of readjusting to do, as they tried to work out what they themselves thought as the system they had grown up in was discredited and displaced by its once-reviled Western rival.[42]

This book will focus on the experiences of East Germans who were born into the GDR after the Berlin Wall was put up on 13 August 1961. This group had known nothing other than growing

up in communist East Germany. To understand what young East
Germans went through following German reunification, it is essential to look back on their experiences under the SED. Just as
the Nazi dictatorship had tried to indoctrinate young people with
their way of thinking in the Hitler Youth, so too had the GDR
through its equivalent youth groups—the Young Pioneers, the
Thälmann Pioneers, and the Free German Youth—which occupied much of the free time of youths aged between 6 and 25.
Young people represented the future of socialism in the eyes of
the SED leadership and it was therefore a top priority to turn
them into socialist personalities. What did this entail? Above all,
it meant belief in the socialist world view, and a commitment as
a collective to working towards a better society. In 1958, Erich
Honecker's predecessor as East German leader of the SED,
Walter Ulbricht, tried to encapsulate the essence of the ideal socialist man by penning the 'Ten Commandments for the New
Socialist Human'. These commandments were phrased like the
Ten Commandments in the Bible and formed an established part
of the SED Party Programme between 1963 and 1979. They give
a flavour of what was expected of citizens, both young and old,
in the GDR:

1. You shall always campaign for the international solidarity of the
   working class and all working people and for the unbreakable
   bond of all socialist countries.
2. You shall love your fatherland and always be ready to deploy all
   your strength and capabilities for the defence of the workers'
   and farmers' power.
3. You shall help to abolish exploitation of man by man.
4. You shall do good deeds for socialism, because socialism leads to
   a better life for all working people.
5. You shall act in the spirit of mutual help and comradely
   cooperation while building up socialism, and also respect the
   collective and heed its critique.

6. You shall protect and enhance state-owned property.
7. You shall always strive to improve your performance, be frugal, and strengthen socialist discipline at work.
8. You shall raise your children in the spirit of peace and socialism to be well educated, highly principled, and physically hardened people.
9. You shall live purely and fairly and respect your family.
10. You shall show solidarity with those who fight for their national liberation and those who defend their national independence.

So how did the regime aim to imbue young people with these socialist values? There was a strong ideological element to belonging to the Young Pioneers. There was a set of commandments, for example, that each 6-year-old had to recite on joining the organization:

Commandments of the Young Pioneers
We Young Pioneers love our German Democratic Republic.
We Young Pioneers love our parents.
We Young Pioneers love peace.
We Young Pioneers are friends with children of the Soviet Union and of all countries.
We Young Pioneers learn diligently, are orderly and disciplined.
We Young Pioneers respect all working people and lend a hand everywhere.
We Young Pioneers are good friends and help each other.
We Young Pioneers like singing and dancing, playing and doing handicrafts.
We Young Pioneers play sports and keep our body clean and healthy.
We Young Pioneers proudly wear the blue neckerchief.
We Young Pioneers prepare to become good Thälmann pioneers.

There was also a uniform, including the blue hat and the blue neckerchief mentioned in the commandments. The three tips of the neckerchief stood for the three institutions of education—the parent's household, school, and the pioneer organization—and the knot symbolized their unity.[43] All of this gave children a sense of importance at a young age.

Alongside the SED's youth movement, schools were of primary importance for inculcating the socialist world view. In fact, the youth movement was integrated into each school's activities, with time set aside for this on a weekly basis. Furthermore, a high point in the formation of the 'socialist personality' was the *Jugendweihe*, the socialist rite of passage for 14-year-olds akin to Christian confirmation. The ceremony involved a procession, a speech, a proclamation of vows, and a presentation, and was yet another chance for the SED to prepare young people to become active participants in the socialist state.[44]

Though the SED was extremely focused on getting young people 'on side', its efforts were more successful at securing outward conformity than active enthusiasm. Some children enjoyed the sense of belonging and the outdoor activities arranged by the youth groups, but many disliked having their free time organized and found the emphasis on ideology boring, participating only to avoid the educational and career blocks which stymied the careers of the uncooperative.[45] Watching Western television to some extent immunized young East Germans against SED propaganda. And Western TV, along with Intershops which sold Western goods in the GDR at extortionate prices, showcased the allure of the brighter, freer, and materially superior West Germany. Also, in the specific context of the 1980s young people in the GDR had raised expectations of reform in light of Gorbachev's pioneering liberalization policies of glasnost and perestroika. All of these factors help to explain why GDR youth policies did not meet with widespread enthusiasm from young people.[46]

What follows explores what young East Germans made of the merging of East and West Germany after the fall of the Berlin Wall. Many of them had been involved in the demonstrations in the autumn of 1989, indicating that in some sense the East German leadership had failed to wholeheartedly win the hearts and minds of young people. But once these young people had unfettered access to the Western consumer world—the delights of Levi's jeans, Coca-Cola, and Milka chocolate—what did they make of the regime change in the years that followed? Had living under socialism actually influenced their outlooks more than they realized?[47] After 1989, many young East Germans initially appear to have been happy to adopt a more materialistic, consumer-oriented outlook. Jana Hensel, who was 13 years old when the Wall fell, describes how life changed for her in her memoir:

> At some point in late '89 or early '90—here, too, I can't remember exactly when—we stopped going to all those state-run extra-curricular events. Saturdays had previously been reserved for community activities, but now most of us preferred to drive across the border to West Germany with our parents...And Wednesdays changed, too. As a pre-teen in the GDR, I used to put on my scarf and pointy cap every Wednesday afternoon at 4 p.m. and head off to meetings of the *Junge Pioniere*, our version of the Scouts, but with a heavy Socialist slant...Seemingly overnight, the endless appointments that had filled our childhood were cancelled...Gone, too, were the Spartacus Track and Field Competitions...Competitive sports were out....Now we rushed home as soon as school was over and parked ourselves in front of the TV...Our interests had moved on...We now collected the free toy surprises that came with McDonald's Happy Meals.[48]

However, despite young people's dissatisfaction with life in the GDR, and their converse attraction to all things Western, after reunification many seemed to miss aspects of life in the former East Germany. Reunification represented a huge change. And, over time, young people felt the social dislocation prompted by the political change a lot more keenly: they developed a more nuanced view than straightforward delight at being able to drink real Coca-Cola. In most cases, political socialization in the GDR *had* influenced East Germans' values and attitudes, and these principles were slow to change.[49] Many East Germans felt that they had cut themselves off from the government's influence by living in niches among like-minded people, but as West German diplomat Günther Gaus pointed out in 1983, 'Niches are not external [to the socialist system], on the contrary they are niches inside GDR socialism...Over the decades more facts, beliefs, and standards of really existing socialism have made themselves at home in private corners than niche dwellers are always aware of.'[50] If, as Gaus suggests, East Germans young and old were far more shaped by life under socialist rule than they had realized, when familiar socialist structures were swept away with reunification, many experienced a deep and unexpected sense of loss. The stories that follow deepen our qualitative understanding of this experience.[51]

In 1990, Leipzig psychologist Walter Friedrich declared that the youth of the GDR was in 'psychological chaos'.[52] Over the space of a few months,

> pupils were confronted with textbooks lauding the praises of the West German state, which only months before had been portrayed as an Imperialist repressor. Normality had been turned on its head. Their country had disappeared and had been replaced by an unfamiliar one, which left them feeling as if they had a black hole in their biographies.[53]

How then, should we try to understand this black hole? First-hand accounts are the starting point for this book which explores contrasting experiences of living across the historical caesura of 1989 and situates each individual's response within the wider context of social, political, and economic developments at the time. From a wider collection of testimony gathered from thirty East Germans who were born from 1961 onwards, eight particularly striking stories have been selected[54]—a large enough number to showcase the multiple and varied experiences of the transition, while equally allowing each story to be explored fully within the confines of a single volume.

To find participants from a combination of urban and rural parts of the GDR, the author placed adverts on noticeboards in supermarkets in former East Germany, pushed leaflets through doors in the Eastern neighbourhoods of Berlin, and advertised on a variety of mailing lists, including the GDR museum in Berlin, the *Dritte Generation Ost* organization (a forum for those East Germans who had not yet reached adulthood when the Wall fell), the academic research centre in Potsdam, the *Zentrum für Zeithistorische Forschung*, the former Stasi prison at Hohenschönhausen, and the *Zeitzeugenbüro*—an eyewitness database of individuals from all over Germany willing to talk about their experiences. The interviewees, too, helped to find new participants in the project, asking among their friends and relatives for willing volunteers.

Each interviewee was sent the same set of questions before the interview. The questions were carefully worded to be as open and neutrally phrased as possible, and they were divided into three sections: life in the GDR, the fall of the Wall and the period of transition between 1989 and 1990, and life since reunification. At the start of each interview, the author explained that she was writing a book about East German experiences of life before, during, and after reunification, with the hope of revealing a variety of responses going beyond the often polarized characterizations of the GDR, cast either as a 'Stasiland' or as a benign paternalistic state. All interviewees answered the same set of questions, as well as further individual questions prompted by their responses. The author used the questions to open up various themes but then let the interviewees speak freely even if they veered away from the question asked, the logic being that this would allow each one to recount things that he or she thought were significant. Alongside these personal testimonies, the book draws on school reports, school work, photographs, reports compiled by the Stasi, and contemporary diaries. This study emphatically does not aim to be representative of what all East Germans went through, but it certainly promises to offer a variety of personal insights into this dramatic time, each of the eight chapters representing one evocation of life in the GDR and its aftermath. And drawn together in one volume, these disparate accounts bring us closer to understanding what young East Germans went through before, during, and after unification.

Though memory is fickle and uncontrollable in nature, the historian can nonetheless reap great rewards by teasing out and analysing unwieldy memories of the past. One of the great advantages of researching the relatively recent past is being able to talk to the participants at first hand. When a historian reads the diaries or letters of people who are dead, there is no opportunity to ask the author further questions or seek clarifications. Using paper sources in the archive, the historian can easily forget that it is real people's lives that they are reading about. Interviews by contrast, unmistakably reinforce this reality. The interviewee becomes much more the subject of history than the object of it.[55] When working with live witnesses and actively producing original historical sources through interviews, there is a valuable and unique opportunity for dialogue.[56] Since all researchers have their own 'baggage', meaning that they cannot help but read sources through the prisms of their own experiences and values, it is surely extremely helpful to meet the protagonists of the story, so that any false impressions which may have been formed from their answers can be corrected. Above all, oral historians can decide which questions to ask of their real, living historical sources, as opposed to historians using paper records, whose questions are inevitably in part dictated by the content of the material they are looking at. And hearing eyewitnesses describe what they went through in their own words has a compelling immediacy which brings the past to life in a way like nothing else.[57]

Certainly, as with many types of evidence, the interview testimonies offer only a partial account.[58] Subconsciously as well as consciously, individuals will have established narratives and explanations of how they have made sense of their recent experiences. And these narratives, these memories, may well discard or exclude facts or incidences that do not fit their overall 'take' on proceedings. This is the reality. But it does not stop what they do remember from being valuable.[59] Each individual will differ in how they decide to prioritize remembering their various experiences. People remember things differently and people had contrasting experiences, both of which help to explain why some accounts contradict as much as they corroborate each other. This does not mean that one account is necessarily more correct or valid than another. One experience might be more typical of the broader experience, but it does not make it more 'right'. The simple fact is that there is more than one historical truth. Each of the life stories told here blends elements of the typical and the exceptional.

Historians interpreting memories must be aware that individual memories evolve as they are slotted into wider narratives that develop long after the event. In the immediate aftermath of reunification, for example, the word *Wendehals* (reunification turncoat) was coined, to describe people who had supported the SED in the GDR but hastily rewrote their own histories to put distance between themselves and the old regime. Since reunification there have certainly been broad shifts in the prevailing memory cultures relating to the SED. Initially, while hopes for a brighter future in a reunited Germany remained high, East Germans appeared happy enough to characterize themselves as victims of an oppressive state, dominated by the Stasi, because emphasizing the repressive nature of the SED helped to justify their conformist behaviour. But as time passed, and disillusion with the reunification process became more widespread, many East Germans began to mourn the loss of their collective past, somehow forgetting or marginalizing the Stasi's activities from their memories in the process. And yet for those who were political dissidents in the GDR, the pervasiveness of *Ostalgie* (nostalgia for the former East Germany), with its attendant rosy memories of the secure and simple life, is understandably a source of great anger, as it conveniently forgets the very real repressive elements of SED rule and emphasizes a cosy past over a dictatorial one.

There are a number of important factors to be aware of when using oral testimony. Firstly, there is no one, monolithic version of events which captures the experiences of all the protagonists. Secondly, the way individuals remember the past may change over time with retelling. Indeed, each individual will likely not have just one version of events that remains static throughout his or her life. This is partly because the way one sees the world at 20 years old is likely to be different to the way one sees the world at 40, and partly to do with the changing context and the prevailing values of the society in which we live.[60] Thirdly, interviewees may well present the past in a way which they believe shows them in the most favourable light. And finally, years after the event interviewees have the benefit of hindsight and, with this, often a fuller understanding of events than was available at the time. Yet in spite of these causes for caution, recollections are usually accurate enough to mean that retrospective interviewing can bring huge rewards. And in some ways memories are *more* authentic than other sources, since they combine an individual's first-hand experience of events with how they have made sense of events subsequently.[61] In fact, it is extremely informative to look at how people have made sense of what they went through.[62]

Individual eyewitnesses may have an axe to grind in the way they recount their experiences, but presenting a collection of accounts helps to reveal the disparate agendas that individuals may have and in so doing illuminates the dichotomized memory culture about the GDR. Indeed, when employing memories as key historical sources for understanding East German perspectives on the transition of 1989, it is helpful to think of the existence of two GDRs: the GDR as it was at the time, and the GDR as we understand it now, which is based on memories of it. Neither historians nor ordinary East Germans will ever recapture the actual GDR that East Germans lived in, because we no longer have access to it. If we accept that the *memory* of the GDR is now what we mean by the GDR, we must acknowledge, too, that there is no single memory of this past. Instead, there are competing and often contradictory versions, which often try to exclude each other. It is therefore important to capture multiple accounts of this past so as not to privilege particular perspectives.[63]

If the GDR as we understand it, is based on disparate accounts of it, this should give no cause for concern. In contrast to historians of the Middle Ages who have relatively few sources from which to tease out readings and rereadings of the past, contemporary historians face the opposite challenge. Instead of having one set of correspondence to tell us about the wider social context of an era, contemporary historians have more information to choose from than they could ever possibly look at. And by doing interviews, historians can learn things that it would not have been possible to discover otherwise. Surely this is a fortunate position to be in, rather than a problem?

Let us briefly consider the cast of characters that form the eight case studies in this book.[64] In the opening chapter we hear from Petra, a 25-year-old Berlin-based PhD student who found herself propelled into high politics after the Wall fell. Petra had been an ardent socialist from her student days in the 1980s but in the transition of 1989/90 she occupied a central position in discussions about how to make reunification happen in practice. Once this was done, Petra was one of only seventeen communist MPs elected to the German parliament in 1990. This chapter explains Petra's continued loyalty to the SED's values in the wake of unification. Unlike Petra, Carola from Eisenach began questioning the regime during her schooldays. She escaped to West Germany when she was 21 years old, mere months before the Wall fell. Chapter 2 focuses on her story and how she felt totally isolated amongst friends who did not seem to mind that SED propaganda was so different from the reality. Carola was angry at the GDR's wanton destruction of the environment and was part of an environmental movement intent on exposing damage the government was keen to keep quiet. This chapter explores her frustration with life in the

GDR, recounts her escape, and includes her reflections on life since reunification.

In Chapter 3 we learn about Lisa, a schoolteacher, who was happy with life in communist East Germany and remains happy with life since the transition of 1989. We hear about her experience of daily life behind the Iron Curtain in Pankow and gain a contented, relatively apolitical perspective on how things changed for the 22-year-old once the Berlin Wall fell. Chapter 4 provides a sharp contrast with Lisa's story: we hear from Mario, a waiter from East Berlin, who was shot at and imprisoned for trying to leave East Germany when he was 20. We learn why Mario was so desperate to leave the GDR, and we hear about his experiences as a political prisoner at the hands of the Stasi, gaining insights into the long-term impact of his persecution. The subject of Chapter 5, 28 year-old Katharina from Brandenburg, was, like Mario, strongly opposed to the socialist set-up in the GDR, but for very different reasons. She was the daughter of a Protestant pastor, and accordingly suffered taunting and other disadvantages at school, and later at work, because of upholding her faith in an increasingly secular society. Katharina married a man who had been imprisoned by the Stasi for disseminating oppositional pamphlets, and as a result, their lives were carefully monitored by the Stasi.

From the oppositional stance of Katharina's family in Chapter 5, in Chapter 6 we move to the Party-loyal family of Robert, who remains a defender of socialist ideals to this day. Robert, who was a 15-year-old schoolboy when the Wall fell, was absolutely content in the GDR system. He felt no envy of West Germans, whom he had learned suffered from high crime and unemployment rates. After the Wall fell, he felt anger at the way everything from East Germany was dismissed as inferior. He believes the West would do well to learn from the policies used in the GDR. Chapter 8's subject, Mirko, was, like Robert, born into a so-called 'Red' (socialist supporter) family. Indeed, Mirko's father was a Stasi informer. For much of his childhood in Dresden, Mirko played the role of a good son, taking on ever-more exalted positions in the government-led youth movement. By his mid-teens however, he had had enough. From the age of 15, he was no longer prepared to toe the Party line and conform in his views and appearance to the state's dictates. Luckily this period of rebellion coincided with the end of the regime, and Mirko faced no serious consequences. As a result of his anti-communist epiphany, he now works with young people to show how damaging the impact of extreme politics can be. In Chapter 8 we learn about Peggy from Frankfurt Oder, who was a 10-year-old schoolgirl when the Wall fell. She had a wonderfully happy childhood in communist East Germany, and remains nostalgic for many aspects of her old life that were simply swept away with reunification. Life was safe and secure in the GDR in contrast to reunited Germany where she has far more worries about money, work, and housing.

Born in the GDR straddles the historical caesura of 1989, focusing on how young East Germans fared in 1989 as their familiar world was all but erased and replaced by a capitalist society. There was extreme and rapid external change to life in East Germany in the days, weeks, months, and years after the Wall fell. What follows asks whether these changes were mirrored internally within these young East Germans? Did they experience a 'revolution of the mind' as they left behind the distinctive GDR culture built up over four decades of socialism or were the values with which they grew up not so easily cast aside?[65] The complex legacy of Germany's second dictatorship comes under the spotlight in the stories that follow, weighing continuity versus change, unity versus division, and loss versus gain.

I

Petra ~ Shaping the Change

Every German has a story to tell about what they were doing on the night that the Berlin Wall fell. Some Berliners did not make it to bed that night as they danced atop the Wall that had divided Germany. Others slept through it, oblivious to the entire affair. Petra Bläss, who had been campaigning for reforms within the GDR, somewhat ironically remained at home when she heard the news. Though she was keen to see what was going on at first hand, her ailing mother was staying overnight, and, having recently suffered from heart problems, could not face negotiating again the four flights of stairs up to Petra's top-floor flat. Instead, Petra hung out of the window to see the Kastanien Allee below thick with traffic as East Berliners drove towards the border crossing on the Bernauer Strasse.[1]

In the week leading up to 9 November, Petra had been glued to her black-and-white television as never before, desperately hoping to learn more about what was afoot. Alongside a million other East Germans, Petra had joined the demonstrators at Alexanderplatz on 4 November with the aim of improving life in the GDR. Many of the protestors carried banners, making demands such as 'freedom, equality, sincerity' and 'privileges for all'. Above all, those who joined the demonstration were seeking free elections, freedom of the press, the resignation of the government, and unrestricted travel.[2] Petra was one of many who hoped that with reform and peaceful revolution in the GDR, it would be possible to have a new socialist republic, offering the 'socialism with a human face' that many of the speakers that day demanded.[3] For Petra, the fourth of November, not the ninth, was the most memorable day of that autumn and the potential for change through peaceful demonstration seemed immense. Looking back on the events of that day, the East German novelist Stefan Heym commented that 'it was like a window had been opened'. At the time, though, it was not clear what all of this would come to. At this stage, reunification was not on the agenda.

When Petra got home from work at around 6 p.m. on 9 November, she switched on the television and caught the start of the press conference in which the SED spokesperson and Berlin Party chief Günther Schabowski vaguely indicated that travel restrictions to the West would be eased. Schabowski talked about the Party's desire to simplify migration, and said that until the East German parliament officially passed such legislation, there would be interim measures to allow East Germans to travel freely to the West. But before it got to the crucial moment where Schabowski famously responded to a journalist's question by saying that the new travel arrangements would come into effect 'immediately' and 'without delay', Petra had to leave as she was meeting her mother and some friends to go and see Gluck's *Orpheus and Eurydice* at the Komische Oper.[4] As they all had something to eat before the performance, Petra and her friends discussed the rumour circulating that the border would be opened up. No one in the group took it seriously and they felt that it must be a joke. None of them had an inkling that a tired and stressed Schabowski had, in his own words, 'only read the damn thing [the SED press release] through once and diagonally at that' and had therefore inadvertently hastened the easing of border controls dramatically.[5]

The performance of *Orpheus and Eurydice* finished at around 9.30 p.m. and there had been no whisper at any point about what was afoot outside. As Petra's mother was staying with her that night, they said goodbye to their friends and made their way from the theatre to Friedrichsstrasse to catch the S-bahn back to Prenzlauer Berg. Petra remembers saying to her mother, 'Something's up. I can feel it in the air.' No one was shouting from the rooftops that the Wall was open, but somehow the atmosphere was different. The S-bahn was fuller than normal. Petra said to her mother that she would turn on the radio as soon as they were back. Once they were home, Petra discovered what had happened and recalls shouting through to the next-door room to tell her mother that the Wall had fallen.

At the time of the *Wende*, Petra was studying for a PhD in German literature at the Humboldt University in Berlin. She was a member of a lively academic community, where students and professors alike were involved in discussions about how to make socialism workable in a modern society. Aged 22, Petra had joined

FIGURE 2 Thousands of people rushed to the Berlin Wall in the days after it opened.

© Robert Wallis/Corbis.

the SED, buoyed by the hope that Gorbachev's more liberal brand of socialism in the Soviet Union might be workable in East Germany too. In any case, Petra points out, given the fact that there were no political parties with real power in the GDR other than the SED,[6] joining the Party was the only option there was to influence political developments.[7] At SED meetings within the university, she explains, they discussed concrete problems relating to teaching and research, as well as the future of socialism. Being a member of the Party did not mean that Petra was slavishly devoted to the SED leaders, however. Quite the contrary, in fact. She often found their political speeches rather crude and uninspiring. But in her experience, there was not a contradiction between being a member of the Party and simultaneously critical of it.

Campaigning to improve the lot of women in East German society was one of Petra's key concerns in the late 1980s. She joined the Independent Women's Association (*Unabhängige Frauenverband*, UFV) in the autumn of 1989 when it was founded. The founding members were critical of what they called *Muttipolitik* in the GDR. Ninety-eight per cent of adult women worked in East Germany at this time, in accordance with communist ideology which presented looking after the home and being in paid employment not as alternatives but rather as two of the core functions expected of women.[8] Symptomatic of this was the song sung by children in kindergartens across the GDR, which contains the lyrics 'When Mummy goes to work early'.[9] Nonetheless, Petra and the other members of the UFV felt that patriarchy still endured in the GDR, and that the politicians who made decisions which influenced women's lives were still overwhelmingly elderly men. In their view, there was much to be done in the fight for gender equality.

The travel restrictions placed on GDR citizens also affected Petra. While studying for her PhD, for example, she was offered a job as a lecturer in GDR literature in Rome, but because of the government's rules she was unable to go. She found this missed opportunity a bit disappointing, but ultimately, she says, she did not dwell on it, as she had plenty of other things going on in her life at this time. Equally, although Petra enjoyed receiving postcards from her West German stepbrother when he travelled around the world, she never really minded that she could not go to these places herself. Others, by contrast, were jealous when Western visitors regaled them with stories of their travels. They were disappointed only to be able to learn about far-flung places from books and other people, frustrated that they would never themselves set foot in non-Eastern bloc territory. Thomas J., for example, a schoolboy from Berlin, later recalled feeling very hemmed in by the travel limitations. He vividly remembers sitting in the classroom on a winter's day in the 1980s, watching birds flying freely out of the window and feeling deeply sad that they could go wherever they wanted while he would never be allowed beyond Eastern Europe.[10]

Petra realizes that her experience was not identical to that of everyone else who lived there, but she overwhelmingly remembers her time growing up in the GDR as a contented one.[11] Crucial, she believes, in explaining how people remember the GDR, is what age and stage they were at, and whether they were able to do a job that they found fulfilling. Petra was able to study German literature—the subject of her choice—for eight years, and remembers being surrounded by fantastic and inspiring academics. Although there was an exhibition in West Berlin at the Hamburger Bahnhof on the exact topic of her dissertation—war and peace in literature—which she could not attend because of the strict travel restrictions, she found this only a minor frustration in the overall context of the stimulating environment in which she worked. She is aware that Christians who felt persecuted or musicians who were restricted in their choice of song lyrics might have different memories of the system, as would those, for example, who were put under pressure to inform for the Stasi. Petra knew that the Stasi existed and that there were probably informants among her circle of acquaintances at university, but she never encountered this herself and never felt that she had to watch what she said.

After people had stopped dancing on top of the Berlin Wall to celebrate the opening-up of the inner German border, a daunting question needed to be answered: what would happen next? With the collapse of communism in Poland and Hungary earlier in the year firmly in mind and with the intention of preventing anarchy and violence, the government quickly set up so-called 'Round Table' discussions with a range of parties and interest groups, such as the Green Party and the recently formed group of dissidents the New Forum, to consider the future. The first of these discussions took place on 7 December and over the next few months they tackled issues such as drafting a new constitution, dissolving the Stasi, and arranging the first free elections in the GDR.[12] In the autumn of 1989 East German protestors had aligned themselves with the New Forum in the hope of fixing the breakdown of communication between the SED state and society; ultimately, they sought to achieve justice, peace, and democracy within the GDR. However, soon after the fall of the Wall, on 28 November, West German Chancellor Helmut Kohl announced a ten-point programme for 'confederation' between the two states,[13] proposing a free market economy, free elections, West German investment in the GDR, and a federation of states—a precursor to reunification. Reunification was never amongst the aims of the East German protestors, and many among their number expressed a desire to merge more slowly with West Germany, voicing fears that the GDR would be swallowed up by a rapid reunification with the Federal Republic. In spite of this, Kohl's proposal soon gained in popularity.[14]

For the first time in GDR history, on 18 March 1990 East Germans participated in free elections. The results of these elections fundamentally shaped the future of their state, as the Christian Democratic Union, which was strongly in favour of rapid reunification, won with 40 per cent of the votes.[15] In preparation for these elections, an Electoral Commission was set up with fifty members, each of whom represented one of the participating political parties.

In a surprising turn of events, 25-year-old Petra was thrust into the limelight: she was selected to be the delegate for the Independent Women's Association on this commission and, shortly after joining, was elected to be its chairperson by the majority of other delegates. She is keen to emphasize that this was not part of some grand plan for her career but was, rather, entirely unforeseen. 'It was a real accident that I ended up running it,' she explains, recounting why she was given this gargantuan responsibility:

> It was partly due to the fact that I was free when I was needed. It was also completely clear that I had not had a political career in the GDR. I told the Secretary of the Electoral Commission that I had been a member of the SED Party for two years at university during the Gorbachev era, but no one was interested in that. They were just interested in the fact that I had been part of the *Bürgerbewegung* [citizens' movement]. They did not want to choose an older person, for fear that bad things would come out about them later.

In this period of uncertainty, she explains, 'normal people like you and me were suddenly thrust into positions of responsibility'. Petra was responsible for delivering free elections—one of the key demands of the demonstrations. 'If I'd really thought about it,' she says looking back, 'I wouldn't have been able to sleep at night because I would have felt so overcome with the scale of responsibility.' At the time, though, there was little space for reflection.

With her focus now on politics, Petra abandoned her PhD. After the elections, she took up a job working for the GDR's second television channel, and was responsible for a live politics programme. As plans took shape for the new Germany, Petra was able to make programmes free from censorship—a sharp contrast with the ideologically filtered offerings of previous decades. Petra's involvement with the plans for reunification was not confined to her day job. When she left work, Petra joined discussion groups with the Independent Women's Association, the Greens, and the New Forum, and sought to determine the best way for the two countries to merge.

FIGURE 3 Petra Bläss as a delegate of the Independent Women's Association on the East German Electoral Commission in 1990.
© Ullstein bild—ADN-Bildarchiv.

'It was an absolutely crazy time', she recalls.[16] She was most concerned with defending and preserving the rights and benefits that women had in the GDR, in light of the fact that far more women worked there than in the West and were used to having freely available childcare, as well as the fact that abortion laws were far more liberal in the East.[17] Petra was outraged, for example, when the first draft of the reunification treaty mentioned only in one short, dismissive sentence that 'the needs of women and the disabled will be taken care of'.

Unlike many East Germans, then, who felt like they had no say or involvement in how the new Germany was formed (including those who had taken to the streets and campaigned for change[18]), Petra was at the heart of decision-making and used her position to try and protect women's rights and social justice. Ultimately though, she was disappointed that drafts of the reunification treaty were much less of a merging of the two existing constitutions of East and West than she had hoped. So when the communist party re-formed as the Party of Democratic Socialism (*Partei des Demokratischen Sozialismus* or PDS) and approached her to stand as an MP in the first elections in reunited Germany, she accepted. Petra was one of a small minority of East Germans who had secured a place to study at university in the GDR, which might explain why she stayed committed to the same path ideologically when most other GDR citizens jumped ship. A year after joining the newly formed Independent Women's Association in late 1989, she was elected as an MP in the first united German parliament. Since the communists only received 2.4 per cent of the vote across Germany, Petra was one of only seventeen out of 662 MPs who were representing the PDS.[19]

When Petra made her political debut, she was 26 and had very little experience of working in national politics. Adding to what was already a huge challenge was the fact that the other politicians in the *Bundestag* were extremely hostile to the PDS MPs. In the preceding Cold War climate, the Western capitalist system had been derided in the East, but communism had been vilified in Western propaganda. The majority of representatives in the *Bundestag* therefore could not abide having anything to do with the former East and appeared to reject the notion that there was anything to be learned from the GDR's approach to things. As representatives of the PDS, Petra recalls, 'we were shut out, we were the evil ones'. When she took to the podium and made speeches, Christian Democrat MPs called out, 'Forty years of Stasi and SED!' One of her PDS colleagues, Gerd Riegel, found this constant hostility hard to bear, and took his own life. Petra, on the other hand, continued to represent the PDS in parliament until 2003 when she decided that she no longer wanted to be bound by loyalty to one particular party and instead wanted to focus on the actual issues that she felt were important. Political categories, she feels, can sometimes be unhelpful. Since then, she has used her experience in parliament to act as a political consultant.

'I realise that my first twelve years [in reunited Germany] weren't typical,' she reflects. 'I was thrown into the polarized political system in the new Germany. You can't experience it in a more extreme way.' Unlike most SED supporters who lost power and experienced a decline in status with the *Wende*, the events of 1989 offered Petra an unprecedented opportunity to pursue a career in politics. While some East Germans were all too keen to put every aspect of life in the GDR behind them, Petra focused on trying to incorporate what she felt were positive elements of the GDR's policies in reunited Germany.[20] During this time, the PDS continued to win seats in the *Bundestag* because those East Germans who still strongly identified themselves with the GDR felt that the PDS best represented East German interests, in contrast to other parties which seemed to distance themselves from the values and policies that came out of the GDR.[21]

Like many others, Petra felt irritated by the Western assumption that in the GDR East Germans had been constantly under pressure from the state and could not express their views. Whenever Petra explained that her own experience was not like this, people responded by saying that she was defending the East—a charge that she vigorously denies. However, one of her motivations for being a PDS MP was that she felt it important not to write off the heritage of the GDR entirely. It was essential, she believed, to include this heritage as part of the new unified Germany while, in her view, the government in reunited Germany sought to establish its authority in part by distancing itself from it. Whilst acknowledging that the Left made a lot of mistakes in former East Germany, Petra feels there should be greater recognition of the things that were good in the GDR, as well as the things that were bad.

Since Petra was fundamentally happy in the GDR, having enough to eat and working in a field that she had chosen, in the months after the *Wende* she felt embarrassed that so many Easterners flocked to buy things in the West. It seemed to give credence to the insulting remarks about East Germans made by West Germans, who said things like 'Look at them! They're shopping again! Don't they have anything better to do?'[22] To Petra, seeing so many

East Germans with West German plastic bags was degrading, and implied that their lives before had been deficient.[23] Bananas, for example, which had scarcely been available in the GDR, came to be a symbol of the gains made by East Germans after unification. West Germans observed how pleased their Eastern counterparts were to have easy access to bananas which had only tended to be available at Christmas in the GDR, and some of them mocked this. 'How do we know that East Germans have descended from apes?' began one joke. 'The banana shelves are always empty after they've been there.'[24] Petra wanted to distance herself from the East Germans who rushed to gain access to Western goods. 'I'd never wanted for food in the GDR,' she explains, 'nor longed for oranges or bananas. I ate them from time to time, but the fact that they were not available all the time was no big deal.' As one of her contemporaries so aptly put it, 'the Wall had fallen and the path to Aldi [a budget West German supermarket] was open'.[25] Similarly disillusioned with the behaviour of her compatriots, another East German penned a diary entry in the wake of November 1989 expressing dismay that her countrymen 'seemed content to slurp Coca-Cola and appeared to aspire to nothing more'.[26] Petra, too, felt shame that so many Easterners had tried to leave the GDR through the West German embassies in Warsaw, Prague, and Budapest.[27] How could she persuade West German politicians that there were good elements in the GDR, if East Germans them-selves were so keen to bury it?

For Petra, the end of socialism in East Germany was not about the increased shopping opportunities it brought. She had been far more excited at the prospect of going to the exhibition on war and peace in literature held in the Hamburger Bahnhof in West Berlin. After the Wall fell, she remembers, a professor came into the sem-inar and threw the prospectus for the exhibition onto the table saying, 'Now you can go yourselves!'

Neither the Stasi-state nor the *Ostalgie* characterizations mean anything to Petra. She certainly does not remember the GDR as a

Stasi-state, but neither is she nostalgic for it, since she believes the principles of socialism were often not well implemented there. Ultimately, though Petra says she is not an opponent of German reunification, she finds many faults with the new political system, which, in her view, is not very humane and is very fixated on money in contrast to the GDR. She wishes that politicians today were more open to learning from things that did work well in the GDR, rather than rubbishing everything about East Germany to make their own actions appear in a better light.

Carola ~ Seeing the Contradictions

In January 1989 Carola left the GDR. In stark contrast to many more dramatic methods East Germans used to escape to the West, be it scaling the Berlin Wall, digging a tunnel under the border, or taking to the water to swim incognito across the border, Carola simply filled out a successful application for a tourist visa to visit West Germany, and never returned.[1]

In February 1982 travel restrictions for East Germans eased somewhat, with GDR citizens regularly gaining permission to visit immediate family in the West, particularly if there was a special occasion like a wedding, a funeral, or a big birthday.[2] Carola had no one that fitted into this category. Her father, though, had a cousin in West Germany. And this cousin just happened to be turning 75 in January 1989. Taking the chance that no one would check her story, Carola filled in a tourist visa application form, claiming that her reason for travel was visiting her aunt to celebrate her 75th birthday. After filling out the application at the police station, an officer quizzed her on the fact that her 'aunt' was 25 years older than her father—an unlikely age gap between siblings. Carola simply played dumb. At one point during this encounter, the officer left the room leaving Carola alone to wonder what would happen next. A simple telephone call could have revealed that Herr Koehler did not have a 75-year-old sister living in West Germany. Carola did not allow herself to think about how the situation might play out. She tried to appear cool, knowing that she had to endure this interview if she was to make it to the West successfully. Luckily for Carola the call was never made. Her gamble had paid off.

Carola was very much in two minds about whether she would stay in the West when she got there. On the one hand, she knew that if she left for good, she might not see her parents for a very long time. She was also concerned that her parents might encounter problems at work as a result of her flight. On the other hand, she felt that she had come to the end of the road with the GDR. She could see no future for herself in the system and had no desire to conform to the regime's expectations. This was a bad situation to be in at the age of 20, she explains. For many, like Carola, who chafed at the bit in East Germany, it was the utter predictability of life in the GDR which they found claustrophobic: 'You graduate from college or professional school and you have nothing

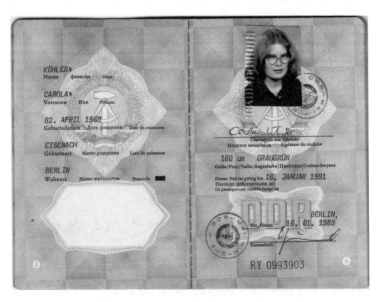

FIGURE 4 Carola's GDR passport.
Courtesy of Carola Koehler.

FIGURE 5 Carola's passport, showing her tourist visa to visit West Germany. Courtesy of Carola Koehler.

to look forward to except thirty-five years of work in the same job. Then you retire; then you can travel to the West; then you die.'[3] The restrictions felt life-inhibiting—'like wearing a corset', Carola ventures. What kind of country had to lock you in to make you stay there? Carola pondered on this as she assessed her options.

Should I stay or should I go? This was the question that nagged at Carola. Could she really up sticks and go, taking only one small backpack of belongings? Was she prepared to leave everything behind that was familiar—her home, her town, her friends, her memories?[4] Others faced a similar dilemma. In an extraordinary case, one of Carola's contemporaries Martin Schneider decided to escape over the wall. When he arrived at the border, he took off his much-loved Western jeans and threw them over the fence to save them from being ripped. Then, in a crisis of confidence, he decided not to flee after all. He was caught and sentenced to one year in prison for attempting to leave the GDR.[5] Martin most likely shared many of Carola's feelings as she was assessing her options.

In a diary entry from November 1988 Carola reveals both how frustrated she was with the GDR and how torn she was about what she should do:

> Restrictions, further repression...this society is becoming less and less humane and harder and harder to live in. Nothing is keeping me here. I'm getting closer and closer to the point of submitting an application to leave the GDR for good. I'm really warming to the idea...We're further than ever from the ideals of freedom, socialism, and democracy. The government has totally deviated from the theories of Marx and Lenin, and has more in common with totalitarian governments like China during the Cultural Revolution or like the present regime in Chile...Is emigration [to the West] giving up? It isn't for me. It would mean a new start for me, a new life, with freedom and individuality.

Carola's preparations for travelling to the West show just how unsure she was about what she would do once she got there. She packed her A level certificates, indicating an intention to leave for good, and yet she only took enough clothing for one week. With a trusted friend from work, she made arrangements for the eventuality that she would not return to the GDR. If, when Carola got to the West, she decided to remain there, she would telephone her friend before the seven-day visa expired. No matter what was said during the conversation, the telephone call itself meant that Carola had decided to stay in the West. The friend would then be responsible for calling Carola's parents to let them know, as well as for arranging the removal of Carola's belongings before the GDR authorities came and cleared the flat, as they did in such circumstances.

Irrespective of what Carola would do in the long term, the first step was to get to the West. Arriving well ahead of time at Berlin-Friedrichstrasse railway station, she hung around nervously, waiting for the night train that would take her across the border. Carola

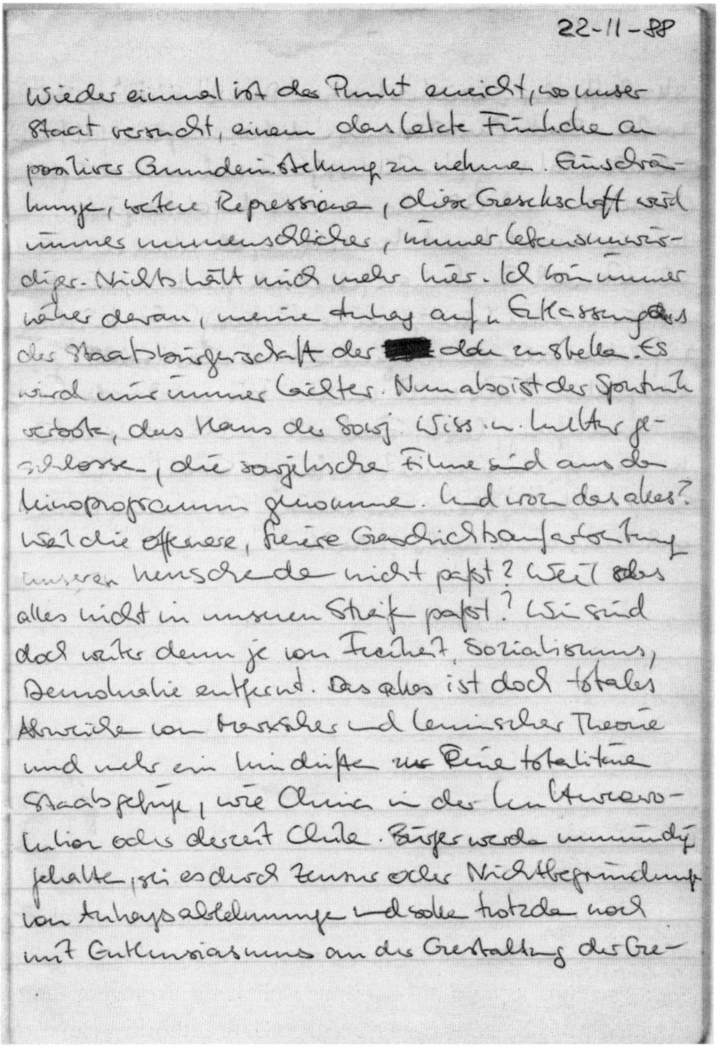

22-11-88

Wieder einmal ist der Punkt erreicht, wo unser Staat versucht, einem das letzte Fünkchen an positiver Grundeinstellung zu nehmen. Einschränkungen, weitere Repressionen, diese Gesellschaft wird immer unmenschlicher, immer lebensunwürdiger. Nichts hält mich mehr hier. Ich bin immer näher daran, meinen Antrag auf Entlassung aus der Staatsbürgerschaft der [redacted] DDR zu stellen. Es wird mir immer leichter. Nun also ist der Sputnik verboten, das Haus der Sowj. Wiss. u. Kultur geschlossen, die sowjetischen Filme sind aus dem Kinoprogramm genommen. Und wozu das alles? Weil die offenere, freiere Geschichtsauffassung unseren Menschen nicht paßt? Weil das alles nicht in unseren Streif paßt? Wir sind doch weiter denn je von Freiheit, Sozialismus, Demokratie entfernt. Das alles ist doch totales Abweichen von Marxscher und Leninscher Theorie und mehr ein Hindriften zu einer totalitären Staatsform, wie China in der Kulturrevolution oder derzeit Chile. Bürger werden unmündig gehalten, sei es durch Zensur oder Nichtbegründung von Antragsablehnungen und sollen trotzdem noch mit Enthusiasmus an der Gestaltung der Ge-

FIGURE 6 Extract from Carola's diary, 22 November 1988.

Courtesy of Carola Koehler.

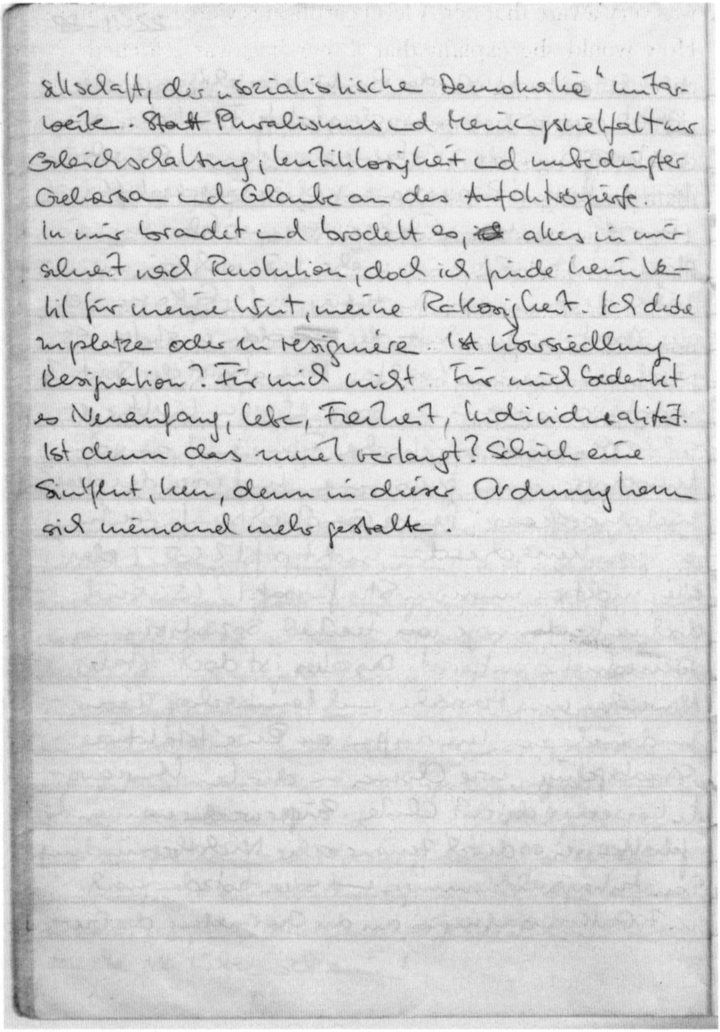

gesellschaft, die „sozialistische Demokratie" unter-
breite. Statt Pluralismus und Meinungsvielfalt nur
Gleichschaltung, Kritiklosigkeit und unbedingter
Gehorsam und Glaube an die Autoritätsgläubige.
In mir brodelt und brodelt es, es alles in mir
schreit nach Resolution, doch ich finde kein Ven-
til für meine Wut, meine Ratlosigkeit. Ich drehe
im Kreise oder ich resigniere. Ist Umsiedlung
Resignation? Für mich nicht. Für mich bedeutet
es Neuanfang, Leben, Freiheit, Individualität.
Ist denn das zuviel verlangt? Schließlich eine
Sintflut, kein, denn in dieser Ordnung kann
sich niemand mehr gestalten.

FIGURE 6 Continued

was very aware that her A level certificates were stashed in her bag. How would she explain that if her bag was searched? No one checked her bag, though. Once settled on the train Carola slept right through to the morning, when she was woken by commuters getting off to go to work in Hessen. She was bursting with excitement, thinking about the new and unknown things that lay ahead. The journey was a necessary evil, which she wanted to get out of the way as quickly as possible, so that she could focus on the future. As Carola crossed the border, she recalls that she deliberately did not dwell on the potential significance of leaving her home behind, instead focusing on what there was to look forward to.

It was never Carola's intention to visit her father's cousin in the West. She had always planned to visit an East German friend who had emigrated to Heidelberg the year previously with the permission of the authorities. Her East German confidante was certain that Carola would stay in the West. Carola had not been so sure. As soon as she got there, though, the prospect of going back just because her parents were in the GDR was not compelling enough.[6] None of her friends in Eisenach had had the same burning desire to escape and they could not understand why she was so unhappy. However, in the six months before her departure, Carola had been living in East Berlin, where she had met others who also wanted to leave the GDR. Most importantly, Carola saw so many new opportunities in the West—the possibility of studying something that she herself had chosen, rather than a choice imposed by government officials, was especially exciting.[7]

Once Carola had made the decision to stay in West Germany, the procedure to make this official was actually quite straightforward. The FRG's Basic Law stated that GDR citizens were also citizens of FRG. All Carola had to do was to go to the refugee registration camp at Giessen. Before long, Carola was studying German literature at Heidelberg University and settling into her new life in the West. Her parents were angry and sad in equal measure when they learned of their daughter's decision. Her father, in particular, had been expecting her to return in time to celebrate his birthday in February. Luckily, however, the severe repercussions that Carola had feared for her parents never came to pass. Her father had to inform his workplace formally and her mother was called to the police station to provide details about Carola's new address, but that was it. And with time Carola's parents came to accept her decision, though it remained sad for all of them that they might not see each other again for years.

It was both the pull of possibilities available in the West as well as the push of the frustrations of life in the East that influenced Carola's decision to stay in the FRG. She was under no illusions that life in the West was perfect—she did not glorify it. She knew that there was poverty in the West in a way that did not exist in the East. And yet, Carola explains, growing up in the East, she had the feeling that everything from the West was somehow more precious; visitors from the FRG even had a certain aura about them. In fact, such was the lure of the West for some young East Germans that when East Berlin schoolboy Ralph H. was asked what he wanted to be when he grew up, instead of saying a train driver or offering another common answer, he said, 'I want to be Grandma because she is the only person in the family who can travel to the West' (permissible because she was a pensioner, the GDR authorities counting on the fact that older people would be less keen to uproot their lives to the West and also being less concerned if they did decide to stay there).[8] Carola loved getting the books, clothes, or records that her grandparents brought back from trips to West Germany. Nevertheless she was less motivated by the material advantages of the West than by the chance life there would give her to focus on what she was really interested in.

Before trying her luck with the falsified tourist visa, Carola had discussed alternative options for leaving the GDR with her best friend. Leaving their parents in a difficult position was one cause for concern. Another worry was that they would not be allowed back to see family and friends in the GDR if they left illegally.

A good option, they agreed, was to find a West German man to marry. They could then live in the West, they reasoned, but visit family in the East when they wanted to.[9] The scheme fell at the first hurdle, however: not only did these girls never meet West German men, the time frame for getting a West German to agree to marriage was also too slow for their purposes.

What frustrated Carola about the GDR above all, it seems, was the impossibility of having an open discussion about anything. As she was growing up, Carola knew that the Stasi were everywhere, observing people in school, in the workplace, and on the street. Occasionally, she explains, she worried that she had said something careless while talking to friends on the train. There was always the fear that people could overhear and misconstrue a conversation conducted in public, leading to problems with the Stasi. Carola craved the intellectual freedom to discuss issues that affected society from every angle, not just a socialist one. Citizenship classes in school, called *Staatsbürgerkunde*, for example, proceeded from the assumption that 'the teachings of Marx are all-powerful because they are true'. These lessons took pupils through history, giving it a Marxist spin from the Ice Age onwards.[10] Socialist ideologues, Carola felt, were trying to fit the circumstances of the late twentieth century with the Marxist teachings from over a hundred years previously.

In marked contrast with Petra, who accepted what she was told in school and believed in the regime's socialist goals, time and again Carola noticed the difference between what she was taught in citizenship lessons and what was happening in daily life. In school, for example, they were always told that the East would soon advance and overtake the West because the socialist system with the economy organized by the state was far superior to the capitalist system of private ownership. Yet, Carola noticed, there were regularly shortages of consumables like fruit, tomato ketchup, and oil, leading to long queues outside shops as people jumped at the opportunities to buy goods as and when they appeared. When the discrepancy was really obvious, she explains, the teachers would say, 'Well, this is what we are working towards. It will be sorted out in a few years.' Carola's doubts about the Party's claims were further reinforced by doing a work-experience placement in a factory, where it became clear to her that loudly trumpeted successes of exceeding production quotas were based on figures plucked from thin air with no basis in reality. The older Carola got, the harder it became for her to ignore the discrepancy between the socialist rhetoric she was taught in school and the reality outside the classroom.[11]

For Carola, church circles provided a release from the relentless need to conform in daily life. Within the safe haven of the church, Carola met other, like-minded young people and had open discussions about how they thought society should be. The church library gave her access to literature that was not widely available in the GDR because it did not reinforce the socialist world view. Carola was very excited to get hold of books by Freud—simply *because* titles by Freud were banned made her think that there must be something really good in them! Everywhere else, Carola says, her mind operated in a schizophrenic way, differentiating between private criticism and public lip-service. It was refreshing, Carola found, to be able to voice views other than those which reinforced Party ideology. Carola's parents, however, were less enthusiastic about their daughter's heavy involvement in the church youth group, and tried to restrict it. Though they were churchgoers themselves, they feared that Carola's close connection with the church might damage her chances of being allowed to study for A levels. This was because only a minority of pupils were able to attend 'extended secondary school' to qualify for university entrance in the GDR (and a mere 10 per cent of each year were then allowed to go to university).

Like many others of her age, Carola was critical of how the East German government airbrushed inconvenient truths which did not fit with the Party image. The deteriorating state of the environment was one of the issues that really bothered Carola. Flying in the face of governmental attempts to suppress the facts, environmental campaigners pointed to the high pollution levels in the GDR caused by heavy industry, be it through releasing waste water from factories into rivers or by polluting the air through the use of brown coal. The chemical plants in Bitterfeld were known to be particularly bad for this. Influenced by the Green Party in the West, more and more informal environmental groups met in the GDR under the protective roofs of the churches. Indeed, by 1989 there were over sixty such groups in East Germany.[12] Since such a high proportion of East Germans worked in industry and construction (48.6 per cent), the GDR was one of the worst polluted countries in Europe in the 1980s.[13] Indeed, by the end of the GDR, seven of the forty-eight types of fish that had existed in East Germany's rivers had died out entirely and a further nine species had become endangered. Furthermore, such was the poor quality of the air in the GDR that the government stopped publishing information about how this damaged the health of its inhabitants in the 1970s.[14] All of this was very worrying for people like Carola who were concerned about protecting the environment.

Frustrated with the GDR government's short-sighted neglect of Green issues, activists like Carola took symbolic action, taking part in the cleaning-up of forests or planting trees. Even if this did not make a massive difference, the rationale was that it was better to do something instead of simply sitting around and bemoaning the state of the environment.[15] Others wrote and disseminated pamphlets highlighting the extent of the pollution in the GDR and raising awareness of the damage caused to the ozone layer by using aerosol cans. Indeed more and more of these pamphlets could be freely accessed at the Environmental Library in the Church of Zion (*Zionskirche*) in East Berlin, which had evaded state control from 1986.[16] The Environmental Library also produced a magazine called *Environmental Pamphlets* (*Umweltblätter*) from April 1987, and this became the most widely circulated underground publication in the GDR. Around this time at the end of the 1980s there were also increasing numbers of protests focused on West German rubbish being transported across the border to be buried in landfill sites in the East.[17] The SED government, like many other dictatorships, was very keen to control its image. Irrespective of the reality, it sought to silence anything that presented the regime in a bad light. It was this that environmental activists sought to change—they hoped to force the government to acknowledge the seriousness of the situation.[18]

Carola also felt restricted by the travel limitations in the GDR from a young age.[19] Living in Eisenach, Carola's family home was only 10 kilometres from the border with West Germany. It was at the end of the motorway for GDR citizens travelling west. From Eisenach, you could travel north, south, or east, but never west. From the age of 12, Carola says, she had a longing to travel further afield, in spite of the fact that her family made use of all the travel options that were permitted, taking holidays in Poland, Romania, Bulgaria, Czechoslovakia, and Hungary.

As Carola got older, she felt the limitations imposed by the East German government all the more keenly. Did she hope for change from within then, I ask her? She certainly wished for greater freedom of travel, greater freedom of expression, and for the government to have more trust in its citizens. But, she says, the regime was so firmly entrenched in its position of power that it was hard to imagine that there would be changes.

So serious were Carola's frustrations with the system that she got to the point of penning a draft application to leave the GDR for good. She wrote:

> This is my urgent application to be released from my GDR citizenship so that I can move to West Germany. I have come to the decision after careful reflection because I feel like an undervalued citizen and therefore feel discriminated against. I find it impossible to live within this governmental set-up, which I see as a totalitarian, Stalinist system, far from the values of socialism, democracy, and individual freedom, far from the theoretical principles of Marx and Lenin, and run by outdated functionaries. I hope to hear about my application very soon. CK.

Interestingly, in the text Carola writes 'ddr' (*Deutsche Demokratische Republik* or German Democratic Republic) in lower case rather than capital letters. This, she explains, was deliberate, and symbolic of the low opinion she had of the East German state.

The minimal prospects for a change in political system also help to explain why Carola and her family consistently conformed to the regime's dictates externally while criticizing it intensely within their own four walls. In private, Carola's parents railed against the ideological narrow-mindedness of the Party. They found the inability to speak freely irksome, and thought the rigged elections a farce. The Koehlers also found the shortages of goods and the limited travel options irritating. However, like everyone else living in East Germany, they had no idea that the Wall would fall and that the regime would crumble. Accordingly, they had to adapt to the situation in which they found themselves. Indeed, as one East German later put it, explaining the overwhelming incentives to conform, 'it is difficult to stand aloof from what supplies your daily bread'.[20] After years of holding out, therefore, Carola's father finally joined the Party in the 1980s to help advance his career. And Carola continued her membership of the East German youth movement, moving from the junior section, the Young Pioneers, to the senior section, the Free German Youth (*Freie Deutsche Jugend* or FDJ), at the age of 14 to enable her to do A levels. In fact, Carola's last school report from 5 July 1986 was full of praise, noting how she was actively engaged in the FDJ and how her views were very much line with those of the state. Carola, then, had obviously been convincing in her outward behaviour at school, in spite of the strong animosity towards the system that she expressed in private.

Getting citizens to toe the line is, of course, precisely what dictators hope to achieve: outward conformity by the majority is essential for the long life of any regime.[21] And if there seems little chance of change in the system, it is understandable that people look to play the system in a way that will advantage them as much as possible.

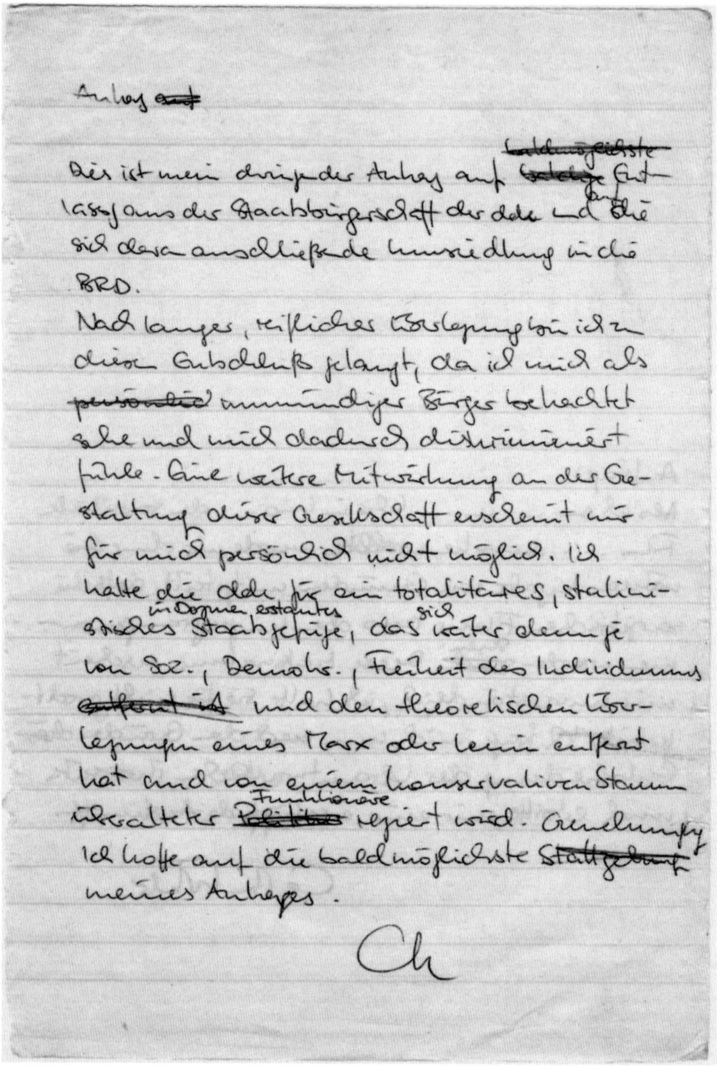
Antrag ~~auf~~

Dies ist mein dringender Antrag auf ~~baldige~~ ~~baldmöglichste~~ Entlassung aus der Staatsbürgerschaft der DDR und auf die
sich daran anschließende Umsiedlung in die
BRD.
Nach langer, reiflicher Überlegung bin ich zu
diesem Entschluß gelangt, da ich mich als
~~persönlich~~ unmündiger Bürger betrachtet
sehe und mich dadurch diskriminiert
fühle. Eine weitere Mitwirkung an der Gestaltung dieser Gesellschaft erscheint mir
für mich persönlich nicht möglich. Ich
halte die DDR für ein totalitäres, stalini-
stisches im Dogma erstarrtes Staatsgefüge, das sich weiter denn je
von Soz., Demokr., Freiheit des Individuums
~~entfernt ist~~ und den theoretischen Über-
legungen eines Marx oder Lenin entfernt
hat und von einem konservativen Stamm
überalteter Funktionäre ~~Politiker~~ regiert wird. Genehmigung
Ich hoffe auf die baldmöglichste ~~Stattgebung~~
meines Antrages.

Ch

FIGURE 7 Carola's draft application to leave the GDR for good. Courtesy of Carola Koehler.

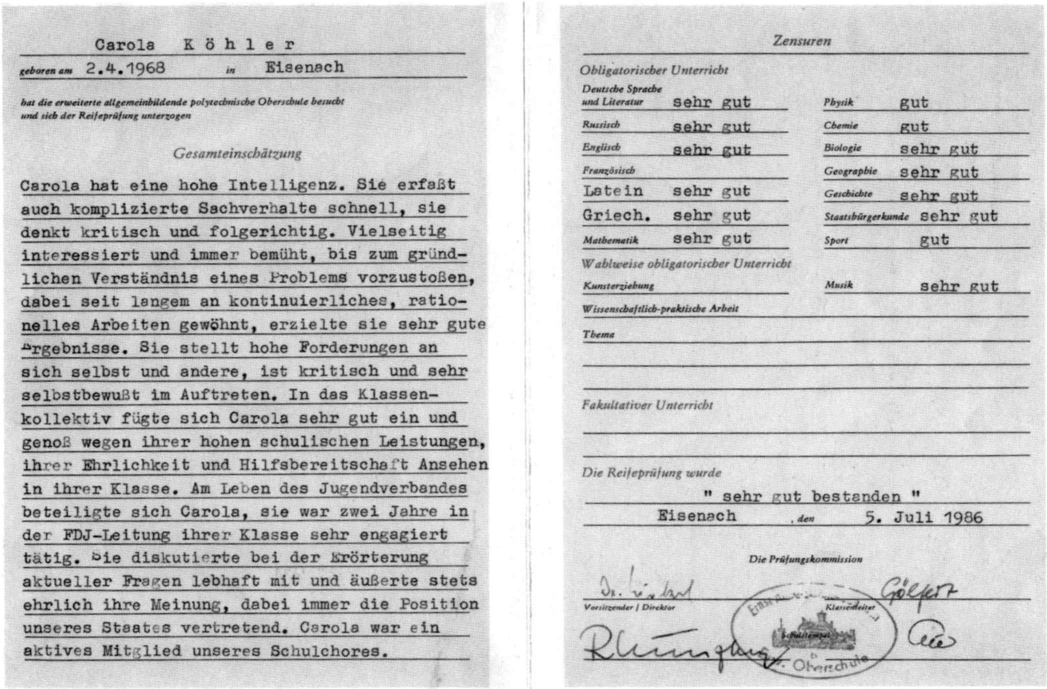

Carola Köhler

geboren am 2.4.1968 in Eisenach

hat die erweiterte allgemeinbildende polytechnische Oberschule besucht und sich der Reifeprüfung unterzogen

Gesamteinschätzung

Carola hat eine hohe Intelligenz. Sie erfaßt auch komplizierte Sachverhalte schnell, sie denkt kritisch und folgerichtig. Vielseitig interessiert und immer bemüht, bis zum gründlichen Verständnis eines Problems vorzustoßen, dabei seit langem an kontinuierliches, rationelles Arbeiten gewöhnt, erzielte sie sehr gute Ergebnisse. Sie stellt hohe Forderungen an sich selbst und andere, ist kritisch und sehr selbstbewußt im Auftreten. In das Klassenkollektiv fügte sich Carola sehr gut ein und genoß wegen ihrer hohen schulischen Leistungen, ihrer Ehrlichkeit und Hilfsbereitschaft Ansehen in ihrer Klasse. Am Leben des Jugendverbandes beteiligte sich Carola, sie war zwei Jahre in der FDJ-Leitung ihrer Klasse sehr engagiert tätig. Sie diskutierte bei der Erörterung aktueller Fragen lebhaft mit und äußerte stets ehrlich ihre Meinung, dabei immer die Position unseres Staates vertretend. Carola war ein aktives Mitglied unseres Schulchores.

Zensuren

Obligatorischer Unterricht

Deutsche Sprache und Literatur	sehr gut
Russisch	sehr gut
Englisch	sehr gut
Französisch	
Latein	sehr gut
Griech.	sehr gut
Mathematik	sehr gut
Physik	gut
Chemie	gut
Biologie	sehr gut
Geographie	sehr gut
Geschichte	sehr gut
Staatsbürgerkunde	sehr gut
Sport	gut

W ahlweise obligatorischer Unterricht

Kunsterziehung	
Wissenschaftlich-praktische Arbeit	
Thema	
Musik	sehr gut

Fakultativer Unterricht

Die Reifeprüfung wurde " sehr gut bestanden "

Eisenach , den 5. Juli 1986

Die Prüfungskommission

Vorsitzender I Direktor   Klassenleiter

FIGURE 8 Carola's last school report from 5 July 1986. Courtesy of Carola Koehler.

So strong was Carola's belief that nothing could change the SED's stranglehold on power that even Honecker's resignation in October 1989 provoked mixed feelings in her.[22] Soon after Carola left the GDR for good in January, her mother booked a trip to Hungary for the autumn, so that they could meet. The news that the General Secretary of the SED was stepping down greeted them on their last day of holiday, and they were unsure what to make of it. In spite of the reforms in Poland and Hungary inspired by Gorbachev's policies of glasnost and perestroika, the GDR leadership had been dogged in resisting such changes, even restricting visits to Poland and Hungary in a bid to stem calls for greater freedom to travel. Kurt Hager, the GDR's ideology chief, summarized the SED's intransigent position regarding the potential for reform by stating, 'just because your neighbour has changed his wallpaper, there is no need to start tearing off your own'.[23] It is unsurprising, then, that Carola and her parents were unsure how to interpret Honecker's resignation. They were concerned, Carola explains, that the Soviets might invade East Germany to stop big changes from taking place. 'In a way,' Carola says, 'we wondered whether it might be better if nothing happened, because we feared that the Party might impose greater restrictions.'[24] Already at this stage, around 14,000 East Germans had taken up the opportunity presented by the opening-up of the Austro-Hungarian border to go to West Germany, so there was definitely a widespread awareness that something was afoot. But there was no sense of inevitability about proceedings. Indeed the decision by the West German *Bild-Zeitung* that same year to stop referring to the GDR in inverted commas was an indicator that West Germans were not expecting the GDR to fall.[25] Events then happened far more quickly than Carola expected.[26]

Living in Heidelberg, Carola was far away from the action when the Wall fell in November 1989. And her life continued relatively unaffected in the months that followed. East Germans did not visit Heidelberg in the same numbers as they did border towns like Kassel. Carola visited West Berlin out of curiosity, but found it totally foreign: both the people and the buildings looked very different. The fall of the Wall did, however, mean that Carola could travel back to East Germany to spend Christmas with her parents in December. And though her father had been initially angry when Carola decided not to return from West Germany earlier in the year, his anger had mellowed into understanding with time. In the years that followed, Carola's decision to leave did not cause long-lasting damage to the relationship with her parents. The whole family were just pleased that they could see each other whenever they wanted.

Six years later, in 1996, Carola moved to Berlin to continue her studies at the Humboldt University. There she found that her East German past was more significant. The GDR, she explains, was a common topic of conversation at the time. She was shocked to find people younger than herself defending the old system; some East Germans were even critical of her decision to leave. At this point, the GDR had no positive associations whatsoever for her.

When Carola first moved to the West in January 1989, she felt that the world was her oyster. So many choices and possibilities were open to her. Though she had not glorified the West as a paradise, she did initially delight in her new-found freedom.[27] Soon, however, she came to realize that freedom is relative, and that even within a democracy there are notable limits. 'Freedom of travel', she explains, 'is only possible if you can actually afford it. And how significant is freedom of speech if no one listens to you and you're not really heard?'

Looking back on the GDR, Carola feels that money played far less of a role there. Within the new capitalist Germany, life is all about making the maximum profit, she finds, which is not a very humane system. Her ideal set-up, she explains, would be a world in which everyone is okay—not necessarily with a really high standard of living, but with enough to eat and drink, access to education and culture, and the possibility of living in peace. Unsurprisingly, freedom of movement is also of central importance in Carola's ideal world. Such a system, she acknowledges, does not exist yet.

Despite enjoying the new opportunities in the West, Carola explains that the transition to a united Germany has been tough for many East Germans. Sometimes, she says, she feels separate from West Germans because they were taught in another culture and another school system. Significantly too, Carola believes that East Germans of her age are still at a disadvantage professionally, several decades after the fall of the Wall. She puts this down to the dominance of West German cultural codes and expectations, as well as West Germans having more established networks of contacts to draw on. So ingrained is this view that when she sees an East German of her generation in an important position of authority, like Angela Merkel as German Chancellor or Joachim Gauck as German President, Carola is always rather surprised.

Reflecting on her GDR past, Carola believes there will always be a difference between Easterners and Westerners of her generation because of their contrasting socialization. Reacting to her GDR past, like many other East Germans Carola recoils from mass organizations, making a conscious decision not to join a political party, for example.[28] Though Carola has successfully integrated into unified Germany, holding down a steady job in publishing, she still says that she finds common ground more easily with East Germans, with whom she feels an immediate sense of connectedness in comparison to people from West Germany. Walls may fall and governments may change, but habits and patterns of behaviour established over decades evidently take longer to shift.

Ultimately, Carola found life in the GDR hugely claustrophobic. It grated on her that the ideology she was fed at school so patently did not tally with her experience of daily life. She found it frustrating that there were so few places where she could voice her opinion freely, and she hankered after a new life with greater room for individuality, as well as greater freedom of travel and freedom of expression. Given that Carola actively chose to move to West Germany before the Berlin Wall fell, it is perhaps unsurprising that she had such a smooth transition into life in reunited Germany.

3
Lisa ~ Accepting the Circumstances

'What's it like with all that unemployment?' Lisa asked her uncle, who was visiting from West Germany in the late 1970s. She was in her early teens at the time and curious to learn more about life on the other side of the Wall. High unemployment was just one of the negative things that Lisa had been taught about West Germany at school. With nothing else to compare it to, she believed the East German propaganda which portrayed West Germany as the enemy, and she genuinely thought that the Berlin Wall was there to protect the GDR from the West.[1]

Since she had known nothing else, Lisa did not find the limited travel opportunities for GDR citizens restrictive. She grew up in the 1960s and 1970s at a time when it was difficult to travel and she operated under the assumption that this would never change.[2] Unlike Carola, who took a great risk when she escaped from the GDR, it did not even cross Lisa's mind to leave. West Germany was simply a country on the map, albeit a country that spoke the same language, but it was just an accepted fact for Lisa that she could not go there. Lisa made the most of the choices that were on offer, visiting Poland, Czechoslovakia, Bulgaria, and Hungary, but she did not feel that she was missing out by not being able to go further afield.[3] 'It is not like I would experience the restrictions if they were put on me now, nearly twenty-five years later', she says.

In that era, Lisa explains, foreign travel was far less of a mass-leisure pursuit than it has become in the age of the Internet and budget airlines, and this was the case in the West as well as East Germany. Like many others of her age, Lisa did not dwell on what she could not do, but rather focused on the things she could do.[4]

Living in East Berlin, the capital of the GDR, where there was lots going on, such as plays and films, parties, and discos, Lisa reasons that there were many distractions on the doorstep and therefore more opportunities to let off steam than elsewhere in the GDR.[5] Everyone could find something to suit their interests, she believes, echoing the conclusion of West German diplomat Günter Gaus, that the SED leadership was able to maintain its stranglehold on power for forty years because there were niches into which ordinary East Germans could withdraw from the demands of the system.[6] While Lisa found many of these in East Berlin, other East Germans found non-political havens in their dachas (small summer houses out in the German countryside), where individuals could retreat from the gaze of the state.[7]

With no other experience of how daily life could be, Lisa felt content in the GDR. She felt no kind of envy towards her Western relatives, she explains, because 'my ideals were not about money or travel, but rather about living humanely together in harmony with others'. There was no reason, she felt, to long to live in the West.[8] Lisa, like many other East Germans I have spoken to, observes that money played far less of an important role in the GDR in comparison to united Germany.[9] With food and rent subsidized, life was affordable in the GDR. More frequently it was a lack of readily available goods, rather than a lack of money, which stopped people getting hold of what they needed.[10] When goods were available, therefore, people often bought them in bulk, irrespective of whether they were running short, not knowing when the supplies would next be available.[11] Frequent shortages, Lisa believes, made people more creative and encouraged a system of bartering in communities. Some people grew vegetables and flowers which they could exchange for items in short supply. Carpenters and mechanics, amongst others, offered their services to locals, knowing that they could call on the help of others when they were lacking certain food or other items.[12] For car owners, keeping on good terms with the local mechanic was wise, as car parts were notoriously difficult to come by in the GDR.

Talking about the shortages at the time, one East German explained, 'We've got masses of cauliflower at the moment. Peppers are in short supply. And fruit—we've got lemons, but bananas and oranges are a rarity, and I've only seen kiwis on Western television. The most important thing for an East German to have to combat shortages is "Vitamin B" ("B" for *Beziehungen*, which means connections).'[13] Living in a society where there were fewer options, there was more to gain from knowing people. All of this, East Germans from both the towns and the countryside later said, created the sense that everyone was in it together—negotiating need and shortages bound them to each other. After the *Wende*, though, when the shortages decreased, so too did the sense of togetherness and connections became less important.[14] In the GDR, an East German might have approached a neighbour with an apple tree to get the essential ingredients for an apple cake. In reunited Germany there are always apples in the supermarkets and so there is less incentive to interact with the neighbours.[15]

Lisa, though, had never felt the need to build up a strong network of connections. She recalls enjoying eating tinned pineapple that she bought in an Intershop,[16] but did not mind that she could not eat it all the time. Even though she now really appreciates the easy access to exotic fresh fruit that did not exist in the GDR, at the time she never wanted for enough to eat. However, she lived in East Berlin, which was generally far better supplied than the rest of the GDR. Her stepfather, furthermore, had relatives in West Berlin, which meant that their family had greater access to Western goods than those without contacts in the West. All of this helps to explain why Lisa, unlike many other East Germans who were envious of the Western consumer world, did not long for a more Western lifestyle.[17]

Looking back over the twenty-five years she spent living in the GDR, Lisa recalls a handful of occasions where state politics entered her daily life. Aged 10, she remembers reading a West German news magazine, *Die Stern*, which her stepfather, a publisher, had brought back from West Germany after attending the international Frankfurt Book Fair. As she was poring over the magazine, Lisa came across a headline that she found puzzling: 'FRG buys 5,000 prisoners from the GDR'. Confused, she asked her stepfather, 'How can West Germany buy people from East Germany?' Although the GDR had thirty-nine newspapers, each of these was controlled by the SED, so it was no wonder that Lisa noticed the West German headline which did not fit with the SED's smooth narrative of the GDR's inherent superiority over the West. Lisa's stepfather was unhappy that she had seen the article, and hastily got up to leave the room to avoid talking about it. Later, Lisa came to understand that it would have been hard for her stepfather to explain the situation to a 10-year-old. At the time, though, Lisa wondered what she had said that was wrong.

Lisa's family contact with West Germany nearly got her in trouble on another occasion. Through her West German uncle, Lisa received a pair of much-coveted Western 'Wrangler' jeans when she was still at school. The GDR did not make 'proper' jeans, Lisa explains, and there was only one other girl in the class who had a pair. So sought-after were they that before wearing her Wranglers to school, Lisa asked the other girl Hanna whether she would mind if she wore hers as well.[18] On 8 May, the day Germany surrendered at the end of the Second World War in 1945, the GDR laid commemorative wreaths at memorials throughout the country, using it as a propaganda opportunity to emphasize how the Russians had 'liberated' ordinary Germans from the Nazis. On that day Lisa's school all went to the local memorial and Hanna had been chosen to lay the wreath. However, when the teacher noticed that Hanna was wearing Western jeans, Lisa was picked instead. Lisa was actually wearing her Wranglers but because they were not so obviously Western the teacher did not notice. Though there were no serious consequences for Hanna on this occasion, the story goes to show how sensitive the Party was about any signs of contact with the West. Wearing Western clothing implied that the clothing provided in the GDR was inadequate and this could not be tolerated by the teachers, irrespective of the reality in which clothing was not always in abundant supply. For the same reason, many East Germans recall turning Western plastic bags inside out before they used them.[19]

On another occasion, Lisa's obliviousness to the regime's rules led to a brush with GDR police. When a friend came from Rostock to visit Lisa in East Berlin in the early 1980s, Lisa gave her a tour around, showing the friend where she had grown up. As it happened, as a child Lisa had always played in the *Grenzgebiet* border area, right next to the Berlin Wall. To give her friend a close-up view, Lisa took her behind the sign forbidding citizens to go any further, whereupon they were accosted by a border guard, who demanded that they get into the police van to be taken for questioning. Though Lisa found the whole thing ludicrous and rather funny, when they were locked into the van, she realized that this was serious. Lisa and her friend were then interrogated separately under the very serious charge of having 'violated the borders' of the GDR. Eventually, however, they were both released. Looking back on the incident, Lisa says, 'I thought the whole thing was hilarious...I was then told that I might not be allowed to continue studying because I had violated the border. But somehow I saw it as amusing and could not take it seriously. It seemed so pointless and illogical. I didn't feel threatened by it.'

In these three episodes, Lisa either asked an awkward question, wore the wrong clothing, or went into forbidden territory. In different contexts these scenarios could all have been much more serious: other East Germans faced far greater penalties for doing similar things. No doubt the fact that Lisa brushed up (admittedly very lightly) against the boundaries of the regime and came away unscathed informs her relatively benign image of the GDR. On these and other occasions, she certainly felt the limits of the system, but as she explains, 'the GDR was my home. I grew up in this country, surrounded by the values it espoused.'

As well as family background, circumstances, and luck, personality too plays a part in explaining how people react to the situation in which they find themselves. Lisa was easy-going by nature, and was content enough with life under SED rule, even though the system made her life harder. She had gone straight into training as a typesetter aged 16 rather than studying for A levels. After a couple of years as a typesetter, Lisa then did her A levels at night school with a view to going on to university. This was an unorthodox career route in the GDR. Since Lisa had trained as a typesetter, in the GDR planned economy it did not make sense for her to be allowed to study again as it was not deemed to be in the interests of society as a whole. Though Lisa actually wanted to study German literature, after several attempts she was finally allocated a place on a course in Berlin preparing her to become an English and German teacher. The whole process had been made much difficult by the government rules and regulations, and she did not even get to study for the degree she wanted. Others might have given up and criticized the regime heavily. Not Lisa. Navigating the constraints of the system, she persevered to find a way of studying at university.

There was another occasion too, which might have caused Lisa to turn against the regime but for her easy-going personality. Aged 16, Lisa had an older boyfriend, Peter,[20] who came from a very 'Red' family on the outskirts of Berlin. Peter's father was an army officer and a loyal supporter of the socialist government. Peter wished to follow in his father's footsteps and train to be an army officer over an extended three-year period, as opposed to the obligatory eighteen-month stint that all young men had to complete after school. When the time came to join up, however, Peter's suitability was called into doubt. Stasi officers tracked down Peter, finding him at Lisa's house, and subjected him to intensive questioning. Lisa's family kept in touch with their relatives in West Germany, and Peter was tainted by his association with Lisa. His dreams of becoming an army officer were brought prematurely to an end. With careers made or lost on such fine margins, it is no wonder that many East German parents kept an eye on whom their children were spending time with.[21]

In the autumn of 1989, Lisa was an active participant in the women's movement. Like many others, including Petra, she had no wish to leave East Germany, but was rather keen to see improvements in the way GDR society was run. It was a busy time for her. Alongside her commitment to the women's movement, she was pregnant with her first child and was also finishing her university degree. The day the Wall fell, Lisa had met a friend early in the evening on the Frankfurter Allee. Soon after she returned home, her partner rushed in at around 9 p.m. and told her what he had heard on the radio. He explained that he was planning to drive across to the West and join the street party on the Kurfürstendamm, West Berlin's most famous shopping street. Lisa explains that she was initially confused about how he was going to travel to West Berlin, but he said, 'Everyone's going. I heard it on the radio!' Her partner, like many others, was eager to make it across to West Berlin quickly for fear that the Wall would be closed up again.[22] With a bit of persuasion, Lisa agreed to join him on the trip. Unlike half the families in the GDR, who were either saving up for a car or waiting (sometimes years) for it to arrive after they had ordered it, Lisa and her partner had a car. Like many East German car owners that night, they sat in a massive traffic jam waiting to cross the border. The streets were packed with people buzzing with anticipation and excitement as they made their way to West Berlin. Once across the Bormholmer Strasse border, they decided to visit Lisa's cousin in Kreuzberg. Not knowing the way, Lisa rolled down her window to ask another driver for directions and he led them

FIGURE 9 East Germans are welcomed as they drive their Trabant into West Berlin on the morning of 10 November 1989.
© Robert Wallis/Corbis.

part of the way there, where they met her cousin, even though it was midnight. They then drove down the Kurfürstendamm and looked at the Brandenburg Gate from the Western side. Some people, who later became known as 'Wall woodpeckers', had taken little hammers and were chipping pieces off the Wall as souvenirs.[23] Others were drinking in the details of West Berlin's streets, which were much more colourful than their East Berlin counterparts, with graffiti and brightly coloured advertising that was not to be found in the GDR.[24] Lisa's boyfriend took lots of photographs and they chatted to others on the street who asked where they were from. Finally, at 3 a.m. they had an early breakfast in West Germany before returning home over the border.

Lisa recalls how exciting the atmosphere was on the night of the *Mauerfall* (fall of the Wall). She had grown up with this Wall and now it was open.[25] 'The West had been a white speck on the horizon when we were living divided by a wall', she explains.

FIGURE 10 'Wall woodpeckers', 12 November 1989.
© Ulrich Hässler/dpa/Corbis.

Suddenly that white speck had become a real place. What followed in the months and years afterwards, Lisa experienced as extremely enriching. Unlike in the GDR, where everything was planned by the state, including what jobs individuals would do, in the FRG life was far less structured and each individual had to forge their own path. This, Lisa says, was quite a shift. For her this was positive, as it gave her many more options, both in her work and in her spare time. She initially worked as a teacher before taking up a job in a publishing house as an editor, alongside her primary job as a novelist.

Lisa, it seems, made the best of the circumstances in which she found herself before and after the *Wende*. The fact that she did not fight the system or hold strongly critical views of the regime in some senses make her story less obviously newsworthy than the more dramatic tales of resistance.[26] Nonetheless, her story is typical of many. Coming to the end of our interview, Lisa says, 'I was brought up in this system. When I was living in the system, there were many things I did not have the distance to challenge. I did not have another perspective.'[27] Everyday life did not feel political: it was about meeting friends, falling in love, and going about your daily business.[28] Ultimately, Lisa knew no other world than the GDR, and therefore quite understandably did not view her situation as especially restricted. It was actually only after the *Wende* that it became clear what she had missed out on.[29]

4
Mario ~ Feeling the Regime's Wrath

The old Stasi prison in Berlin now has a café and a shop where you can buy postcards of the prison. Who would you send these to? I wonder as I wait for Mario, a former inmate, who has agreed to meet me for an interview. Shortly after half past ten a tall lean man comes in, dog in tow. He deposits the dog behind the counter with the receptionists before greeting me and leading me down a long corridor to a quiet room for our interview. Mario comes to the prison three times a month to give tours. All the guides at Hohenschönhausen prison were once incarcerated here. Each of them tells their story to remind people of the brutal side of the East German dictatorship, which is so often remembered with nostalgia as a paternalistic state providing employment and a safety net for all.

Mario, who is now 43, turns the clock back to when he was 16 to begin his story. He explains that on leaving school, he, like all his other peers who were not going on to do A levels, had to get a job within a limited number of weeks or risk prison. With this in mind, his father arranged a position for him as a waiter. Mario was not thrilled at the prospect, having set his sights on becoming an actor, but he gradually grew accustomed to his work and found release by dancing the night away in various gay clubs in East Berlin. Being homosexual was not explicitly forbidden but it was still a sign of deviance, a sign of being part of a subculture not controlled by the

FIGURE 11 Sixteen-year-old Mario on holiday in 1984.
Courtesy of Mario Röllig.

state.[1] There were always Stasi informants, colloquially known as *Horch und Guck* (Eyes and Ears), amid the partygoers.[2] Nonetheless it was not specifically Mario's sexuality which brought him into conflict with the regime.

After some time training as a waiter, Mario took up a position serving customers at Schönefeld, East Berlin's main airport. There he became friendly with a politician from West Berlin called Gottfried who travelled through regularly, and they started a relationship.[3] It might seem surprising that Mario and Gottfried were able to sustain their relationship, given that they lived on opposite sides of the Berlin Wall. However, for West German citizens in the 1980s, it was actually quite straightforward to get a day visa or even a longer one, provided that you were not a former Nazi or a former citizen of the GDR who might seek to undermine the basic tenets of the socialist state. West Berliners could go to several offices to apply for a visa to visit the GDR. One such place was behind Zoo railway station, another was in a shopping centre in Steglitz.[4] Applicants would then hear if they had permission for their visit within two to fourteen days. On the day of travel, West Berliner visitors to the GDR like Gottfried would take their passports to the border, where their name would be checked on a computer by a border guard to ensure that they were allowed to travel. They would then hand over 25 West German Marks for each day that they were spending in the GDR and they would receive 25 East German Marks for each day in return. These were the conditions of travel and West German travellers had to comply, in spite of the fact that 25 West German Marks was worth a lot more in real terms than 25 East German Marks. Not only this, but West German visitors either had to spend all the money they exchanged or hand over their remaining cash when returning to the West by 'donating' it to the Red Cross in the GDR. Since the GDR was always short of West German currency and American dollars, the GDR visa authorities were generally quite lenient about which West Germans were allowed to travel across the border. Gottfried travelled across to the GDR quite often on day visas to see Mario, and together they would eat in restaurants, go for walks, and dance in discos. In this way they were able to sustain their relationship. However, like all those West Berliners who travelled across to East Berlin on day visas, Gottfried had to leave the GDR by two o'clock the following morning. Mario recalls many a time when he said a regretful goodbye to Gottfried at the so-called Palace of Tears (*Tränenpalast*)—the colloquial name given to the former border crossing at Berlin-Friedrichsstrasse railway station, because it was where so many East Germans said goodbye to Western friends and relatives travelling back to the FRG and West Berlin.[5]

Picking up on Mario's relationship with a West German politician, the Stasi approached him and asked him to pass on information about Gottfried. The Stasi was particularly keen to find out about what was happening in West German politics, because in the competitive Cold War climate, they hoped to use this information

to the GDR's advantage. Mario explains that the Stasi had opera-
tives in West Germany who would bribe West German politicians
to vote a certain way on parliamentary policies, with the aim of
undermining and influencing politics there. Mario, however, declined
the Stasi's request, and this is where his problems with the state
began.

Following his refusal to collaborate, Mario was demoted from his
job as a waiter to doing the washing-up. He was also followed by the
Stasi. They were blatant about it, he explains. They would get their
camera out very ostentatiously so that Mario knew he was being
photographed and under observation.[6] It was around this time that
Mario decided to try to leave the GDR: 'It was at this point that I
thought even if there's a 90 per cent chance that I'll be shot, I want
to leave. I can't stand it for one more day. I thought, even if I have to
sleep under a bridge in the West it would be better than continuing
to live here.' It was actually illegal for East Germans to leave the
GDR permanently and the Stasi went to great lengths to enforce
this, even though the GDR had signed the Helsinki Treaty in August
1975, which stated that it was a basic right to be able to leave one's
own country. The only change for East Germans after Helsinki was
a slight relaxation in the travel restrictions: they were allowed to
apply for a tourist visa to visit relatives in the West but whether this
visa would be granted was entirely up to the authorities.[7] These visa
conditions were of no use to Mario, however, who wanted to leave
for good.

Mario's solution was to escape illegally. Given that the border
with West Germany was observed by approximately 50,000 border
guards in watchtowers and on the ground who were sanctioned to
shoot anyone trying to escape, not to mention the land mines and
self-firing devices placed on the border strip as deterrents, Mario
decided not to try and breach the Wall in Germany. Instead, he
chose to go through the Eastern bloc, specifically to Yugoslavia via
Hungary. He settled on Yugoslavia because it was not a Warsaw
Pact country, and therefore was not bound by the 1955 terms which

assured mutual defence between eight of the communist states within the Eastern bloc. This meant that Yugoslavia had a more liberal brand of socialism under Tito.[8] Staying with a friend in Hungary, Mario concocted a plan to swim across the River Donau at its narrowest point to Yugoslavia.[9] He then planned to travel to West Germany from there.

When the day of his escape came, 25 June 1987, he changed into his swimming kit and began to make his way towards the border. All of a sudden he was under fire, bullets whizzing past. He made a run for it but was caught—not, it turns out, by the border police but by a local man not far off his own age of 19, who had been bribed to guard the border. Mario begged his captor to let him go. The young Hungarian was clearly torn about what to do, but with tears in his eyes he explained that if he let Mario go, he himself would be sent to prison. Understandably, as he was handed over to the border police, Mario felt extremely scared. When he planned his escape, Mario explained, he had considered two outcomes— either that he would be successful or that he would be shot dead. Around 1,000 people were shot dead attempting to escape across the Berlin Wall or the 1,378-kilometre inner German border, and between 200,000 and 250,000 East Germans were imprisoned for political reasons between 1961 and 1989—most commonly for trying to escape the GDR, the crime being *Republikflucht* (flight from the Republic).[10]

After sharing a cell overnight with a Romanian prisoner who was too scared to talk to him, Mario and eight other young people who had attempted to escape were flown handcuffed back to Berlin. Upon arrival, Mario was bundled into a windowless vehicle disguised as a van from the East Berlin department store 'Centrum Warenhaus', alongside a handful of others. It was 30 degrees centigrade outside, but inside the van it was probably 10 degrees hotter. Like the other prisoners, Mario was locked into a box smaller than a wardrobe, forcing him to be hunched up with very little breathing space. In the pitch-black, the prisoners silently made their journey into the unknown, with armed Stasi officers guarding them menacingly with large guns. Mario could tell that they were on the motorway to start with because the road was smooth, and then he sensed that they were in a town, because the roads were bumpier. At one point, he says, the van stopped at crossroads and he could hear pedestrians talking outside. He thought about screaming, he explains, but he was afraid of being shot by the guard. The fear of the unknown is what Mario remembers. All the guards said was 'We're from the *Staatssicherheit* [Stasi] and you're being taken to our special prison', but, as Mario explains, 'You couldn't help fearing for the worst, that they'd take us into a wood and shoot us.' About four hours later, sleep-deprived, hungry, and scared, the prisoners arrived at what later turned out to be Hohenschönhausen Stasi prison in East Berlin. At the time, they had little idea of where they were, but given the length of the journey, Mario assumed that they were in some remote part of the German countryside. If the van had driven directly from the airport to the prison, this would have taken forty minutes. The long drive was all part of a deliberate tactic of disorientation.

Wherever Mario thought he was, the scene upon arrival was not a pleasant one. Looking back, he felt like he had walked onto the set of a Nazi horror film: uniformed men with large rubber batons glowered menacingly as he disembarked from the van which was already parked inside a garage so as not to disclose the location. Blindingly strong, bright lights fell on the prisoners, disorientating them further in the otherwise dark garage. Mario had never been treated anything like this before. He was totally taken aback and shocked to his core. He was then strip-searched by a Stasi officer, who stood there in uniform with rubber gloves on, shouting, 'Take your clothes off!' Mario took his clothes off down to his underwear whereupon the guard shouted, 'Everything!' Why is this necessary? Mario wondered. 'I had to spread my arms and legs wide and the guard explored every orifice of my body with his hands in rubber gloves,' Mario recalls. 'It was very painful.' At this point the officer gave Mario a piece of paper to read which stated his rights. In his shocked and disorientated state, the only thing Mario was able to take in was that he had the right to wear his own clothes. He raised this with the officer who said, 'You should have thought of that before. Now you're just prisoner 328, the number of your cell on the third floor.' Mario was then given the prison uniform: a dark blue tracksuit and brown shoes, as well as red underpants. On the shelves Mario noticed that most of the underpants were blue, so he did wonder why he had red ones. Perhaps, he thinks, it was because he was a gay man. Mario remembers that he was given trousers that were far too big, so he had to hold them up, causing the guards to laugh at him. Walking to his cell for the first time,

FIGURE 12 Photograph of Mario on his arrival at the Stasi prison in Hohenschönhausen, Berlin on 3 July 1987. This picture was in Mario's Stasi file which he gained access to at the Stasi Archives (BStU) after the Wall fell.
Courtesy of Mario Röllig.

Mario recalls that the corridor seemed incredibly long. In retrospect he thinks that this was deliberate, so that prisoners felt the overwhelming power of the system. The building as a whole, he believes, was designed to make you feel like a really small person.

Eventually he arrived at cell 328, where he would spend the next three months alone, alongside a bed and a latrine. There were certain 'House Rules' in the prison, all designed to make the experience unpleasant and uncomfortable. During the day, prisoners were not allowed to sit or lie on their beds. There was no fresh air and the cell windows were frosted to prevent the prisoners from seeing outside. At night, however, they were not allowed to sleep on their sides and were required to have their arms out of the covers and to each side of the body when sleeping. If prisoners turned onto their sides during sleep guards would bang on the cell door violently until they moved onto their backs. A 100-watt light bulb would come on at random through the night, jolting prisoners from their sleep. All this contributed to many broken nights and sleep deprivation.[11]

When the cell door was opened, prisoners were expected to stand in a certain position and identify themselves by number.[12] The guards interacted with the prisoners like robots, Mario says. They issued short, set commands that they had learned: 'Stand up!', 'Turn around!', 'Come!', 'Go!' Mario would always try to talk to them, asking things like 'Have you got children?' Mostly these questions were met with silence or Mario was told to be quiet. Mario later heard the story of a guard who opened the door and asked 'Can I help you?' when he heard that the inmate was crying. This guard was immediately switched to work in another place. In the corridor there were video cameras, and the cells were bugged. It seems, then, that if guards were ever friendly, they were replaced.

A traffic light system operated in the prison. It was designed to ensure that prisoners never saw one another. When a guard saw a red light it meant that the corridor was occupied: another guard was moving a prisoner. A green light meant the corridor was free and the next prisoner could be moved. One time, Mario remembers vividly, the traffic light system did not work and the guard told him to stand facing the wall with his hands behind his back. Nonetheless Mario and the other prisoner caught each other's eye and grinned triumphantly, because they knew the system had not worked and they had seen each other.

By all accounts there was enough to eat as a prisoner, but the food was always the same and extremely fatty in content. Each day was punctuated by three meals at 8 a.m., 12 noon, and 6 p.m. This is how Mario knew what time of day it was. For breakfast there was white bread, with margarine and jam, as well as bitter coffee. For lunch there was a portion of fatty meat in gravy, alongside potatoes which, in Mario's memory, were either half raw or totally overcooked. In the evenings prisoners received white bread, margarine, salami and blood sausage, and tea to drink. The only opportunity prisoners had to eat something else was in the interrogation room: sometimes prisoners would be given their favourite food if they gave their interrogators useful information about others.

Since it was forbidden to exercise in the cell, Mario recalls putting on weight. He tried to counteract this by running laps, doing sit-ups and lunges during the two sessions a week he was allowed to spend outside in open-air cages. These sessions varied in duration from ten to thirty minutes. Some prisoners disliked going into the outdoor boxes because they felt like caged wild animals as armed guards watched them from above.[13] Mario liked to get the fresh air and exercise, however. When you were in the outdoor box, Mario explains, you were not allowed to look at the sky, but sometimes he did. The armed guards shouted '*Kopf runter!*' ('Head down!') The best thing, Mario recalls, was when he took a sneaky look up at the sky and saw a plane. He remembers seeing Pan Am planes with the blue-cross symbol on the aircraft body, and thinking 'One day I'll sit in one of those planes'. Mostly, however, Mario did look down because he was worried that the guards would shoot him. Fear and uncertainty were always there as a prisoner. When the guards patrolled the other outdoor cells, Mario explains, then he could look up at the sky. And when he had seen the sky he felt great and the day was saved.

The prison rules dictated that it was strictly forbidden for prisoners to sing. Mario recalls two occasions when he defied this rule. Once, in July 1987 he sang the Udo Jürgens song *'Ich war niemals in New York'* ('I've never been to New York'), symbolic, of course, because of the travel restrictions on East Germans. After a minute a guard opened the cell door and hit him twice with a rubber baton. Shortly afterwards, a prisoner in another cell started singing the same song very loudly. 'The guards seemed totally shocked that we were disobeying orders in spite of the threat of being beaten', Mario recalls. After that, Mario was not allowed outside for the next few weeks. On 13 August 1987, the anniversary of the building of the Wall, Mario was allowed outside again. On this occasion, he chose to sing the West German national anthem, including the lyrics *'Einigkeit und Recht und Freiheit für das deutsche Vaterland'* ('Unity and justice and freedom for the German Fatherland'), which was highly provocative in the context of divided Germany. The guards above quickly came down from their observation posts, by which time Mario had almost finished the song. He was taken back to his cell in handcuffs and forbidden from going outside for the next four weeks. 'When I sang,' he recalls, 'the guards shouted "Quiet!"' On this occasion too, a prisoner in the cell next door started to sing loudly as well. These were extraordinary, unusual moments.

For all that there were a few occasions where Mario showed youthful defiance of the prison rules, there were other times where his total vulnerability to the whims of his guards was made particularly clear. One such example was when he was taken for his weekly shower. Normally, he would undress in an antechamber and then go into the shower, which would then be locked behind him. The guard outside would control the water. One time, Mario got undressed as normal, leaving his clothes and towel in the antechamber. He was locked into the shower and washed as normal.

The water then stopped, but no one unlocked the door. Mario called out, 'I would like to come out now', but there was no one there. He did not shout out, because this was against prison rules and prisoners who screamed were threatened with being taken to the arrest cell in the basement. Instead, he stood there, cold and dripping, and wondering why no one was coming. Twenty minutes went by, then forty minutes... after one and a half hours a guard came and said 'Oh, you're still here. We forgot all about you.' It was really humiliating, Mario says. He firmly believes that there was nothing that went on at the prison that was not deliberate. Such an experience, he thinks, was designed to make him feel powerless against the regime.[14]

With hour upon hour to kill, Mario played mind games with himself. He did mental arithmetic, recited poems to himself, and tried to think of nice things. There were no distractions—no newspapers, no books, no radio, no television. At one point, seven weeks into his imprisonment, he was so severely depressed that the guards acceded to his request for some books to read. They gave him crime novels, about GDR border police arresting people trying to flee, and books about travelling—a deliberate and cruel move psychologically for someone who has no freedom. Mario likened this to giving a starving person a cookbook. He soon stopped reading the books as they only exacerbated his longing to be free again. Echoing what Mario recalls of his time in Hohenschönhausen, another political prisoner in the GDR gave voice to some of his feelings in a letter to his wife on 15 November 1984: 'It's hard to keep track of time. I've become like a machine... The world is a hive of activity outside... and I know nothing about it... I long for company, for work and for a battle in which I have a fair chance.'[15]

So long were the stretches of time that prisoners spent alone, that many were finally glad to talk to someone when they were hauled out to be interrogated.[16] This was a deliberate tactic employed by the interrogators to get prisoners to confess. Mario recalls that in these interrogations, there was usually a good cop and a bad cop.[17]

The bad cop might shout and be really threatening while the good cop maintained a low profile. The bad cop would leave the room and the good cop would say, 'Now then, I think we can deal with this in a more calm and civilized manner.' But Mario said the good cop was almost worse than the bad cop, because despite his superficial friendliness, you knew he was working for the other side. When he first arrived at the prison, Mario said, 'I want to call my lawyer!', to which the prison guard replied, 'You've been watching too much West German television. You can't have a lawyer, you can't afford a lawyer, and even if you could afford one, the lawyer would be working on the side of the state.' The fact was that there was no independent judiciary in the GDR, and the Stasi sometimes even suggested sentences to the judges in court.

First and foremost, the interrogators were trying to extract a confession from Mario—a confession that he was trying to escape from the GDR. He held out through many sessions, resisting answering by instead counting the leaves on the wallpaper behind the interrogator—there were 582 leaves, it turns out—a fact he was able to establish on several occasions. A comfy chair was left vacant at the table. Only if you answered certain questions or if it was your birthday did you get to sit on this chair. Sometimes the interrogator turned off the tape recorder and said, 'We can't use anything that you say now. Who organized your escape?' Later, Mario found out, there was another tape recorder running in the cupboard. The interrogators tried to tempt Mario into confessing, saying that things would be easier for him if he confided in them. 'Don't worry, we have plenty of time', said the interrogator repeatedly, the last thing a sleep-deprived Mario wanted to hear after days on end sitting in his cell with nothing to read and no one to talk to. The interrogator always sat by the window, which in Mario's eyes represented freedom and the outside world. The curtains were almost always closed, so prisoners could not see out, but sometimes, Mario says, a crack was open and wind from the open window blew the curtains. 'When I saw out of the window,' Mario recalls, 'I thought of being on holiday. You had to come up with strategies to kill time. The interrogator would sit there reading the paper and would repeat the same question for hours. It was really draining.' The interrogators only ever saw the prisoners in the interrogation room. They had nothing to do with what happened to the prisoners the rest of the time. They did not see the conditions in which the prisoners spent most of their time—a deliberate strategy so that they felt no empathy for them. Eventually Mario conceded that he had attempted to leave the GDR, whereupon his interrogators showed him clause 213 of the GDR statute book, which stated: 'Anyone who leaves the GDR illegally...will be punished...by imprisonment or a fine.' They said, 'Well, you will be imprisoned for at least two to eight years now.'[18]

Having extracted a confession, the interrogators produced a list of Mario's family, friends, and acquaintances and exhorted him to provide information about them. Time after time he resisted telling them anything significant, stringing them along by providing minor pieces of useless information about the people on the list. For a long time after he was released, Mario had a guilty conscience about what he had told the interrogators. But he was so afraid that his knees shook and he had to hold them down with his hands to hide it. 'I was never beaten and I was never tied up', Mario explains, but the interrogators inflicted damage on prisoners without physically hurting them.[19] They began to tire of his lack of cooperation. When the phone rang in one session, he was shepherded out of the room by one of the guards, but not before overhearing the interrogator on the phone say, 'Alright then, we'll bring his parents in.' This, of course, sent Mario into a panic, fearing for the fate of his parents. He pleaded with the guard, saying, 'You can't bring my parents in, don't bring my parents in!' before the guard replied, 'They weren't talking about your parents this time, but they easily could have been. Maybe you'll be more cooperative next time.' Mario recalls that the interrogators made other implicit threats relating to the well-being of his sister, who had a small daughter.

They said, 'Do you care about your niece? It would be a shame, wouldn't it, if your sister was killed in a car accident and your niece had to go into a state children's home.' The interrogators seemed to know everything about Mario's life and they used this information to exert power over him. Another East German dissident recounted a similar experience at the hands of the Stasi, recalling, 'they knew which foods I prefer to eat, when I typically took the children to school, even the toothpaste I usually buy'.[20] The Stasi's knowledge of every little detail about a prisoner's life was disconcerting and could help break down their resistance to confess. These were the pressures that Mario faced when being asked to inform on his friends and acquaintances.

FIGURE 13 An interrogation room at the Stasi prison in Hohenschönhausen, Berlin.

© Ineke Kamps/Flikr/Getty Images.

In the outside world, Mario's parents were treated like social outcasts by many friends and colleagues once word got out that their son had tried to escape. No one would sit with Mario's father in the canteen at lunchtime, so fearful were they of being associated with him.[21] For Mario's parents, their son's treatment at the hands of the Stasi opened up a whole new way of looking at the communist regime, which they had previously loyally supported as Party members, and their dream of working with the state for a better Germany was over. At the point of Mario's incarceration, Stasi officers said that Mario's parents should sign a declaration saying that they would break off all contact with their son. Disillusioned, they refused, and left the Party.

Soon after Mario's imprisonment, Maria, a friend from West Berlin, rang up his parents asking where he was, as she hadn't seen him at the club where they so often met. Like many other East Germans, Mario's father was aware that their phone call might be listened to.[22] Choosing his words carefully, he suggested that Maria travel across to East Berlin on a day visa so that they could meet for a walk in a forested area, where they could talk more freely. There he explained about Mario's escape attempt. As a Westerner Maria was able to enlist the help of Barbara von der Schulenburg, a lawyer who specialized in securing the release of political prisoners in the GDR. The system of exchanging East German prisoners for West German money had been in operation since the 1950s but in the 1980s, with the thawing of relations between Eastern and Western political leaders and with East German politicians facing ever-deterioriating economic conditions, the GDR seemed particularly open to selling the freedom of certain political prisoners to the West. The West, for their part, were keen to help remove their fellow Germans from Stasi captivity, even if the money did help the SED. Overall, between 1963 and 1990, 3.8 million West German Marks was paid by humanitarian organizations, such as Amnesty International, as well as by churches, other charities, and private donors, for almost 34,000 political prisoners. The cost of freedom from the GDR did not come cheap. The average prisoner cost 100–120,000 West German Marks to free, but this varied hugely depending on factors such as the prisoner's education and length of sentence.[23]

As luck would have it for Mario, his friend's connections led to his representation by one of the most prestigious legal minds in East Germany, Professor Wolfgang Vogel, who was a key figure in negotiating with the Interior Ministry in the GDR for the release of East German political prisoners.[24] By this stroke of good fortune Mario's freedom was secured on 18 September 1987 for the relatively low sum of 40,000 West German Marks. Initially, the conditions of his release were that he had to live in East Berlin at his parents' address, he had to report to the police station every week, and he was not allowed to go out at night. Mario also had to sign a confidentiality agreement, promising not to talk about his experiences in prison.[25] The release officers explained that if he went back on this agreement and talked, he would either be rearrested or 'taken care of' in a car accident. Then suddenly one day, on 7 March 1988, papers came through giving Mario permission to leave the GDR for West Germany. This was a great relief for Mario since it had been difficult since his release to live in the country which had put him behind bars.[26] Arriving at the police station that afternoon, they said, 'You have until midnight to be out of the GDR or else we'll arrest you and put you in prison again.' Mario quickly replied that he could be out of East Berlin and into West Berlin in 45 minutes, but then the policemen explained that he could not cross directly through to West Berlin, but had to go the long way into West Germany and use the train.

Mario lost no time in setting out. He bade a hasty farewell to his parents, not knowing whether or not he would see them ever again, and set off on his journey. Just before the border with West Germany the train was halted, his papers were checked, and he was thoroughly searched. He made it into West Germany with only minutes to spare before the midnight cut-off. Four minutes after crossing the border the train came to a halt at Wolfsburg, the first stop on the Western side. The platform was brightly lit but completely deserted. Suddenly Mario saw a large nun wearing a black habit running along the platform and shouting his name. Forewarned of his arrival by Maria, Sister Hildegard, a nun from the *Bahnhofsmission*, a Christian charitable organization which helps travellers in need, had come to meet him. She took him to the mission and gave him somewhere to sleep.

A strong part of Mario's motivation for leaving the GDR had been a desire to be with his West German boyfriend, who had been very pleased to hear the news that Mario had been released from prison, even though they had only managed to talk on the phone since then. Eager to be reunited with him, Mario took a flight to West Berlin and headed straight for his boyfriend's house. When he arrived, a small child answered the door. Some very awkward moments passed as Mario came to realize that his boyfriend in fact had a whole other life with a wife and family. Downcast and dejected that the future he had longed for with this man was no longer to be, he sought out his West Berliner friend Maria who had played such an important part in his release. And by May 1988 Mario had secured a job he had often dreamed of, being a waiter at one of the top hotels in Berlin.

On the night that the Wall came down, Mario had worked a long shift. His father rang him from East Berlin to tell him what had happened. 'Young man, the Wall has fallen,' his father said. 'Shall we come over?' Mario's initial reaction was that it was a sick joke: 'I'd had a hard day of work behind me and I said "Are you drunk? What kind of joke is this?" and then hung up. My father rang back and said, "Put the television on." So then I turned on the TV and saw that he wasn't joking.' For other East Germans, who had campaigned for change, this was a happy moment. They hoped for a relaxing of social control in a free, independent Germany. Mario's first reaction, however, was fear. While the Wall had been up, he was safe from the Stasi officials who had ruthlessly

FIGURE 14 Free at last! Mario standing in front of the Berlin Wall in Kreuzberg, West Berlin in March 1988.
Courtesy of Mario Röllig.

pursued and imprisoned him. Now he was not. Rightly as it turned
out, Mario was afraid of running into his Stasi interrogators. In
fact, fear and trepidation about what would happen next were very
common among East Germans, not all of whom were as euphoric
about the collapse of the SED as the pictures of people dancing on
the newly opened Berlin Wall might suggest.[27] Some, like Mario,
who had battled to escape the GDR prior to November 1989, felt
resentful that their compatriots could now simply walk over the
border without any personal risk.[28]

In the ten years that followed, Mario was able to put his trau-
matic experiences behind him. That is, until quite by chance he
encountered one of his interrogators on 17 January 1999. Mario

was working behind the cigar counter in KaDeWe, an upmarket department store in West Berlin. As he was serving a customer, he had the feeling that he recognized him—he certainly recognized the way this man cleared his throat and touched his nose. Finally the penny dropped and he realized that he was serving his interrogator. Mario coolly looked the man in the eye and said, 'I think you owe me an apology. You interrogated me at Hohenschönhausen.' The interrogator, though briefly taken aback, snarled, 'I owe you nothing. You were a criminal!' Enraged at the interrogator's lack of remorse, Mario lunged towards him aggressively, only to be restrained by his colleagues at KaDeWe. The managers there did not take kindly to this kind of disruption on the shop floor and Mario lost his job. He was deeply shaken by this encounter. When the Wall fell he had been worried about once again walking the same streets as his persecutors. Now, in KaDeWe, his nightmare scenario had become a reality. Overwhelmed by feelings of fear and insecurity, Mario tried to kill himself. Luckily a friend found him before it was too late, and he was taken to a mental hospital, where he spent the next ten years in intensive therapy to try and get over his treatment at the hands of the Stasi.

Like many others, Mario took up the opportunity to view his Stasi file once the German government decreed that this should be possible. From December 1991 former citizens of the GDR have been able to write to the BStU (*Die Bundesbeauftragte für die Unterlagen des Staatssicherheitsdienstes der ehemaligen DDR* or GDR State Security Records) and if they have a file they will be sent a copy of it. The decision came a full two years after the Wall fell, and in the interim many former Stasi officials had a hand in destroying the paper trail the regime had left. Overall, one-third of all the Stasi files were eradicated in this period. It is only due to the technological backwardness of the GDR that more files were not destroyed.

The decision to open up the files was and still is a controversial issue.[29] Historians are of course delighted that this material is available as it gives them unparalleled insights into the modus operandi of the Stasi. For many ordinary people, however, access to their files has fuelled accusations of betrayal and has sometimes led to painful discoveries of being informed on by friends, acquaintances, colleagues, and even family members.[30] Mario's file was over 2,000 pages long. Within it, he discovered that his oldest and best friend Torsten had tipped off the Stasi about his relationship with a West German politician, which is what prompted them to start hounding Mario.

Once he discovered his best friend's betrayal, Mario arranged to meet up with Torsten. Sitting across from him, Mario placed his Stasi file on the table. Torsten was lost for words and turned bright red with embarrassment. Finally he spoke. 'Well what do you want me to say? It's all in the past now.' By now it was clear to Mario that his friend was not going to apologize. He therefore simply stood up and walked out, and has never seen him again. Though it is unclear what motivated Torsten to inform on Mario, there were many reasons that a person might work for the Stasi—in some cases it was blackmail for an ill-judged drunken criticism of the regime or for an extramarital affair, in other cases patients were denied medicine unless they collected information for the Stasi about their neighbours. Like many others, Mario discovered betrayal by his nearest and dearest after the Wall fell, and this continues to contribute to his difficulties in forming close relationships with other people. He explains that though he has been in a relationship for the past two years, as a result of his experiences in the GDR, it took him a long time to open up fully and trust his partner. Very early on in their relationship, he confides, Mario actually did some research into his boyfriend and his family to make sure that they had no connection with the Stasi. And, of course, living in the GDR also had a long-term impact on those East Germans who had less extreme experiences than Mario. Indeed in 1990, the East German psychoanalyst Hans-Joachim Maaz put together a psychological portrait of East Germans in the wake of the *Wende*, concluding that, as a result of living in a dictatorship, former citizens of the GDR were well practised at blocking emotional responses instinctively. 'We were', he says 'as walled in emotionally as our country was blocked off physically from the outside world by the Berlin Wall.'[31]

While Mario was still recovering from his breakdown in 2004, a friend called him, asking him to hurry over to Kreuzberg. The police were in the process of confiscating a dog from an alcoholic homeless man, his friend explained. And if someone did not take the dog, it would be put down. When Mario arrived at the scene, the dog, who was kicking up a fuss about being separated from her owner, suddenly trotted over to Mario. And she has now been in Mario's care for eight years. Mario explains that he does not even really like dogs but that it has been amazingly therapeutic looking after Daphne. Whilst in the mental hospital, suffering from severe depression, Mario recalls his sense of hopelessness, of not wanting to get up, of not wanting to see anyone. Now that he has a dog he has no choice, he has to get up and take her out, and through their walks he talks to lots of other dog owners, helping to restore his faith in other humans.

Though when I met Mario he looked fit and well and no longer lives in a mental hospital, the deep impact of his experiences in the GDR means that he will never be able to do a 'normal' full-time job. In this sense, the Stasi, who aimed to destroy their opponents psychologically, were regrettably successful.[32] Mario talks of the psychological scars of imprisonment. Even before the encounter with his former interrogator in KaDeWe, Mario used to change his job every few months. When everything was going well, when he had established a good routine, he felt like a prisoner. The routine reminded him of being behind bars. Since 2003, Mario has received a pension as compensation for the severe mental trauma caused by his time in Hohenschönhausen. This pension is the equivalent to a head waiter's salary, as this is what Mario might well have worked as, had it not been for the psychological impact of his imprisonment. No longer is he constrained by a working routine that reminds him of the worst time in his life. 'My greatest luxury today', he says, 'is that I can plan my own day and if I'm not feeling mentally strong, I don't have to do anything.' In the early 2000s, Mario did tours of the Stasi prison several times a week, because he needed the money to make ends meet. At a certain point, though, he found doing all the tours meant that he felt like he was never escaping from the prison in his head. He was consequently readmitted into hospital. 'It felt', he says, 'like my personality was bound up with talking about this topic.' Ever since Mario has received the pension, 'a large part of my worries have gone', he explains. 'Previously I was constantly worried that my past would threaten my future.' The pension means that Mario will have enough money to survive even if he suffers from further psychological problems in the future.

In some senses, Mario feels that life is all the sweeter, having had such a horrendous experience in prison followed by a mental breakdown. 'I have a heightened sense of pleasure,' he says. 'When I was imprisoned, there were times when I thought I'd never get out. Not many times, but a few times. When I was lonely in my cell, at night, alone, I doubted whether I would survive at all. The difference is noticeable only because I've had these horrible experiences. A good wine, good conversation—I take particular pleasure in these simple things.' Mario explains that travelling freely abroad is something that he particularly appreciates because he was unable to do this from the GDR. Sitting in a café in France on holiday is all the more pleasurable with the memory of what it was like to be walled in.[33]

Some aspects of daily life are unavoidable, however, and the experience of being imprisoned and interrogated makes them especially hard. When Mario goes into a bank or other administrative offices there are similarities, for example the official sits behind the counter like in an interrogation. It is now very difficult for Mario to go into such places and he has to take a friend with him because the associations with the interrogation situation are so strong in his head. For other former prisoners, too, people in authority like bank

FIGURE 15 Mario on holiday in Sweden, August 2010.
Courtesy of Mario Röllig.

managers, traffic wardens, or policemen, can instil fear. Other things that Mario encounters in daily life can also trigger horrible memories. He explains, 'Sometimes when I see a van on the road similar to the one that took me from Schönefeld airport to Hohenschönhausen prison I have to sit down because it makes me panic. Even smelling GDR lino flooring is enough to put me on edge because of its associations.'[34] The ongoing impact of imprisonment therefore manifests itself in multiple and perhaps surprising ways in daily life.

Mario has made it his mission to raise awareness about the brutal side of the East German dictatorship. As well as giving tours of the prison, he talks about his experiences to schoolchildren and to journalists. In all of these contexts, recounting his story can be difficult. When schoolchildren come on the tour of the prison, for example, they sometimes appear bored and are easily distracted. Mario finds this very bad for his nerves. His story is too painful, he explains, to tell to people who are indifferent to hearing it. He recalls revisiting the prison in December 1998 for the first time since his release. There was a group of schoolchildren doing a tour at the same time. But while they were laughing and mucking about, Mario had tears in his eyes. He recalls, 'I couldn't believe that they were laughing.' But they noticed how upset Mario was and they asked their teacher, 'Why is he crying?' Mario explained that he had spent the worst time of his life imprisoned there. The schoolchildren were then quiet and paid much closer attention to the tour. Today, Mario explains, he does not react so emotionally to such things. If visitors laugh, he rationalizes, they are trying to distance themselves from the situation. When he does a tour with quite young schoolchildren, at the start he says, 'Anyone who doesn't want to come can stay behind here'. And then the pupils are surprised and think, 'Ahaa, if I don't have to do it there might be something interesting in it.' Mario asks students to put their phones on silent, but there are always some who talk on the phone. Once, he recalls, he reprimanded a pupil for this and said, 'I asked you to turn your phone off and remain quiet, and you haven't done this, so I'd like you to leave', leaving the student very shocked.

Sometimes too, Mario encounters a frosty reception from teachers when he goes to talk in schools. He puts this down to fear that he may raise unwanted and difficult questions about what the teachers themselves did in the GDR. In spite of the challenges, however, Mario remains undeterred in his mission to raise awareness of the darker side of communist East Germany. He finds it very satisfying when he feels that young children take his message on board. After his talks, he explains, students sometimes say, 'I'd always thought communism would be great. But when we see that everyone's forced to be the same, then it's awful.' This perspective was not clear to them before. Sometimes, he says, teachers ring up to say that pupils who used to be skinheads are letting their hair grow long again, and that they are not wearing army boots anymore. The teachers explain that as a result of Mario's talk the pupils no longer identify with extreme ideology. This is his goal.

Mario is also writing a memoir. This, he explains, is a slow process, and part of his therapy. He has written most of it—his childhood in East Berlin, his experiences being pursued by the Stasi, his failed attempt to escape, and life after the Wall fell. The one part he finds almost impossible to write about is the three months he spent in the Stasi prison. So painful are his memories that he says it is very hard to find the words to capture what he went through and how he passed the time. For four years, Mario's agent has been eager to know when the manuscript will finally be finished but when he sits down to write about his experience in prison, Mario says he always finds lots of other things to do—anything but that. It is just so difficult to even think about it. Another reason he has not published his story yet is out of fear about how the perpetrators will react. He is afraid that they will buy the book and say it is all lies because their memories will be different. All of this goes to show how tough it is to write a personal account of such a controversial and politically charged topic in recent history.

The whole course of Mario's life has been dictated by his ill-fated escape attempt in June 1987. It is hard to imagine that the man I am talking to has been through so much, but the absolutely enormous impact of living in the GDR is abundantly clear in his story. He will not rest from his mission, he says, until every school textbook acknowledges the brutal side to life in East Germany. A survey conducted twenty years after his imprisonment in 2007 showed that 31 per cent of former East Germans do not think that the GDR was a dictatorship. Such figures merely underline to Mario the importance of his work. Furthermore, under the terms of German unification, those East Germans who worked for the Stasi could not be prosecuted. 'The biggest shock for me was that hardly anyone was punished', Mario explains. Erich Mielke, who had been Minister of State Security (Head of the Stasi) for thirty-two years from 1957 to 1989, was imprisoned for less than three years, and notionally he was not being punished for his Stasi activities, but rather for murdering two policemen many years previously in the Weimar Republic.

He was one of only three Stasi officials who served a jail sentence in unified Germany.[35] Erich Honecker, who had ruled East Germany for twenty-eight years from 1971 to 1989, also evaded prosecution for violating human rights on the grounds of his poor health and his advanced age, and in 1993 he moved to Chile where he died a year later.[36] What a farce, one might think, that so few people have been brought to justice for their actions. Mario certainly takes this view. The scale of involvement with the regime was so vast, however, with an estimated one in six East Germans working for the Stasi in some capacity, that punishment was simply not practical. At least this is what decision-makers at the time of the *Wende* claimed. The level of complicity with the regime is certainly often difficult to quantify and categorize.[37] A central difficulty in untangling this challenging situation was the fact that actions which were legal in the GDR could not be termed illegal retrospectively in the united Germany.[38] It is also important to avoid the dangers of hindsight, in that those who lived in the GDR did not know that communism would break down. From their perspective at the time, communism was the system they would be living within in the long term. It is therefore understandable in some sense that the vast majority of East Germans sought ways to align themselves with the prevailing system.[39]

From the perspective of someone like Mario, however, whose life in many ways has been ruined by the SED regime, it seems grotesque that so many who were perpetrators retain positions of power, in the police or in local government, for example, in the new Germany. As historian Cornelia Heins so aptly puts it, 'Nobody wants to be responsible for stirring up a political and legal hornets' nest, but sweeping the Stasi past under the carpet is a slap in the face both of all of its victims and of justice.'[40] Anger at this injustice will get him nowhere, Mario explains, but by doing tours and raising awareness of the crimes against humanity in the GDR, he aims to counteract the whitewashing of Germany's past.

5
Katharina ~ Believing in God under Pressure

The Stasi prison Hohenschönhausen is in an area of East Berlin known for the high number of ex-Stasi officials who live there. Rumours abound of old socialists giving misleading directions to enquiring tourists who are hoping to visit the prison.[1] Having got wind of this, I decided to embark on one of the more ludicrous activities connected with this project: doing a mailshot in the area in the hope of drumming up some interesting candidates to talk to. As an afterthought, I also put up a poster outside the prison itself. A few days later, I received an email from a tour guide at the prison, offering his wife as a suitable candidate. We exchanged a few jovial messages, in which he signed off 'Gilbert Furian, the Private Secretary'. His wife Katharina is now a very busy parish vicar, and so he made all the arrangements for her.

In the same year that the Berlin Wall was built, Katharina was born into a family that opposed the socialist regime. Her father was a vicar, leading a Protestant congregation in a country village called Golzow on the eastern side of the River Oder in the Seelow area. Whereas some Protestants made small concessions to the regime to make their own lives easier, Katharina's family stuck uncompromisingly to their beliefs, having faith that God would protect them. Her parents consistently refused to vote in elections in the GDR, for example, risking the wrath of the Stasi. Under normal circumstances, voters who approved of the one available candidate simply had to put their voting slip into a sealed box at the polling station. Those who risked voting against the candidate had to step into a separate booth in front of all the polling officials and cross out the name of the candidate. There were usually huge costs to stepping out of line in this way—costs that included losing one's job and often close surveillance by the Stasi.[2] Fully aware of the potential consequences, Katharina's parents remained adamant that they would not vote while the elections were rigged. And when Stasi officers knocked on the vicarage door offering them a lift to the polling station, they simply said no.

Many Christian parents chose to enrol their children in the government-led youth movement, the Young Pioneers, irrespective of their reservations about it. They rightly feared that not joining would adversely affect their children's chances of taking A levels or going into higher education. Katharina's parents, by contrast, were clear from the start that this was not something that they would bend on. Teachers tried to encourage children like Katharina to join, pointing out the nice uniform and the camaraderie as selling points. 'You would make such a good Pioneer,' they said. 'Don't you want to wear the uniform like everyone else?'[3] In spite of the pressure, Katharina did not join. She was one of only three children in her class who had opted out and as a result she was an outcast at school. 'Other children could tell that I did not fit in,' she explains. 'They sensed that I was best avoided.'[4] Like the 8 million other Christians living in the GDR during the 1980s, Katharina faced many difficulties on account of upholding her faith in an increasingly secular society.[5]

As in other dictatorships, the East German government was keen to remove any rival claims to the loyalty of its people. Religion was therefore never welcomed by the SED, even if it paid lip-service to toleration in the early years after the war. From the 1950s onwards the government began to take away youth work from the churches, bringing it under state control. The state also decreed that, instead of confirmation, from 1955 young people should prepare for a *Jugendweihe* ceremony: a secular ritual which marked a young person's development into a socialist citizen. Swimming against the secularizing tide came at a cost and those who persisted in their loyalty to the church were subject to penalties: many were barred from doing A levels and few were allowed to study at university. Perhaps surprisingly, given the state's position on religion, Christians in the GDR were able to read theology at university—a move that was likely a half-hearted attempt to demonstrate religious tolerance. Nonetheless, once out in the wider world, Christians were discriminated against in the workplace.[6]

School was the most difficult time in Katharina's life. 'The teachers who supported the Party tended to be the worst,' Katharina recalls. 'They hated religion and projected that hatred onto me.' When Katharina failed to give the correct answer to a question, those teachers would humiliate her, asking in a mocking tone, 'Where is your God then?' Katharina believes she was also given worse marks and school reports as a result of her Christianity.[7] And on one notable occasion, when the young Katharina refused to take off her crucifix in class, the school called in uniformed Stasi officers to reprimand her. 'I was treated like I was a serious criminal', she recalls. Normally, Katharina's mother expected Katharina to fight her own battles at school, explaining that Katharina should trust in God that nothing bad would happen to her. However on this occasion, she came to the school to defend her daughter against the authorities.

Anne-Marie B., a schoolgirl in the GDR like Katharina, also ran into difficulties with the Stasi as a result of her Christian faith. She later recounted that a Stasi car had drawn up beside her as she was leaving school one day. Anne-Marie was told to get in and was driven to a forest, where they would not meet or see anyone. There she was asked to inform on the Christian community she lived in. The Stasi worker mentioned that he knew Anne-Marie wanted to study medicine at university. If she informed for the Stasi, he explained, he would make this possible. Conversely, he said, if she did not comply, her path to higher education would be blocked for good. Anne-Marie's parents, however, had prepared her for this eventuality. She said to the Stasi worker, 'The community I live in is so close-knit that if I started keeping secrets or changing my behaviour, they would notice.' Because of what she had said, the Stasi let Anne-Marie go and she did not have to act as an informer. A rejection letter in response to her university application did, however, follow shortly afterwards.[8]

It is a common misconception that many East Germans were forced into informing for the Stasi. The Stasi did ask some East Germans to spy on friends and acquaintances and threatened career blocks and other penalties for refusing to comply. However, this applied only to a minority as most informants were voluntary, the thinking being that genuine supporters of the Party would provide more reliable information than informers who were forced into it. If people did not want to refuse the request directly, they could simply tell friends and acquaintances that they had been asked to inform, meaning that they would no longer be able to report their views or monitor their behaviour unsuspectingly. This would render them useless to the Stasi and the recruited informant would be released from his duties.[9]

Having heard about the challenges that Christian children experienced out in the wider world, one vicar was so concerned that he decided to delay his daughter Angela's schooling by a year.[10] He reasoned that when she was a year older she would be better equipped to withstand the disparaging remarks made about her family's values and beliefs. Angela's father took other steps to shield his daughter from the regime, by encouraging her to pursue an interest in music. Whereas the Party took a keen interest in the physical prowess of young people, either so that they could wow the world with the GDR's brilliance in international sports events, or as a good basis to serve the country in a military capacity as a soldier, they were less interested in music. Parents from nonconformist backgrounds like Angela's and Katharina's therefore often sent their children to music classes instead of sport practices in the hope of avoiding the gaze of the state as far as possible.[11] However, in spite of such efforts to protect his daughter, Angela was singled out in class on the basis of her family's faith. Once, for example, her class was studying a poem in class which made reference to eternal life, and Angela remembers that the teacher said, 'That's the kind of nonsense that Angela and her family believe in.' It was hard being an outsider at school, and there were times when Christian children like Katharina, Angela, and Anne-Marie wished they could just blend in with their conforming peers.[12]

Looking back on her childhood in the GDR, Katharina remembers how important it was to watch what she said, in public, at school, and above all when talking to Party members. If she breathed one word too many, she knew that her parents could be sent to prison and she and her siblings could be sent to a children's home.[13] Coming from an oppositional background, it was more likely that children like Katharina would speak out of turn inadvertently and land themselves in trouble with the regime. Christian parents therefore counselled their children very carefully, explaining what they could and could not say outside the home. Katharina explains that her parents did not want to raise her as a liar, but they advised her to be careful about repeating what she heard at home. 'I did not want to harm my parents,' she says. 'I sensed when I could or could not say certain things.' As a young child, however, it was sometimes difficult to know what might get you in trouble. The contexts of conversations were always shifting, so no hard-and-fast rules could apply about when it was safe to talk freely and when it was not. 'I was often silent rather than saying yes to something I disagreed with', Katharina remembers. From a young age she got used to 'double thinking'. What was said at the supper table within the four walls of home could be open and frank, but such conversations were not for repetition outside. Katharina did not grow up expecting to be able to express her opinions freely.[14]

Interestingly, although in some senses Katharina had to be more careful about what she said in public than children from regime-supporting families, in other senses she had more freedom about what she could say. As a vicar's child, it was not really expected that she would toe the Party line and therefore she could more boldly overstep the boundaries of acceptability. Katharina also felt that the regime could not really touch her because she felt protected by the church.

Throughout the 1980s in particular, the Protestant Church provided a shelter for dissidents, whether or not they were religious. As a vicar, Katharina's father believed it was the church's duty to protect freedom of speech and therefore to protect those who wanted to discuss their ideas freely. He therefore opened his church to anyone who wanted to talk about reforming GDR society. This became more feasible following the uneasy truce agreed between church and state in the Concordat of 1978. The Concordat allowed the church greater freedom of action which it used to allow campaigners for peace, freedom, and environmental matters to meet on its premises.[15] Within the church, too, Christians became increasingly vocal in their criticism of the militarization of GDR society, following the introduction of compulsory 'defence education' in schools in the 1970s. As part of the so-called Swords into Ploughshares peace movement, they criticized the regime's insistence that peace could only be maintained with weapons and complained that pacifists who did not want to be conscripted for compulsory military service were discriminated against. Later, in 1989, it was this movement that began the weekly peace prayers in the Nikolaikirche in Leipzig which contributed to the collapse of communism in the GDR.[16]

Given that the SED had aimed to create a state without churches and a society without Christianity from the very outset (albeit with nominal religious toleration in the 1949 constitution), and had harassed and discriminated against Christians, the thawing in SED policy towards the church in the Honecker era was certainly surprising. This was yet another example of the contradictions between the Party's stated aims and its policies in practice. Crucial to this policy shift was the fact that the East German Protestant Church, which had remained a member of the all-German *Evangelische Kirche Deutschlands* (EKD) until 1969, reorganized itself and became formally independent from the West.[17] Offering the church some latitude in the 1970s, it seems, was part of a wider strategy of the SED which was seeking to shore up East Germany's identity as distinct from West Germany. With this in mind, the regime allowed the church a freer hand in its own matters in return for acceptance of the SED's political authority. Teaching about Martin Luther was apparently also reinstated as part of the GDR's plan to differentiate its cultural heritage from the FRG. This reflected the fact that SED leaders, who had paid lip-service to the idea of German unification in the 1950s and 1960s, abandoned this commitment in the GDR constitution of October 1974, which no longer had references to the 'German nation' and instead stated that the GDR was 'forever and irrevocably allied with the USSR'. There were profound consequences of this change of policy, particularly in terms of how this filtered down to GDR policy towards the church.[18]

From the 1970s, small groups took advantage of the safety of the church to print underground journals, which covered topics including the environment, freedom, and human rights.[19] And in an unusual turn of events, Blues musician Günter Holwas collaborated with Protestant pastor Rainer Eppelmann to put on so-called 'Blues Masses', gatherings where East Berliners came to hear Blues music intermingled with Bible readings. From 1979 onwards these 'Blues Masses' attracted large crowds, their subcultural and increasingly political character led to trouble with the state and tension within the church, and they were abandoned in 1986.[20] Overall, though, the SED's acceptance of 'the church in socialism' and the subsequent Concordat of 1978 meant that churches offered unprecedented opportunities for opposition activists to meet and organize, which in turn played a crucial role in the events of November 1989 and beyond.[21]

Despite its increasing role as a haven for nonconformists in the GDR, the church could not protect Katharina from all the Party's discriminatory measures. With only a limited number of places for pupils to do A levels available, there certainly was not room for a Christian nonconformist. School therefore ended for Katharina aged 16.[22] She began training to be a nurse, but switched tack when she found out that it was possible for her to do A levels in the humanities from home, with a view to later studying theology. Katharina received nowhere near the amount of guidance that pupils got at school, but she prepared for her A levels privately, learning from textbooks, and passed her exams in 1983. She then studied theology for five years, before taking up her first job as a vicar. 'Being a housewife was never an option for me', Katharina tells me. Growing up in the GDR, where 97 per cent of women were employed, it was simply the norm for women to work. Given her Christian faith, alongside the restricted opportunities available to her as an outcast in society, a career in the church seemed the obvious next step.[23]

It was through her connection to the church that Katharina gained a more detailed knowledge of life in West Germany than many other East Germans were exposed to. From 1950 onwards, every town and village in the GDR had a partner church in the West. West German congregations came to visit their sister parishes in the East, and discussed religious practices in each community. This led many East German Christians to forge friendships with people on the other side of the Wall.[24] Through this scheme Katharina's church welcomed many West German Protestants to their parish every year. The visitors appeared happy and more relaxed than the people from the East. They smelled of a mixture of good things such as perfume, chocolate, and coffee, Katharina remembers. It was 'like they came from another planet', one young boy later recalled.[25] Such impressions created a sense of wonder about the West for many Easterners. East Germans in general were curious and eager to know more about the West, as the following anecdote shows:

> I remember when people who were allowed to visit the West came back and said the toilet paper there was soft, that it had double sheets and was decorated with flowers. 'My God,' we thought, 'can you imagine?' And we couldn't! We couldn't imagine a world where the toilet paper was decorated with flowers![26]

Like many other East Germans who received visitors from the West, Katharina remembers feeling in awe of them. 'Wow! The big wide world has come to visit!' she thought. Above all, though, these visitors contradicted the government portrayal of the West. The East German government presented the FRG as a society in which the gulf between rich and poor was enormous, where crime, homelessness, and drugs posed big social problems because the state did not look out for its inhabitants. However, through meeting and talking to West Germans Katharina was immune to such propaganda.[27] Unlike others with little or no contact with the West, Katharina was aware of an alternative discourse to that of the state from early in her life. When teachers of the ideologically marked citizenship lessons taught the history of the world from a socialist perspective in terms of class struggle, Katharina knew that there were alternative ways of looking at it from her home life, be it from a Christian perspective or a Western perspective.[28] And through this church partnership with the West, Katharina developed friends on the other side of the Wall who shared the same fundamental beliefs.

Katharina's family also gained an insight into the Western consumer world through the parcels they received from Christian friends and relatives in the West. Though not usually explicitly forbidden by the regime, such contact with Western Germany was frowned upon by the Party, as in the Cold War context, the FRG and the GDR were locked in an ideological battle of communism versus capitalism. Wearing Western clothes in the GDR, as we saw in Lisa's story, was therefore taken to be a betrayal of socialism. The reality, however, was that many families like Katharina's relied on parcels from Western relatives to clothe themselves. Illustrating this is the astonishing fact that the number of blouses posted from West to East Germany was almost double the number sold in GDR shops. On average, it seems that West Germans sent around 25 million packages a year to their compatriots in the GDR.[29] Not all of the presents from the West actually arrived because the Stasi often opened parcels and confiscated books, magazines, and money. Nonetheless the items that did arrive were certainly useful to Easterners. As well as clothes, other popular items in parcels included soap, tights, chocolate, and coffee.[30]

Families in the GDR frequently delighted in wearing, eating, or drinking things that they simply could not get hold of in the East. In one rather amusing case, an East German doctor attended an international conference in Pilsen, in the Czech Republic—a town famous for its beer. Over drinks that evening the East German fell into conversation with a doctor from West Germany. The Westerner was surprised that the Easterner was drinking Coca-Cola all night instead of the local speciality. When the Easterner explained that they did not get Coca-Cola in the GDR, the Westerner promised to send him a regular supply of Coke—a promise he kept until the Wall came down.[31] As well as Western consumables, some Western clothes were particularly sought-after in the East, such as Levi's jeans and Adidas trainers, which were not available to buy in the GDR.[32] Most East Germans were simply delighted and grateful to receive such gifts, but for some, these parcels made them feel like beggars, or at least second-class citizens.[33] The clothes that East Germans like Katharina received tended to be worn-out, second-hand items. Nonetheless when this clothing was worn at school it was taken as yet another sign of Katharina's family's deviance from the ideal socialist model.

Katharina enjoyed the friendships she developed with the West Germans who came to visit, and she was grateful for the parcels that her family received from the West, but she had no burning

desire to live there. 'You need to imagine that I did not know anything else,' she explains. 'I was born at a time when it was not possible to travel to the West and I operated under the assumption that
that would never change.' Katharina had vague dreams of visiting
beautiful cities like Heidelberg, London, and Paris, but she always
knew that they were dreams. And having built up these places in
her mind, after the Wall fell, she found Heidelberg something of a
disappointment. 'It's not that it wasn't pretty', she explains, 'but at
the end of the day, Heidelberg is just a town!' Katharina was
always excited to receive the Westerners when they came, but she
never thought about fleeing to the West. 'I knew that I would never
be able to come back to the GDR,' she explains. 'That would have
meant leaving all my family behind.'

Delving back into her childhood, Katharina recalls going on
holiday with her family outside the GDR. Like all other inhabitants
of the socialist state, their options were limited. Of the Eastern bloc
countries that they were permitted to visit, Poland and Czechoslovakia were the most popular with East Germans. The majority,
though, travelled within the GDR to the Baltic, Tübingen, or the
Harz mountains. Unlike Carola, who found the limited travel
opportunities in the GDR particularly suffocating, Katharina did
not find this aspect of socialist rule problematic at the time. Her
family travelled in Czechoslovakia, Hungary, Bulgaria, Romania,
and Poland, enjoying the differing scenery that the trips provided.
Within the Eastern bloc, Katharina noticed that the host countries
always differentiated between East and West German tourists, with
East Germans getting inferior treatment at every turn. This was
because hard West Germany currency was far more desirable to
tourist traders than the East German Mark.[34] But while this meant
that it was not ideal to be a tourist from East Germany, it never
occurred to Katharina to wish she was from the West.

Katharina did not expect that the GDR set-up would change,
but that does not mean she was content with every aspect of it.
Like Mario, Katharina experienced the Stasi's activities as very

intrusive in her day-to-day life. This was especially the case after she married Gilbert, a former inmate of the Stasi prisons at Cottbus and Hohenschönhausen.[35] Gilbert and Katharina first met in 1983. They had just got together when suddenly Katharina heard no more from him. Initially she assumed that Gilbert had decided to end their relationship, until she heard through friends that he had been arrested by the Stasi at work. The authorities had discovered that Gilbert was involved in writing and disseminating dissident leaflets, along with a group of punks who were critical of the regime. It was when Gilbert sent some of these leaflets by post to the West that his role was discovered. Slandering the state had severe penalties, and Gilbert spent two years in prison. When he was released in 1985, Gilbert tracked down Katharina in her student flat and they married soon after in 1987.

Gilbert's two-year probationary period was a nervous time for both of them. Not only did he suffer regularly from nightmares, he had to behave impeccably or risk imprisonment again. Minor offences, such as going out without taking his passport or jumping a red light in his car, could have cost Gilbert his freedom once more. Both Gilbert and Katharina felt under pressure constantly to watch particularly carefully who they talked to and what they said. Though they did not know it at the time, Gilbert and Katharina were heavily observed by the Stasi in the early years of their marriage. Gilbert's Stasi file later revealed a day-to-day chronicle of their activities, noting who their friends were, who visited the house, what conversations were had inside the house, as well as other observations including the fact that Gilbert was a nonconformist because he did not regularly eat a cooked lunch when he was at home. Sometimes Stasi officers took a more active approach when dealing with dissidents, attempting to disturb and confuse the dissidents' minds by breaking into their apartments and moving things around—be it adjusting the pictures on the walls until they were slightly askew or empting the tea caddy and refilling it with an inferior brand.[36] This, at least, Gilbert and Katharina were spared.

FIGURE 16 Katharina and Gilbert at the registry office in Prenzlauer Berg, East Berlin, on their wedding day, 23 October 1987.
Courtesy of Gilbert and Katharina Furian.

Looking back at her life in the GDR, Katharina remembers the power and control that the government tried to exert over each individual. In contrast to Lisa's carefree experience, Katharina's life in the GDR was marked by fear.

Both Katharina and Gilbert had a stake in seeing the GDR system reformed. Along with thousands of others in the autumn of

FIGURE 17 Katharina and Gilbert on holiday in 1987 on Rügen, an island off East Germany in the Baltic Sea. Gilbert had injured his eye whilst drilling holes into sheets of metal—the job he had been allocated upon release from prison in 1985.
Courtesy of Gilbert and Katharina Furian.

1989, they attended a demonstration agitating for change. Katharina had only recently given birth to her first child, so her thoughts were mainly focused on caring for her newborn son. Gilbert, by contrast, was much stronger in his feelings of opposition. Nonetheless, Katharina was interested to notice that people were starting to say things out loud that had previously been thought but left unsaid. That had not happened before. 'I am not sure I believed we would change anything,' Katharina later confessed. 'But I still wanted to be there.' It was increasingly clear that something was afoot. Indicative of this was the observation of one young girl about this time: 'Suddenly Western films were shown in the East German cinemas a lot earlier than normal.' Before, it had taken about two years for new Western films to appear in the East, but when this girl was able to see *Dirty Dancing* just a few months after it was released in the West, she thought, 'Wow! Something really must be happening!'[37]

So how did Katharina feel when she learned that the Wall had fallen? She felt free. 'I knew that no one was going to lock us up anymore.' Like Carola, though, she had mixed emotions. She was concerned about what would happen next and in particular how the Russians might respond. On the evening of 9 November, she and Gilbert and their newborn baby were staying at a dacha deep in the forested countryside. Nobody else was around and they were totally isolated. The dacha had no television but there was a radio. That evening, Gilbert heard Günter Schabowski on the radio talking about the eased travel restrictions. Calling to Katharina, he said, 'Did you hear that?' She had not been listening but thought Gilbert must have got the wrong end of the stick. 'Nonsense! You misheard!', she replied. 'Let's go to bed.' Gilbert and Katharina therefore slept through the dramatic events of that night entirely, only to learn the full story on the radio in the morning. 'We were both stunned,' Katharina explains. 'We couldn't believe it.' They quickly packed up their things and travelled directly to Berlin, keen to get across to the other side in case the border was closed up again. They were just one small family among the 2.5 million East Germans who visited the West within six weeks of the Wall's fall.[38] Thousands of East Germans like them were pouring across the border into West Berlin, picking up the 100 West German Marks of Welcome Money (*Begrüssungsgeld*) that every East German citizen was entitled to when they visited the West.[39] Convinced that the border opening was only temporary, Katharina used the opportunity to stock up on vitamins. And then she and Gilbert sat in a café in Kreuzberg drinking fresh coffee, which was not easily available in the GDR.

Katharina, it seems, was quite calm and collected in response to accessing the Western consumer world for the first time. Others, by contrast, were more overawed by the experience. As one East German woman said shortly after the Wall fell, 'We are probably the only region in the industrialized world where a soap or detergent commercial trumpeting how one brand can outperform another can be the sole subject of a dinner conversation.'[40] Typically, East Germans recount their first visit to a West German supermarket, where the range of goods was overwhelming in comparison to the GDR. Angela, for example, remembers visiting a West German supermarket for the first time with a West German family friend. The friend was looking for clementines and was rather put out that there were none to be had. 'It must be because of the floods in Spain', the friend said. Angela was amazed by this episode: firstly that this lady could link the absence of food on the shelf with events in another country and secondly that she clearly expected to be able to eat clementines regularly—a fruit that was a rare luxury in the GDR.[41]

Whilst 28-year-old Katharina had a practical response to the wider range of goods in the West and took the chance to buy essentials that were more readily available in the West, and 11-year-old Angela was amazed by the availability of fresh fruit from abroad, other East Germans were more excited to sink their teeth into a bona fide Big Mac for the first time. In a letter sent to friends in the West on 13 November 1989 describing his first visit over the border, East German Thorsten Mueller explained that while he felt completely overwhelmed by drinking in all the details of the West, his girlfriend was absolutely focused on going straight to McDonald's:

> Katje absolutely wanted to go to a McDonald's restaurant. She stormed in, and I stood outside just opening my eyes as wide as I could. I was shaking so. It was all so modern, white and made of glass, the windows were so amazing, the roof was constructed in a way that's only familiar to us through western newspapers. Katje pulled me inside. I felt like a lost convict who'd just spent twenty-five years in prison. Katje had some money that we used to buy a Big Mac. I'm sure we behaved in such a way that everyone could see where we came from. Above all, I was in such a state of shock that I was stumbling over everything.[42]

For others who were a bit younger when the Wall fell, the most exciting thing was access to 'real' Western chocolate. In the GDR, children and adults alike had gone to Intershops. For most East Germans, visits were mainly to window-shop and look longingly at the wider range of sweets and other food that was available to Westerners. Families like Katharina's received West German Marks from visitors which they could then exchange at the East German State Bank (*Staatsbank der DDR*) for special 'Forum cheques' to spend at the Intershops. It was only then that they would get to choose some Western goodies. For many like Katharina growing up in the GDR, Intershops were a kind of 'childhood Mecca', a paradisiacal 'Garden of Eden of excesses', far away from the reality of daily life.[43]

For adults who were loyal Party members, it was of course important not to seem to be longing for anything from the West, since this would imply that the East was deficient in some respects. So what did the Party make of so many of its members visiting Intershops? In one recorded case, an SED member recounted his dilemma. He had received some Western currency from relatives and was unsure what the right thing to do with it was from the Party's perspective. Should he spend the money in an Intershop or should he do nothing at all with the money? he pondered. At a Party meeting, he raised the issue, asking for guidance as to how to proceed. He received the answer that since the GDR was short of Western currency, it was his patriotic duty to spend the money in an Intershop. The advice, however, was caveated with the fact that he should not, under any circumstances, visit an Intershop in his Party uniform! For many East Germans who had no access to Western currency, visiting Intershops was simply a matter of window-shopping and gave them a glimpse into the other world, beyond the Wall.

After reunification though, Katharina, like Petra, was embarrassed by the way East Germans rushed to fill their plastic bags with Western products. She was not a fan of the rampant consumerism, aware that she had done just fine in the GDR with much less. Echoing this view, Thomas S., who was a teenager when the Wall fell, reflects on his reaction to the new abundance of choice. He says, 'I ask myself how we had enough to eat in the GDR if we need everything that is on offer today.'[44] Other East Germans have also cast doubt on whether the greater choice of goods now available to East Germans was inherently beneficial. As one East German woman put it, 'Who needs so many different types of chocolate?'[45] For Katharina certainly, the greater access to material goods from the West was not the most significant aspect of the transition to reunited Germany.

In the wake of reunification, many East Germans tried to conceal their Eastern origins. They wanted to blend in with their more prosperous and modern-looking West German counterparts. Many felt self-conscious about their washed-out jeans, their generic grey shoes, and their acrylic shopping bags, all of which made them stand out from the apparently well-groomed West Germans. Although shopping in the West was in some ways novel and exciting for East Germans after reunification, it was also stressful, as they did not want to make choices that singled them out as being from the GDR. In fact, a small number of East Germans were so keen to blend in that when they bought a new car, they had it registered to the address of a Western friend or relative, so that the car would have a Western number plate.[46] It was not only their external apparel that marked out East Germans, however.

Each day in reunited Germany revealed new ignorance for East Germans feeling their way on unfamiliar territory—ignorance that they were keen but understandably ill-equipped to hide. With new street names, new money, and new shops—to name but a few changes—it could feel overwhelming to get to grips with the new system. No one took East Germans by the hand and guided them through. And many felt shame that they did not know all the answers automatically: how to pronounce the food they wanted to order in McDonald's, how the supermarket trolleys worked in the West, what to wear to be sure to blend in with Westerners. The wider choices that were available to East Germans after unification were certainly advantageous, but the interim, as they learned to navigate and fit in with the new modus operandi, was not without stress.[47]

East Germans found that their behaviour, too, was quite different from West Germans. Though it would be a gross simplification to say that all East Germans conform to the stereotype of the so-called *Jammerossi* (moaning Easterner), and not all West Germans conform to the *Besserwessi* label (arrogant, know-it-all Westerner), in some cases these clichés appear to have had some validity. Katharina recounts one such occasion. In her parish, two new vicars came to work at the church. One was from the West and the other from the East. The first time they were working together, the West German vicar said to her East German colleague, 'Take that chair away and bring me that book!' And though the vicars were of exactly the same seniority, the East German vicar silently complied with the orders. Only afterwards did she approach Katharina, saying 'That Wessi (West German) is unbelievable!' In this instance, they both conformed to the stereotypes. Behaviour, it seems, can be as much a giveaway of Eastern or Western origins as appearance. And behaviour, which is subconscious as well as conscious, is arguably far more difficult to change.

Though Katharina is without doubt glad that the GDR is no more, she identifies three sources of personal disappointment about reunification. Firstly, she has observed West Germans exploiting the naivety of East Germans to further their business interests. Unlike other East German children who grew up fearing the West due to socialist propaganda, in Katharina's Protestant circles, West Germans were understood to be 'the good guys'. 'We, who had not had a great deal materially and longed for more, opened our doors to West German conmen', she explains. Katharina felt disappointed that the 'ruthless capitalists' from West Germany could not see the human consequences of their exploitation. And while East Germans gradually learned the rules of a Western consumer society in the early years after the *Wende*, Katharina felt that the West's relationship with the East was almost colonial in style.

Disintegration of relationships with West Germans which had endured while Germany was divided was the second negative consequence of reunification that Katharina experienced. Perhaps surprisingly, the solidarity across the border between East and West Germans appeared to falter in many cases once the Wall fell. Katharina's friendships with West Germans forged through the church exchanges seemed to peter out after the transition. She wonders if this is because the West German Christians no longer occupied an inherently superior position, meaning that their friendships with East Germans no longer had a benevolent and charitable purpose. Equally, Katharina's mixed reaction to unification, which was comprised of some pleasure at the new freedoms but also some critiques of the new regime, led her to fall out with her West German aunt who could not understand why her niece was not greeting the *Wende* with a big hurrah and instead was unhappy about Kohl's victory and rapid reunification. When Katharina dared to mention in a letter how West German conmen had been ripping off naive East Germans, her aunt went ballistic, angrily replying: 'You are a Communist! You are all the same!' Katharina explains that her aunt simply could not understand why she was not celebrating the reunification more, although she feels that most West Germans were more understanding of the difficulties East Germans faced after 1989.

The failure of the government in reunited Germany to punish Stasi officers and informers is the final major disappointment Katharina mentions in relation to the transition of 1989. She understands the legal difficulty of prosecuting crimes that were not against the law in the GDR. But, like Mario, as someone who suffered as a result of the Stasi, the seeming absence of consequences for their actions seems deeply unsatisfactory. 'I don't think we should have to work with people who spied on their colleagues, friends, and relatives for the Stasi,' she explains. 'Can we really accept that they thought they were working for the good of the system? Can we really accept that we should let sleeping dogs lie because it was so long ago? I am not convinced.' In spite of her wish for greater punishment for Stasi workers, she does believe that people can change. A number of former SED supporters have joined her church in the years since reunification—a development that has provoked a mixed and sometimes even hostile reaction from members of the Protestant congregation. Interestingly, Katharina finds that these SED supporters do not see themselves as having been on the other side in the GDR. They present themselves as victims of the regime too, claiming that they were put under pressure to act as informers. 'How creative the mind can be!' Katharina remarks wryly as she recounts this tale.

Katharina feels no nostalgia for life in the GDR, but she can understand why some East Germans remember it so fondly. 'I did not find anything good about it', she says, 'but others remember the job security and the material security and the fact that everything was very cheap.' This security, she explains, came at a price. Everyone also appeared to be more equal in the GDR, she says, but it was a forced equality rather than a voluntary one. Other East Germans have also harked back to a sense of togetherness in the GDR, but in Katharina's experience this feeling of 'belonging together' only counted for those with the correct ideological views.[48] Indeed, unlike others who enjoyed the sense of belonging in the Young Pioneers, Katharina was made to feel an outsider at school because she was not a member. Therefore for all of the difficulties inherent in the transition from one system to another, and for all of the flaws in the new system that she sees, Katharina definitely does not want the old system back.

Katharina spent the first twenty-eight years of her life as an outcast in the GDR because of her Protestant background. At the time of interview, this is longer than she has lived in reunited Germany. The shelter and comfort she found within the church during these years of ostracization means that she feels that whatever the future holds, the church will always offer her refuge. And living through the transition of 1989 has made her aware of the fact that all political systems have their downsides. Casting her mind back to life in the GDR, Katharina says she often wonders whether life really was that bad there. 'There were things that annoyed me. But there are things that annoy me today. There was a lack of freedom. But I did not feel hemmed in or restricted in my daily life.' Ultimately, she concludes, 'living in the system was not nearly as bad as outsiders generally seem to think'.

6

Robert ~ Supporting the Idea of Socialism

The way people recall life in the GDR is just so different that it is surprising to find that they lived in the same country.[1] The constant hounding by the Stasi drove Mario to an escape attempt, landing him in prison and leaving him with a lifetime of psychological scars. It is understandable, then, that the Stasi features prominently in his memories of the GDR. In Katharina's case, her experience of discrimination by the state on account of her faith helps to explain why stories of Stasi intimidation also form a significant part of her testimony about life in the GDR.[2] For some East Germans, however, who had little or no contact with East Germany's state security apparatus, the Stasi forms little part in their recollections of living under socialism. Robert, who spent the first fifteen years of his life growing up in communist East Germany, is one of these. Looking back now, he feels that the GDR has been totally demonized by histories that are overly focused on Stasi activities. It creates a false impression, he explains, of what life was like.

Sensationalist media interest in the Stasi has portrayed the GDR as a highly regulated surveillance society in which freedom of speech and freedom of travel were severely curtailed. Not so, says Robert. As the son of a Free German Youth (FDJ) functionary Robert grew up in Berlin-Marzahn in a family that believed in the proclaimed goals of a socialist state: eliminating inequalities and working together collectively for the overall good of the GDR. Robert's father was one of the leading figures in the *Org-Büro*, the events management department of the FDJ, and, though he sometimes criticized the reality of East German politics, on the whole he believed in the principles of communism. Growing up in a family which supported the state and not holding views that clashed with the Party's ideology, Robert did not feel many constraints on his freedom of speech. 'After all,' he explains, 'I was a child, and most of my friends in Berlin-Marzahn came from families which supported the system.'

Nor were travel restrictions a significant problem for Robert's family. Within the bounds of what was possible for GDR citizens, Robert and his family went on many trips abroad, visiting Hungary, Poland, Bulgaria, and Czechoslovakia. All of this meant that Robert and his family were not knocking up against the state's boundaries of acceptability. They felt to some degree free.

In fact, in contrast to the portrayals of the GDR as strictly regimented, Robert insists that there was actually plenty of scope to do your own thing and that it would be wrong to overemphasize the influence of the Stasi in day-to-day life. East Germans adapted

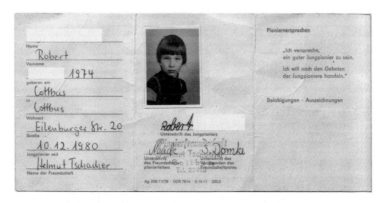

FIGURE 18 Robert's membership card for the socialist Young Pioneers Organization (*Pionierausweiss*).

Courtesy of Robert S.

their behaviour to conform where necessary, for example not shouting out criticism of the system on the street. And this was obviously more easily done if you supported the regime. But within the bounds of cautionary, sensible behaviour, Robert recalls, there were ways of sidestepping state control.[3] Like many others who lived in areas of the GDR where FRG broadcasts could be received, Robert watched Western TV daily—for instance American detective and action series such as *The Fall Guy*, *Magnum PI*, *Airwolf*, and *MacGyver*, which gave him an impression of life on the other side of the Iron Curtain.[4] Robert's cousins, however, were part of a wider group of people in Dresden and its surrounding villages who lived in the reception black spot where the TV aerial did not pick up West German television. This area was known as the *Tal der Ahnungslosen*—the Valley of the Clueless— as the people there had even fewer ways than most to learn about life beyond the Eastern bloc. Consequently, when his cousins came to stay in Berlin during the holidays, Robert remembers that they sat glued to the television, so keen were they to make up for what they could not access at home. It was not actually forbidden to watch Western TV in the 1980s, but the regime frowned upon it, especially if the viewers in question were political functionaries like Robert's father.[5] In the Cold War context, showing any interest in the West—the enemy—was considered a betrayal of the GDR. There were ways of getting around this, however. One way was not to talk about watching Western TV outside the home. Another way was to close the blinds to hide the screen when watching Western programmes but to open the blinds when watching Eastern programmes, so that anyone looking into the apartment would see that you were loyal to the Party.[6] There was only a small compromise when it came to watching TV in Robert's house: he and his brother were allowed to watch Western programmes, but their parents made them turn off the sound during the breaks so that they would not be caught off-guard, humming the tunes to Western adverts at school or in other public places. Through being a bit flexible and innovative, he contends, East Germans could and did retain a certain amount of freedom.[7]

Even if you knew someone was an informer for the Stasi, you were simply more careful than normal when talking about politics and you would alter your behaviour, Robert explains. He describes one such incident: in July 1989, Robert's father went to the communist International World Youth Meeting in Pyongyang to run the GDR pavilion and to represent the FDJ. Quite naturally, on a few occasions, Robert's father rang home to speak to his family. On the way to school one day, his best friend Alex came up to Robert and said, 'Your father is in North Korea. I know because my father listened in to your parents' phone conversation last night.' This is how Robert and his family learned that their telephone was tapped. A shocking revelation, and cause, one might think, for Robert to break off his friendship with Alex. Not so. Robert already knew that Alex's father had been working for the Stasi. As a result of the incident, however, Robert's mother cautioned him again not to talk about politics with Alex, and told him not to speak to Alex on the phone at all. 'This was easy, though,' Robert recalls. 'We didn't really talk about politics anyway and in any case I supported the regime.'

Robert was well aware that fellow East Germans were shot at and sometimes killed trying to flee the GDR. At the time, though, Robert explains, he was just a teenager, and like most others in his social environment, he accepted the state's view that these people were enemies, trying to damage the borders of the GDR, and he therefore thought it was right that they should be punished. Robert's acceptance of the state and its values is echoed in the experience of Jorge Seidel, who worked for the Stasi in his twenties. Looking back, he explains,

> When I worked for the Stasi, I was absolutely convinced of the political need for my work. I was also absolutely convinced of the evil of the western bloc countries. When I read American documents, I saw them as being tools of the devil. Today I'm not proud of it, but until the very end I was convinced that I was serving my country and protecting it.[8]

All of this creates a strikingly different picture to the one put forward by Mario, and helps to explain why Robert is insistent that the GDR cannot be compared to Hitler's dictatorship. As a historian specializing in Nazi concentration camps, Robert cannot relate the brutality and inhumanity meted out by the Nazis to what he experienced or what he learned later about the GDR:

> For someone like me who researches National Socialism, I look at places like Hohenschönhausen [prison] and by comparison it is like my school. I do not want to belittle it [what happened at the prison]. It is important that there are tours of the prison, but one should not compare the two [Nazi Germany and the GDR] because they are completely different things.

From the outside, there are certainly some obvious parallels between the organization and function of the two dictatorships, with ostentatious military displays, state-run institutions for social control, and the repression of opposition. There are also some obvious differences between the ideological aims of the NSDAP and the SED, and between the targets of state-sanctioned violence. Robert is keen to emphasize that the scale of discrimination and violence used by the Nazis was far more widespread. Comparing the number of Germans incarcerated under the two regimes, he says, the higher level of persecution under the Nazis becomes evident. In twelve years of power, the Nazis imprisoned 3.5 million political prisoners versus 225,000 during the forty years of SED rule.[9] 'How', he asks, 'can one compare 138 victims of the Berlin Wall to the 6 million murdered Jews? The GDR never ran extermination camps, nor attacked and destroyed countries all over Europe.'

Robert has become a defender of a differentiated view of the GDR, because he feels that since reunification Westerners see nothing more to his old country than it being the home of the Stasi.[10] 'When I do tours in the GDR Museum [in Berlin]', Robert explains, 'and I tell stories from my life in the GDR, I notice that Westerners come in with the expectation of learning about the baddies, the Stasi. Yes, it did exist, but the GDR was much more than this.' This perception has perhaps been perpetuated by the opening-up of Stasi files showing the extent to which East Germans spied on each other.[11] Tabloid newspapers in the 1990s gave a great deal of coverage to stories of scandal and betrayal from the GDR. Unsure about whether he wanted his happy memories of childhood spoilt, Robert did not apply for his file initially. Finally, curiosity won out and he applied to see it...only to find out that he did not have one. He was, after all, only 15 when the Wall fell. His father incidentally, recently discovered that he had a file, and is waiting to see a copy of it. Robert says that some people were desperately disappointed not to have a file, since in the new context of reunited Germany, it would show how much they had resisted the regime. He also believes that 'in some senses, it [the opening up of the Stasi files] has created pointless work. Around 2,000 people have had legal cases brought against them for contravening human rights in the GDR.' In moving forward, in seeking to build a joint future for the two Germanies, the legal authorities were faced with a serious dilemma about how to deal with such cases. Robert says, 'Only a couple of people have been found guilty, but they say we must do this to face up to the second dictatorship.' It is clear why people like Mario might want to seek justice, but from the perspective of Robert, it seems that overemphasizing the importance of the Stasi is a political strategy to reinforce a wholly negative Western view of the GDR. For Robert, who supported the regime's goals and had no direct contact with the Stasi, their existence gave him no cause to question the regime.[12]

Above all, Robert is extremely exercised about the ignorance and assumptions of West Germans about the former East. 'Were you starving?' some ask. 'November 1989 must have been such a relief for you. You could finally escape.'[13] 'No!' Robert wants to shout from the rooftops with frustration! 'We may not have had as much choice about what to eat, but we always had enough to eat. And no—I didn't want to escape the GDR: it was my home!'

Westerners assume that everything in the GDR was awful, he finds, and that all Easterners wanted to leave.[14] 'Being anti-communist and being anti-GDR had been a key preoccupation of the FRG. The GDR was an evil enemy whom they presented in a bad light, saying, for example, that everyone was poor there,' Robert asserts. 'So it is impossible for anyone from the FRG to think that there was anything good about the GDR because the basic point of departure of the FRG was anti-communism.'

For sure there were certain things that Robert would have liked to have from the West: as a child it was Milka chocolate and Matchbox toy cars that he coveted in the Intershops, which he describes as being like 'a gate to heaven', and as a teenager it was leather or bomber jackets, West German military boots, literature, and records.[15] However, this did not mean he wanted to move to the West. At school he was taught that Westerners were the enemy, and teachers underlined the disadvantages of living in a capitalist society, such as unemployment, homelessness, drugs, and crime, so he had no desire to go there.[16] When he visited his aunt who lived in a flat in Baumschulenweg, the train would pass near the Berlin Wall. From the train window, he could see part of Neukölln in the West. Robert recalls that he thought, 'Oh, that's the West. I have no interest in that.' Other young East Germans were even more oblivious to the division of Germany. Felix R. from Pankow in East Berlin remembers marking his seventh birthday by going to see the view from the top of the TV tower (*Fernsehtum*). Far from noticing the Wall that divided the city below in two, he remembers spotting a shiny slide and begging his father to take him there.[17] Robert was that much older, but still the division did not consciously intrude on his daily life.

When Robert heard bands like *Die Toten Hosen*—a popular punk rock band from Düsseldorf—playing on West German radio, he explains, he wished that he could go to such concerts, but ultimately he felt at home in the GDR, surrounded by family and friends. And besides, he reasons, it was all but impossible to get over the

Wall, so why waste energy thinking about it? Young people a little older than Robert did begin to challenge the restrictions imposed by the regime. Why couldn't *Die Toten Hosen* play in the GDR, for example? A growing number found the answers they received to such questions both odd and unsatisfactory, leading to disaffection with the regime. Robert believes he may well have shared these feelings if the Wall had not fallen when it did. Certainly the period around 1990 was a time when he began to grow curious about the world beyond Eastern Europe. Others, a few years older than Robert, could not believe that they would have to wait until they were retired to visit Paris or Rome.[18]

Robert loves to confound the assumptions of Westerners about life in the East by talking about the punk rock concerts he went to as a teenager. Westerners, he explains, cannot believe that such a counterculture existed in the GDR.[19] However, it was a different matter in the late 1970s and the early 1980s when punk rock music and the associated nonconformist scene were not tolerated by the SED. Young people who seemed to prefer Western music and lifestyle epitomized the antithesis of the 'socialist personality' that the SED had tried to instil in young East Germans. East German punks' unruly hair and casual clothing further grated with the authorities, which had a much smarter, tidier, and crucially military ideal in mind for their young people. Punks therefore were considered a menace to society, and the Stasi monitored their activities carefully. Unlike subversive literature, access to which could be controlled relatively easily, it was harder for the government to limit access to alternative music which East Germans could tune into on the radio, although it did not stop them trying. Bands had to submit lyrics to the authorities for approval ahead of performances, to ensure that the words did no damage to the socialist cause. And when they did get permission to perform, it was on the condition that a maximum of 40 per cent of the music they played was of Western origin, and the rest was produced under socialism.

These were just a few of the rules that the SED government enforced to regulate popular music.[20]

In the context of perestroika (the easing and restructuring of socialist rule initiated by Mikhail Gorbachev from 1985 onwards), however, when Robert was coming of age, there was a greater acceptance of punk music, which was played by the likes of Party member and radio DJ Lutz Schramm during his show *Parocktikum* on East Germany's youth radio station DT64.[21] In some senses, then, the regime did not exert as much control over society as the 'Stasi-state' label would suggest.

Symptomatic of this was the room that existed for rebellion among Robert's age group. In the late 1980s, Robert explains, there was a growing problem with neo-Nazi gangs, especially where he lived in Marzahn, the home of many elite party functionaries. Children of loyal Party members were rejecting the values of their parents, saying 'My father is a socialist, therefore I'll be a Nazi.' This was something that Robert particularly noticed when he went on a youth camp to Czechoslovakia in early 1989. It was customary in the GDR for youth camps to be arranged by the workplace of one of the parents. Because his father was an FDJ functionary, the camp Robert attended was for FDJ functionaries' children.

It was only here that Robert noticed how popular neo-Nazism was becoming amongst this group, when they sang Nazi songs and did the Hitler salute. This was not for Robert. Having been brought up under socialism, he said, he could never support Nazism. Instead, his generational rebellion was to become a punk rocker who, whilst remaining left wing, believed in anarchism. For Robert and his friends, being anarchists did not mean being violent or committing terrorist crimes, it rather meant being free of regimented leadership and replacing this way of doing things with peaceful discussion.[22] Looking at the experiences of Robert and his cohort, it becomes clear why Stasi-centred portrayals of GDR inhabitants as passive conformers are inadequate, undifferentiated, and reductive.

FIGURE 19 Robert's ticket to an alternative rock concert organized by the FDJ in the summer of 1989.

Courtesy of Robert S.

FIGURE 20 Robert as a teenager, on the day of his *Jugendweihe* (the socialist state's equivalent to confirmation) in 1988.
Courtesy of Robert S.

It is not only the misrepresentation of the GDR in reunited Germany that bothers Robert; the manner of unification itself is a sore point. When East German demonstrators took to the streets in the autumn of 1989, he is keen to point out, unification was not on their minds. They wanted to reform socialism from within, to make it more democratic, with an easing of restrictions on the press and on travelling. In previous years campaigners for reform had carefully

FIGURE 21 Postcard from the Young Pioneers' holiday camp 'M. I. Kalinin' near Berlin in the 1980s.
Courtesy of Robert S.

negotiated the borders of acceptability and asked each other 'How far can we go?'[23] In the months preceding the *Wende* they became bolder, however, and started saying out loud what many people had thought but not dared to say previously.[24] As we saw in Petra's story, many wanted the practice of socialism to better reflect its ideals. Shortly after the elections in March 1990, Robert recalls taking part in an unofficial left-wing demonstration on the Kollwitzplatz where people were chanting 'Nie wieder Deutschland' and someone burnt the Prussian flag. So although East Germans voted overwhelmingly in favour of unity, it was neither the original intention of the demonstrators nor was it unanimously supported when it happened. Furthermore, Robert believes, the election results show that the majority of East Berliners were against Helmut Kohl's plan for East Germany to join the West German federation. Campaigners, then, did not really get where they wanted to be. They felt that the little steps forward they had made, the little improvements, were all swept away and no longer had any meaning.[25] Ulrike Poppe, one of the founding members of the New Forum, who was involved in leading the 'Peaceful Revolution' (*friedliche Revolution*) in the autumn of 1989, later explained that when campaining in the lead-up to November 1989, 'I looked upon it more as two people walking towards one another with mutual respect than as one taking the other by the hand and going in the direction that only the one wants to go.'[26] Most East Germans did not know what they were signing up to, Robert thinks.

FIGURE 22 Robert's passport bearing the stamp of his first visit to West Berlin on 12 November 1989.

Courtesy of Robert S.

They formed their impressions of the West from TV adverts showing smiling children eating Milka chocolate and playing with Lego.

When they voted yes to unification, Robert argues, East Germans were voting to merge the two cultures of East and West Germany. The reality, he says, is a type of cultural colonization or, as some East Germans wittily put it, 'Kohl-onization', referring to Helmut Kohl's central role in bringing about rapid reunification of Germany:

> The idea was that the two countries would accommodate each other. The reality has been that the one eliminates the other. So as an East German I feel keenly the elimination of my own culture…No one talks about any of this in Germany. Everyone carries on as if nothing has happened.[27]

Perhaps West German politicians could see no reason why East Germans would object to a straight substitution of West German culture for East German culture. However, Robert and Petra, like other East Germans, have subsequently felt angry that their culture has been marginalized and eliminated. They felt angry, too, that the naivety of GDR inhabitants was exploited by West German businessmen who saw opportunities for quick profits in the East, be it through disreputable mail order offers or dubious door-to-door sales.[28] One of Robert's contemporaries, Hans-Michael S., reflected on his dislike of the 'cold capitalism' shown by these Western entrepreneurs, saying, 'in the 1990s I had the feeling that Westerners were just out to make a profit: that they didn't have anything good in mind. Even if we weren't as successful economically, I definitely had the feeling that we were morally superior to our Western counterparts.'[29] Overall, Robert certainly concurs with the view of East German historian Stefan Wolle that 'socialism was drowned in Coca-Cola and stoned with Haribo gummi-bears'.[30]

Robert and his peers grew up in a very distinctive environment within the GDR, and now, a quarter of a century after reunification, barely a trace of that culture remains. The GDR was Robert's childhood home and that home no longer exists. In the media—on the television, on the radio, in newspapers—when journalists refer to Germany's history, Germany's past, they invariably refer to West Germany's past. It is true that East Germans represented a minority in reunited Germany as the GDR had 16 million people in comparison to the 63 million people living in West Germany.[31] But they were a significant minority, nonetheless. They represented a fifth of the population of reunited Germany. And if their distinctive past is marginalized and denigrated, it is easy to see why people like Robert feel disenchanted. 'Every day another bit of GDR culture disappears,' he confides. 'I feel that things are moving further and further away from my own world. It is very difficult to describe. It is a bit like growing up in a building that is knocked down and turned into a supermarket. I feel that my own country isn't there anymore…I still feel that I'm a foreigner here.' It is not that he wants to return to the GDR—he concedes the many benefits he has profited from in the new system: the freedom to travel, the freedom to study what you want, and the freedom to buy what you want. The reality of unification, however, from Robert's perspective, has been a cultural takeover by the West, with little or no room for East German ways, leaving many East Germans like him bereft of the familiar, communal basis of life in the GDR. Robert, like many others, thinks that even after reunification, the West could have learned from the East, as well as the other way around. And even twenty-five years on, he regrets the fact that unification did not represent more of a mixture of the two systems.[32]

The feelings many East Germans share, of missing their old lives, do not necessarily have anything to do with the political change. Everything was suddenly different. *Ostalgie* therefore represents East Germans' longing for the comfort and security of what they knew—the GDR. An East German saying goes as follows: 'When a West German talks fondly of his early years, this is called his childhood. When an East German talks fondly of his early years, this is branded *Ostalgie*.'[33] When East Germans mention any of the advantages of their old system, this is often met with accusations of being 'Red' or 'one of them', when really what it shows is an affinity not with the SED state but with the familiar and secure life in the past that happened to be in the GDR.[34] The saying furthermore suggests that Westerners believe Easterners are not able to assess accurately what they lived through in the GDR and the knock-on impact of this is that the GDR is now evaluated almost exclusively through a Western lens.[35] In fact, many East Germans were simply used to daily life in the GDR, and have no desire to be told by FRG inhabitants how they should view their former lives. It is the apparent preponderance of Western views on the GDR, often epitomized by a focus on Stasi activities, which irks so many who lived in the GDR and who experienced it as much more than this.[36]

This, and the fact that in reunited Germany there appears to be a self-perpetuating system of West Germans being winners and East Germans losers, means that there remain significant feelings of difference, even a quarter of a century after the two states were reunited. From the perspective of many Easterners like Robert, the entrepreneurial activities of West Germans who bought up cheap property in the East soon after the *Wende*, simply priced them out of a housing market in which they were already severely disadvantaged, given communist policies on property ownership and wealth distribution.[37] Equally too, where forging a career was concerned, East Germans felt at a distinct disadvantage. With reunification, the whole way in which employment was organized for East Germans changed dramatically from being state-controlled to being much more individually determined.

Easterners like Robert, who were coming of age when the Wall fell, had to feel their way in an unfamiliar new system. Their parents were no more experienced in the new system than they were and thus, unlike West German teenagers who could seek advice from their parents, young East Germans had to work it all out for themselves with limited or sometimes understandably ill-informed guidance from their elders.[38] Although, theoretically, living in reunited Germany has created more opportunities for Easterners, in reality it seems that these opportunities are not accessible for all and certainly leave some 'trapped at the lower end of the newly competitive social ladder'.[39] Perhaps this explains why, five years after the Wall fell, T-shirts emblazoned with the message 'I want my Wall back' rapidly sold out.[40] For Robert, though, it is definitely not a case of wanting to return to the GDR: he fully appreciates the new freedoms and possibilities available to him in reunited Germany. He simply wishes that the reunification process had been more of a mixture of the two political systems.

7

Mirko ~ Rejecting the Party Line

Thirty-nine-year-old Mirko is a man of slight build with long black hair held back by a headband. We sit across the table in Mirko's kitchen and turn the clock back to the late 1980s when Mirko was a teenager. On 1 October 1989, a crowd gathered at the station in Freiberg, Saxony, to watch six special trains go past. The trains were special because they were carrying East German refugees from Prague to the Federal Republic. Desperate to escape life in the GDR, these refugees had thrown themselves on the mercy of the West German Embassy in Prague, asking to be repatriated to West Germany. Marking a key moment in the demise of the GDR, West German Foreign Minister Hans-Dietrich Genscher addressed the crowds from the Embassy's balcony on the evening of 30 September. He began his speech by saying 'I have come to you to tell you that today your exit…', but before he could finish speaking the crowd had drowned him out with cheers. The result was this convoy of trains. Only a month before the Wall came down, these 4,500 East Germans travelled by train across the East–West border, arriving on Western soil at Hof railway station.[1]

Mirko was in the crowd at Freiberg that day. He was as curious as the next man to see what was going on. The East German police on the other hand were keen to deter such interest, and used brutal methods, including dogs, water cannons, and rubber batons to disperse the crowd. Aged 15, it was the first time that Mirko had seen this aggressive side to the police, and it made a lasting impression.

FIGURE 23 GDR refugees on the train leaving Prague for West Germany in
the autumn of 1989.
© CTK/DPA/Press Association Images.

Twenty years later, Mirko organized a commemorative train
journey between Prague and Hof to remember this important
moment in GDR history. Some of the original passengers joined
the train, alongside many young Europeans who were born in
1989. The purpose was both to mark this symbolic action in the
final stages of the GDR's demise and to raise awareness among
young people about Germany and wider Europe's divided past.

Growing up, Mirko's family life was dominated by his father who
was an ardent supporter of the SED and its ideology. Not only was
his father a Party member, he was also a university lecturer specializing in the ideology of Marxist-Leninism. Academics in this subject tended to be particularly ardent in their commitment to
socialism. Beyond communicating the essence of Marxist-Leninist
doctrine in his work, Mirko's father also acted as an IM (*Informelle
Mitarbeiter* or informer) to support the SED, collecting detailed
information about a man in the local mining society, which he then

passed onto Stasi officers.[2] Mirko was unaware of his father's role as an informer at the time, and he is unsure if the information his father collected was ever used. But informers tended to give the Stasi reams of detail that they could potentially use to their advantage at a later date. Out of commitment to the Party and dedication to the East German cause, Mirko's father also cut all contact with his Western relatives, which included his three siblings, regarding everything relating to the West as having a malevolent influence.[3] And, whilst watching Western television was not strictly forbidden for Mirko and his sister, his father made it clear that he thought it to be nothing more than Western propaganda.

How did his father's views affect Mirko? What did he himself make of life in the GDR? In his early years, it appears that Mirko was neither fiercely loyal to the regime nor violently opposed to it. Aged 14, he took part in the socialist *Jugendweihe* ceremony, marking his passage into adulthood. For Mirko, this was an event which held little heartfelt significance. Like others his age, he was pleased to be recognized as a young adult, pleased to be able to go out alone for the first time, and pleased to be able to drink his first glass of wine, but in his memory the *Jugendweihe* was as much about receiving presents from the family as it was about making a serious ideological commitment to the state.[4] In spite of his seeming ambivalence to the ceremony, Mirko was given the position of *Agitator* (speech-maker) in the FDJ at school and was later its leader there too. His father was delighted. It reflected well on his parents that their son was progressing within the junior ranks of the official youth organization. On a fundamental level, Mirko does not have particularly fond memories of the FDJ. It was obvious that it was compulsory, he explains, and many pupils were clearly bored by the activities. He recalls little emotional attachment to the ideas expounded by the FDJ leaders, and, like many others of his age, he wore the uniform and took part in the youth movement's activities until the autumn of 1989 because his parents told him not to make a fuss or irritate the authorities.[5] They were only too aware of how serious it would be for their child to be an enemy of the state, since it could affect his career prospects in the future and their own in the present.[6]

Despite his lack of enthusiasm for the FDJ, in 1987 Mirko did derive satisfaction from being selected to go on a four-week 'Pioneer Republic Camp'. It was not the lectures, workshops, military, or leadership training at the camp that appealed to Mirko. It was rather the fact that he had been picked over others in his year, and that he got to miss regular school. At the time, Mirko says, the ideological and military emphasis of the camp did not seem strange in the least. Two years later, in the summer of 1989, Mirko attended a military training camp for all boys his age living in the Freiberg area. Here he was filled with horror at the emphasis on the military. Looking back, he finds it weird to think that the leaders were all working to groom him into the perfect socialist personality. The unquestioning way in which he and the majority of his contemporaries participated in the FDJ activities, Mirko reflects, makes it easier for him to understand how so many Germans participated in the Hitler Youth during the 1930s.[7]

Growing up in the GDR felt normal to Mirko. His family were comfortably off and he certainly had enough to eat, contrary to what Westerners had learned through Cold War era propaganda. Some of his friends' families had contacts in the West who sent over parcels of scarce or expensive goods but since Mirko's family had very little contact with their Western relatives, they had to make do with what was available in the GDR. None of this bothered Mirko, he says. He was not jealous of his contemporaries who had Western things, he says, because, like Lisa, he has never been that interested in material things.

Likewise, Mirko did not feel constrained by the travel restrictions imposed on GDR citizens. Having greater freedom to explore other countries would have been nice, he remembers thinking, but it did not make him unhappy. As a lover of aeroplanes though, he remembers going to watch planes take off: 'It was a funny feeling to see the planes leaving for places I would never be able to travel to.' For most of Mirko's childhood, then, with no benchmark for comparison, he accepted uncritically the circumstances in which he lived.[8]

Despite having no contact with the West, Mirko began to view the East German regime in a more critical light in his teenage years. A number of things he had been told either in school or by his parents no longer added up. Everyone seemed to be so keen to tell him how terrible life in the West was, yet when his friends' relatives came over from the Federal Republic they arrived in amazingly smart, modern cars. For Mirko this cast doubt on the anti-Western propaganda he had been fed. He also began to wonder why there was such a strong military presence in the GDR, given that its leaders claimed to champion peace.[9]

The demand for conformity, too, began to grate on Mirko. As he grew older, he wanted to express himself as an individual rather than as an unthinking, regime-supporting robot. There were many times, Mirko says, when he stopped himself from voicing his true opinion, aware that it did not fit within the accepted socialist narrative. There were certain topics, he explains, that he just knew not to mention, including the Stasi, the army, relations with the Soviet Union, the poor conditions that pensioners were forced to live in, and the fact that East German hospitals were outdated in comparison to West German ones.[10] In school therefore, it was easiest to trot out approved stock phrases, which would guarantee good marks.[11] Mirko's contemporary, Robert Ide, also recalls watching what he said at school very carefully: 'Silence, I quickly learned, was the best way of avoiding trouble', he explains. He took further steps to find out who it was safe to talk to. Exploiting a quiet moment at break time, he looked through his class's register, where all the students' names were listed. Next to each student, there was a column which detailed what job his or her parents did. Scanning the register in haste, Robert noticed that next to some of these entries about the parents were the big red letters 'SED', indicating

FIGURE 24 Mirko as a teenager on his first solo visits to East Berlin. (above) aged 16; (below) aged 15.

Courtesy of Mirko Sennewald.

that they were Party members. This, he remembers, was really useful information, because when he went on school trips afterwards, he knew which parents he could talk to about his love of certain West German TV series, and which parents to avoid.[12]

The political pressure on Mirko intensified in the final years of the regime. He was put into a so-called *S-Klasse* (*Spezialklasse* or

Special Class) when he transferred to the *Erweiterte Oberschule* (German equivalent to a sixth form college) to study for his A levels and this coincided with the period when he began to question the regime. Being in the elite class came with a particular political pressure: Mirko and his classmates were meant to be good examples of socialist citizens. It did not work too well in his class, Mirko explains. His teacher was duty-bound to try to encourage the boys in the class to sign up for more than the obligatory eighteen months of GDR military service. It was a well-known fact that those who had served in the army for three years instead of eighteen months were far more likely to be offered a place on a university course of their choice. Nonetheless, when Mirko's teacher raised the subject of military service with the seven boys in his class, none of them wanted to sign up for officer training. A Stasi representative came to the school to interview each of the boys in the hope of persuading a few to sign up. It was made very clear in the interview that unless the boys signed up for three years of military service, they would not get a place to study at university. None of the boys changed their minds, but, Mirko said, this pressure was very stressful at the time.[13]

At school, too, although he got good marks, Mirko ran into difficulties for having long hair and for refusing to remove his headband when the teacher asked him to. Of course all schools are familiar with pupils pushing the boundaries of dress codes but teachers in the GDR were duty-bound to root out anything that deviated from the socialist norm—unusual hairstyles or clothing were indicative of nonconformity.[14] Mirko, like Robert in Chapter 6, had dared to be different. Perhaps the reason why Mirko dug his heels in lies in the fact that so much of his life had already come to feel controlled by the authorities.

Seeing the police violence in dealing with the crowds who had come to watch the refugee train pass was a crystallizing moment for Mirko. Even without provoking the policemen or being aggressive, it was difficult to avoid being beaten, Mirko recalls. And whilst

Mirko was witnessing this state-sanctioned violence for the first time amid the crowds on Freiberg station platform, his father was actually part of the official operation to keep East Germans from getting too close to the trains as they passed. The next day in school a teacher asked the class who had been at the station, leaving Mirko feeling worried after he had confessed to being there. Prompted by his experience on the station platform, Mirko went along to the *Nikolaikirche* in Freiberg where there were discussions about reforming the GDR. It was around this time too that Mirko left the FDJ and joined an alternative political group with liberal values called LILA (*links liberale Alternative*, the Liberal Left Alternative).[15] LILA's belief system was very different to the FDJ as it was keen to support East Germans in their growing demands for freedom in various forms. Their ideals far better matched Mirko's own ideas and seemed far more convincing to him than those the FDJ, which appeared outdated and inflexible. Consequently, Mirko was very engaged in politics at the time of the *Wende*, supporting LILA's position on rapid reunification rather than the FDJ's preference for reform within the GDR.

Mirko slept through the night of 9 November, only learning of the fall of the Wall on the radio the next day. 'It was unimaginable to me that this would happen,' he explains:

> From September onward, it was clear that something would change, but it was still surprising how things developed in November. The system which had seemed invincible was suddenly gone. I had hoped for reform, he said, but neither the opening up of the Wall nor reunification was predictable. What followed was a period of uncertainty; there was a lack of direction and people wondered what would happen next. There was also a sense of breathing out, of relaxing.

Mirko went to school as normal on 10 November. All lessons were cancelled and many pupils did not turn up. This merely intensified an existing trend as, from May 1989 onwards, when the border between

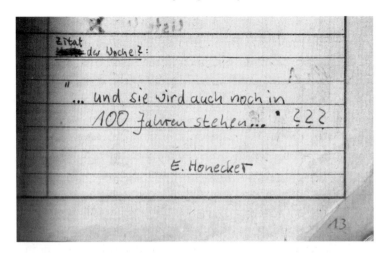

Zitat der Woche?:

"... und sie wird auch noch in 100 Jahren stehen..." ???

E. Honecker

FIGURE 25 '…and it [the Wall] will still be standing in a hundred years…'
Erich Honecker speaking in Berlin on 19 January 1989.
Courtesy of Mirko Sennewald.

Austria and Hungary had been opened up, more and more children
across the GDR simply failed to come to school since their families
had fled to the West.[16] On 10 November, however, Mirko remembers
that those who did come to school sat around discussing what had
happened and what would happen next. Around this time, Mirko
jotted down some of the more absurd quotations of the socialist
leaders, reflecting his growing scepticism towards the SED. Demonstrating a particularly detailed knowledge of current affairs, even for
a 15-year-old growing up in the heavily politicized GDR, Mirko cited
Erich Honecker's declaration from a speech on 19 January 1989 that
'The Wall will be standing in fifty and even in a hundred years, if the
reasons for it are not yet removed', poking fun at the former General
Secretary of the SED who had clearly been proven wrong.

Throughout its forty-year existence, adults and children alike
told jokes at the expense of the regime. Such jokes were dangerous,
but were an excellent way to let off steam about the frustrations of
daily life in the GDR. A common joke in schools, which alluded to

the limited meal options at lunchtime, was 'Our canteen offers a choice. Either you eat it, or you leave it.' Numerous other jokes involved the three statesmen Ronald Reagan, Mikhail Gorbachev, and Erich Honecker meeting God in heaven. Erich Honecker, it seems, was always the butt of the joke:

> Erich Honecker, Ronald Reagan, and Mikhail Gorbachev meet God in heaven and ask him what the future of their countries will be. 'The USA', God says, 'will become a communist state.' Reagan turns around and begins to cry bitterly. 'The Soviet Union', God continues, 'will disappear altogether.' Gorbachev too turns around and begins to cry bitterly. 'And what about the DDR?' Honecker asks. God looks at him, turns round, and begins to cry bitterly.

> Erich Honecker has lost his watch. He calls the Minister for State Security and asks him to investigate. The next day Honecker finds his watch under the bed. He immediately calls the minister to tell him to stop the investigation. 'Too late,' the minister replies, 'We have already arrested ten people, all of whom have confessed.'

> Erich Honecker, General Secretary of the Communist Party, is delivering a speech. He asks the people: 'Who is your mother?'— 'The German Democratic Republic'—'Who is your father?'— 'You!'—'And what do you want to become.'—'Orphans!'[17]

Despite his evidently keen sense of irony in the *Wende* period, Mirko was extremely serious about his desire for reunification with West Germany rather than reform within East Germany. To emphasize this point, he drew a sketch of the GDR flag in his exercise book and then scribbled it out. (See Figure 28.)

Mirko's exercise book further demonstrates his contempt for the regime by referring to the moment when Erich Mielke, head of the Stasi, was jeered and booed in the East German parliament for the first time on 13 November 1989. (See Figure 29.) Criticized for addressing his colleagues as comrades, Mielke was taken aback by the hostility against him and apologized, explaining 'But I love you all'—an embarrassing utterance that fell on deaf ears in the *Volkskammer* and was captured live on television. The doodled hangmen in Mirko's notebook are quite prophetic. This moment marked the abrupt end to Mielke's power, and by 7 December he had been detained in custody.

Over the following months, after reunification was decided upon, East German schools experienced rather a hiatus. Ideological components of the old syllabus such as citizenship lessons and the FDJ were quickly dropped, and strongly socialist teachers swiftly disappeared from the classrooms, but it was unclear what the new syllabus would be. Schools suddenly adopted a Western approach to education, but as most of the teachers were from the old system, they lacked confidence in using these new teaching methods.[18] Over the coming years Mirko sat his A levels in reunited Germany, before taking a job working for Airbus building aeroplanes.

While for young people like Mirko there were more options and greater choice in reunited Germany, this was not the case for everybody. His father, for example, lost his job teaching the regime's

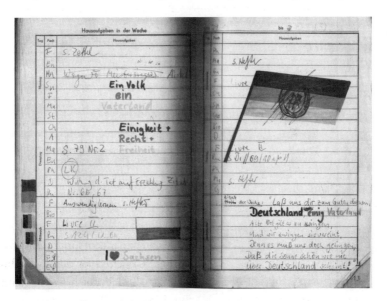

FIGURE 26 Extract from Mirko's exercise book.
Courtesy of Mirko Sennewald.

FIGURE 27 'But I love you all…' Erick Mielke addressing the *Volkskammer* on 13 November 1989.
Courtesy of Mirko Sennewald.

ideology, and, as a firm believer in socialism, felt like a fish out of water, holding views contrary to those of the prevailing government (much as opponents of the SED had felt in the GDR). Since Mirko holds very different political views to his father, he chooses not to talk about politics with him, knowing that it will lead to arguments. He simply says, 'We hardly ever have discussions about politics because we disagree. It is easier that way.'[19]

Much of Mirko's life story after 1989 seems to have been shaped by growing up in communist East Germany. For the past few years, for example, he has run a cultural institute which arranges exchanges for young Germans with young people from Eastern Europe. The participants learn about foreign cultures and different types of government through their visits abroad. Through this work, Mirko has also given talks to local governments in the Balkans, presenting the developments in Saxony after 1990 as a model for transforming a cultural sector from a socialist system to a

Western one. Motivated by the lack of freedom in Belarus, Mirko has worked with an oppositional youth movement there, sharing his experiences from East Germany in 1989 and the transition that followed afterwards. For Mirko this is in part a political mission, driven by his own experience of living in the GDR.

Unlike many of his contemporaries, including Carola, who avoid having any formal political affiliation, due to their toxic memories of the dictatorial set-up in the GDR, Mirko is actively involved in politics at a local level, striving to improve the situation in his community as a member of the liberal Free Democratic Party of Germany (*Freie Demokratische Partei* or FDP) in Dresden Neustadt. Growing up in the GDR and living through the transition to unification, Mirko explains, has encouraged his belief that individuals have an important part to play in shaping their circumstances.

Mirko is not the least bit nostalgic for life in the GDR. He views the possibilities as much greater in reunited Germany but at the same time believes that freedoms are more limited currently than is widely acknowledged: 'You have a lot more choice about what you do, but it's not like there aren't any barriers and boundaries in re-unified Germany.' In theory, of course, all Germans can now travel around the world, all Germans can now say what they want without fear of reproach, and all Germans can now live their lives free of close monitoring from the likes of the Stasi. Mirko concurs that it is much better to be able to travel freely, explaining, 'Whenever I fly anywhere, I am aware that it is a great freedom and I am grateful.' However, 'Freedom to travel for example is fantastic in theory, but a lack of money prevents many people from exploiting this freedom.'[20] He adds, 'There can be bureaucratic or financial limitations, for example, which mean you can't do certain things, so in some cases self-determination comes to an end relatively quickly.' Indeed, as one East German noted, looking back on the high hopes pinned on the West German capitalist model, 'When we drove in our Trabant to West Berlin, I had the feeling that we could buy whatever we wanted. I soon realized, however, that everything cost a lot more money than we had.'[21] Freedom of speech is another much-vaunted virtue of modern democracies, but are we really free to say what we think? The existence of predominantly accepted views means that it can still be a challenge to voice unpopular or unusual ones. Also, though the Stasi no longer collects detailed information, in Mirko's experience the state in united Germany holds a great deal of information about every individual, and, in order to receive state benefits for example, one has no choice but to give this information. In fact, as one contemporary wrote, concurring with Mirko's views on the shortcomings of the new system, 'the search for individual happiness is possible in both systems. Only under capitalism it is harder to explain why you sometimes do not find it.'[22] In the wake of communism's collapse in Europe, triumphalist narratives endure about the virtues of democracy versus the pitfalls of socialism. For Mirko, who has lived in both systems, this binary distinction is too simple and serves to mask discussion about how the status quo could be improved.

Overall, spending the first sixteen years of life living in a socialist system has had a profound impact on Mirko. In direct reaction to the shortcomings of the East German state, as an adult Mirko remains active politically. Having experienced first-hand how extreme politics can shape daily life for the worse, through his work in countries like Belarus, Mirko is determined to protect individuality, freedom, and privacy where possible. As a teenager Mirko questioned and challenged the established structures of the GDR and after its demise he has retained a critical stance towards state authority in united Germany.

8

Peggy ~ Feeling Safe and Secure

When Peggy woke up on the morning of 10 November 1989, she knew that something was amiss. As she lay in bed, she could hear the familiar splutter of the coffee machine and smell the aroma of bread rolls as it wafted into the bedroom. Normally, though, Peggy's mother would come into the bedroom, open the curtains, and then sit by her on the bed, talking to her and stroking her face until she was finally awake. That day, her mother did not come in. Confused, Peggy slipped out of bed, careful not to disturb her two younger sisters who were sleeping in the beds next to hers. She found her mother sitting at the kitchen table, hands wrapped around a cup of coffee and staring into space. 'Why didn't you wake us?' was Peggy's first question. 'The Wall's fallen', her mother replied laconically. Peggy was unsure what her mother meant. She followed her mother's gaze out of the window, expecting to see the fence at the end of their garden in small-town Prenzlau knocked down. 'Not that wall,' her mother explained, 'the Wall in Berlin!'

A number of thoughts passed through the head of 10-year-old Peggy. She had heard about the West being rife with unemployment and homelessness, so one of the first things she thought was 'I hope we get to keep our flat and I hope my parents don't lose their jobs'.[1] Much like Lisa, Peggy believed what she had been taught in school about the long queues outside the (un)employment centres in West Germany, where people were not guaranteed work, despite having good qualifications.[2] She accepted what she had

been taught about West Germany being the enemy, a society with
an imperialist, capitalist, and allegedly inhuman world view.[3] Fear
much more than hope, then, characterized Peggy's initial reaction
to the news. She had no inkling that the change would bring new
opportunities for her. She certainly did not feel relief or a sense of
freedom at last.[4] And a more pressing concern was whether her
school camp which was scheduled to start the next day would still
happen. The class had been looking forward to going to Templin
together as a reward for their 'good socialist behaviour'. Now,
events in Berlin called the trip into doubt. Peggy was relieved to
learn from her mother that the trip was still on.

Peggy had noticed the rumblings of discontent in the year running up to the fall of the Wall. Before her family had moved to Prenzlau that autumn, they had lived right on the market square in
Frankfurt Oder. She and her sisters had a great view of the protestors who were calling for change below with their big banners. Her
mother was philosophical about the situation in the GDR: it might
not be perfect, but she was equally sure that the Western way with its
unemployment and lack of social security had its downsides too. Her
father, by contrast, frequently complained about the state of play in
the GDR, and took part in the demonstrations. He even left his
family behind to travel to the Prague Embassy in September 1989,
hoping to secure safe passage to the West, only to change his mind
and return to his family the day before the West German Foreign
Minister Genscher said that all the applicants would be let through.[5]

The weekend after the Wall fell, Peggy's family decided to drive
to West Berlin. Since Peggy was away, her family took a 40-kilo-
metre detour via her camp to see if she wanted to go with them.
When they arrived, however, Peggy decided to stay with her
friends—there was a disco happening that night to celebrate *Fasch-
ing*, the start of the carnival period celebrated in Germany between
the middle of November and the start of Lent each year, and
Peggy and her classmates were going to wear fancy dress. She
asked her parents to bring her back one thing above all: a Hanuta

wafer biscuit. For years, Peggy had watched the TV adverts singing the praises of Hanuta. They were made to seem so heavenly that Peggy had long felt aggrieved that she was not able to eat them: 'When I saw Western adverts, I thought it was really mean that I couldn't eat Hanuta. How come I don't have the pleasure of eating those? I always thought. After the Wall fell one of my biggest priorities was to eat a Hanuta.'[6] When she finally got to taste this biscuit a few days later, the Hanuta was something of a disappointment. This was Peggy's first step towards a realization of how exaggerated Western advertisements were.[7] In our interview she says this is indicative of her experience of dealing with West Germans generally: they are good at presenting themselves in the most favourable light possible, but this promising presentation is not always a true reflection of their abilities.[8]

Peggy's first visit to the West in February 1990 made a favourable impression on her. En route to Hamburg, Peggy's eyes gaped at the huge Western cars she saw on the motorway. What would it be like, she wondered, to be so rich that you could drive around in cars like the ones she saw? These cars looked so different from the Trabant her family were driving in. When they were about to park up, a big Mercedes rushed in and took their parking bay. Was this just typical arrogant Wessi (West German) behaviour? Peggy's family wondered. But no! The driver had not seen them and was profusely apologetic when he realized. He backed out and found another bay so that Peggy's family could park where they had intended. This man then came over and introduced himself. He was fascinated by the Trabant and joined the family for a spin around the car park. He was a local man and was keen to take the family on a guided tour around the city in his Mercedes. Once the family had seen the cultural highlights of Hamburg, the kindly West German took them to McDonalds, insisting that he order one of everything on the menu so that the family could taste all that was on offer. Peggy could not believe it when she saw that the total bill for the food was 120 West German Marks—more than the 100 West German Marks of Welcome

Money that East Germans received when they visited the West. The whole experience was very exciting. West Germany seemed wonderful and new but it also felt quite different.

Of course not all East Germans had such positive initial encounters with their West German counterparts. Felix R. from Pankow in East Berlin was a young teenager in the early 1990s. He and a friend took a shopping trip to 'Zoo' in West Berlin, whereupon they were accosted by an old man. The old man showed the boys needle marks in his arm, while claiming that he had a knife in his pocket which he would use to kill them if they did not hand over all their money. Fearing for their lives, Felix and his friend ran to the nearest underground station and only felt safe when they got to the Eastern part of the city. In mere moments, East German propaganda about the problems with drugs and crime in the West had been confirmed to these boys as true.[9]

Other East Germans, who did not have such extreme experiences on their first visit to the West, nonetheless frequently commented on how foreign West Germany felt. Once they had satisfied their curiosity by venturing over the border, many retreated to their own half of Germany, later explaining that, although it was interesting to see the FRG, it was all very unfamiliar and simply did not feel like home.[10] Fourteen-year-old Robert Ide noticed in particular how different the food was: 'The bread rolls from the lurid yellow bakery chain tasted bland and looked like they'd been pumped full of air. The macaroni seemed too fat and the spaghetti too thin.'[11]

Small differences like these were accompanied by so many other big changes that in the years that followed, some East Germans like Peggy came to feel that they had lost their homeland.[12] They also had the impression that West Germans looked down on their education system as inferior and treated them as though they were unquestioning supporters of socialist values or, at the very least, might have some strange opinions and beliefs.[13] This feeling was often even more pronounced among those East Germans who experienced the transition to unification at a later stage in life. Nina

Benedict, a woman in her sixties, for example, sank into a deep depression following the amalgamation of East Germany into the West: 'No one asks me for my advice any more,' she wrote. 'Who today wants still to hear, or indeed ever to have heard, a body of thought that was once "infected" by socialism?'[14] Another lady, who had been mayor of a town called Kella between 1980 and 1990, echoes Benedict's dejection, describing what it was like to have her beliefs and actions challenged so fundamentally: 'When I think of how hard I worked and how I fought for every little thing...And now to think that was all wrong. Everything I did! For this village! I didn't necessarily want that [communist] system, but simply to help make life somewhat more bearable for the people here.'[15]

Although Peggy was only a young girl when the Wall fell, and was therefore not challenged to justify her past actions in the way that many of her elders were, she nonetheless has a sense that Westerners may take her views less seriously if they know that she grew up in the GDR. 'I can't speak High German,' Peggy adds. 'It makes me feel fake.'[16] This in itself marks her out from West Germans. 'In part it is the way they talk and the words they use, but it is also the fact that their whole way of behaving is different', she says.[17] To this day, Peggy feels like an outsider if she is in a group of West Germans and is more comfortable in East German settings.[18]

Long before the fall of the Wall, the German-speaking Czech novelist Franz Kafka articulated the negative impact on a friendship of very different experiences:

> Once there were two friends. One had spent six weeks in a hospital bed. The other had spent the same time travelling. When the traveller visited his friend, he would talk of nothing but the fabulous time he had. Although the two had been friends for a long time, they could no longer communicate. Their recent experience made them strangers.[19]

For those East Germans like Peggy who had had little or no contact with people in West Germany, it understandably took a long time to build friendships with Germans who had lived on the other side of the Wall.[20] In the early years of transition many of them observed that the West German way of life was faster, louder, and more colourful but simultaneously also very alien. The cultural norms of everyday life were simply very different, and many missed the sense of security and shared mission that they had felt in the GDR. It therefore took many East Germans quite a while before they felt at home in their newly reunited country, and for some, like Peggy, this remains an ongoing process of adjustment.[21] It was with some foresight, then, that Erich Honecker, as General Secretary of the SED, declared, 'Ideological work has lasting influence on the development of the people.'[22]

Looking back on her childhood in the GDR, Peggy has over-whelmingly positive memories. Too young to feel the impact of the travel restrictions, she simply recalls happy times with her family on holidays, close to home, organized through her mother's work.[23] Most workplaces in the GDR organized holidays for their em-ployees within East Germany and since these affiliated holidays were subsidized, they were much cheaper than taking a holiday independently. Peggy's best family holiday, she says, was in a forest near a lake only 20 kilometres away from their home, but it still provided a change of scene, nice weather, and parents with spare time. What more does a child need on a holiday, she asks? In today's world, by contrast, Peggy questions whether it makes sense for people to fly halfway around the world for their holidays when they don't even know the places of natural beauty on their doorstep.

Peggy also remembers her time as a member of the socialist Young Pioneers as great fun. What with the uniform, the singsongs, and the regular outings, there were plenty of things to enjoy with friends.[24] 'I have positive memories of the Pioneers,' she says. 'We went on excursions, days out visiting museums and going swim-ming.' She and her friends used to collect old material to be recycled, and they would receive money for the cloth, paper, and

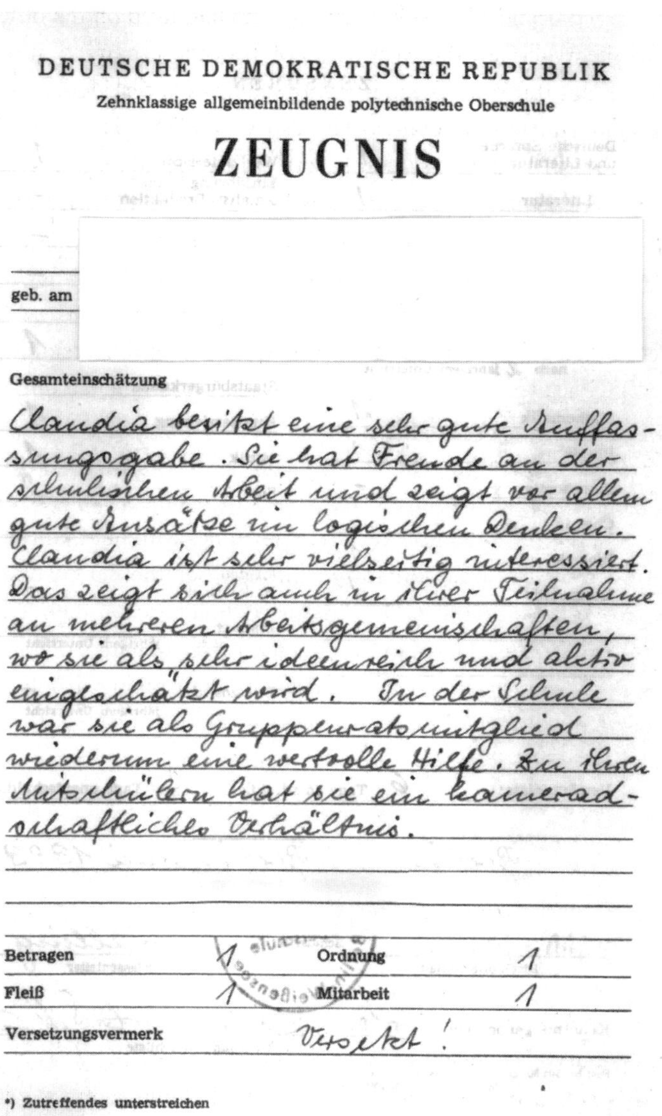

DEUTSCHE DEMOKRATISCHE REPUBLIK

Zehnklassige allgemeinbildende polytechnische Oberschule

ZEUGNIS

geb. am

Gesamteinschätzung

Claudia besitzt eine sehr gute Auffassungsgabe. Sie hat Freude an der schulischen Arbeit und zeigt vor allem gute Ansätze im logischen Denken. Claudia ist sehr vielseitig interessiert. Das zeigt sich auch in ihrer Teilnahme an mehreren Arbeitsgemeinschaften, wo sie als sehr ideenreich und aktiv eingeschätzt wird. In der Schule war sie als Gruppenratsmitglied wiederum eine wertvolle Hilfe. Zu ihren Mitschülern hat sie ein kameradschaftliches Verhältnis.

Betragen	1	Ordnung	1
Fleiß	1	Mitarbeit	1
Versetzungsvermerk		Versetzt !	

*) Zutreffendes unterstreichen

FIGURE 28 Claudia's school report from 1989.
Courtesy of Claudia S.

glass which would go into the class fund.[25] In her spare time, Peggy sometimes collected cloth as a way of getting a bit more pocket money. One time, she earned 10 East German Marks through her efforts. When her teacher got wind of this, she asked Peggy in front of the whole class whether she was going to donate any of her gains to the class fund. Feeling under pressure, Peggy gave 8 East German Marks to the fund and kept just 2 for herself. This is a small example of the values that pervaded GDR society and in particular the rejection of private interest and ownership.

The school report from 1989 belonging to Claudia S., a girl two years older than Peggy, tells us a lot about the values that the regime wished to instil in young people, in particular about the importance of working together as a society, with a far greater importance placed on the collective than the individual. It praises Claudia's active contribution to 'working groups' within the school, and states that 'She interacts with her fellow pupils in a comradely manner'.

Unlike other children in her class, Peggy did not have many relatives from the West, and this was a source of envy. Though her father's relatives had sent a parcel once, she explains,

> I always wanted more Western relatives. I was jealous of others in my class who had more relatives in the West. They got clothing from the West, or sweets. My grandmother was almost of the age when she could go over, but then the Wall fell. I was looking forward to when she could go over, aged 60, because a friend of mine had a granny who brought things over from the West. But I did not want to go to the West. I was not aware that it was an option. It seemed like an absurd idea.

Only one truly negative memory of the GDR sticks out for Peggy, and this relates to the corruption of authorities. Each Saturday morning, Peggy's class went swimming. The girls had their lesson first and then the boys came after so that the girls could go home to dry their hair before returning to school. Peggy enjoyed swimming and had a good rapport with the sports teacher who was quite authoritarian in his teaching style. Sport was a serious matter in the GDR. Its founding father, Walther Ulbricht, had declared that 'Everybody, Everywhere, Should Play Sports Every Week'.[26] Sport was viewed by the Party leadership as the key vehicle for transforming East Germans into socialist citizens. Success in sport at an international level, so the thinking went, would raise the profile of the country throughout the world and instil pride and loyalty in its citizens. Training young hopefuls was a key stepping stone on this path to socialist glory.[27] At swimming training one Saturday, Peggy had been joking around with the teacher. As the lesson progressed, he got frustrated with the girls who could not swim and chucked a bucket of cold water over them. Emboldened by their jokey rapport, but also cross at the way the teacher had been mean to the struggling swimmers, Peggy soaked the teacher with a bucket of water. Taken aback by her behaviour, the teacher took a swing at her with his arm which sent her flying across the room—an act that was seen by all the girls in the pool and by all the boys who were crowding to look through the window while they waited for their lesson. When she got home, Peggy told her parents what had happened. They went straight to the school to report the incident to the head teacher. The head teacher was not inclined to listen to such a story and after several meetings it was decreed that Peggy should retract her claims and apologize to the sports teacher in front of the whole class, saying that she had lied about what happened. At the time Peggy realized that something was not right about this situation. Children these days, she believes, would not be so easily manipulated.

Despite her clash with the school authorities in the third grade, a more positive experience with another teacher helped to even out Peggy's opinion of those in charge. Every parents' evening at school, the best exercise books would go on display. Parents who were in the Stasi were often particularly anxious to see their children excel academically and would take an active role in ensuring that the work was neat and that the pictures were stuck in as tidily as possible. One parents' evening, the teacher chose to display Peggy's work, despite it looking less perfect than some of the other books. The teacher explained that she chose it because it was clear that Peggy had done the work herself. This example helped Peggy to retain her trust in the system.

As our conversation turns to the *Wende*, Peggy tells me that in many ways she believes reunification has worsened the quality of life for East Germans. Fundamentally, her values remain those of the state in which she was born. Peggy's stance is not taken out of a feeling of envy or resentment, nor because she has failed to thrive in the new circumstances. She is perfectly content with her lot. However, she genuinely believes that the GDR system had some real benefits. In keeping with many East German women, Peggy began having children relatively young by Western standards, aged 26.[28] Like Lisa and 95 per cent of East Germans who responded to a major opinion poll in the early 1990s, Peggy feels that too much emphasis and import is placed on money and material goods in reunited Germany, and she notices this particularly in reference to raising children.[29] Whereas she had her first child while she was still a student, so that she would have lots of time with it, and now works very reduced hours as a freelance historian so that she can pick her children up from school and spend time with them every day, Westerners that she knows put off having children until their mid-thirties when they were materially more established, and then they remained focused on work after having children with the aim of providing expensive equipment and toys for their offspring. For Peggy, having more money is not the answer and life in a consumer society does not nurture the values that she considers important. 'I don't need lots of money,' she says. 'I just need enough money. Apart from that I want free time to spend with my family.'

Nor has greater access to the Western consumer world made East Germans happier people, Peggy contends. Certainly in the wake of reunification, the new range of choices open to East

Germans was often as much a source of anxiety as it was pleasure. As one girl who was two years older than Peggy later explained,

> Throughout my childhood I had worn cast-off clothes sent by Western relatives through the post. Now I could go into shops like H and M, where the choice was abundant. Before, I'd never had to think about what suited me or what was appropriate to wear. With a complete absence of criteria for what to pick, I was overwhelmed.[30]

Another of Peggy's contemporaries, Angelique L. from East Berlin, who was 15 when the Wall fell, had a similarly stressful recollection of how her mother simply burst into tears in the 'Europa' shopping centre, so bewildered was she by the choice of so many pairs of shoes—and bags to match.[31]

Another aspect of life in reunified Germany causes Peggy concern. In her eyes, a private market economy for housing simply is not fair.[32] 'Why', she asks, 'should someone with rich parents have more choice about where they live?' She rails against inherited privileges. She and her husband live in accommodation provided by the state—a flat they were allocated as students when they were expecting their first child. They are fearful, she explains, that they will be cast out from their home if the state sells their flat. They live in the Prenzlauer Berg area of Berlin, which has become increasingly trendy with West Berliners and expats alike. If Peggy's family did have to leave the flat, they could never afford to stay in the area. This worry, this fear of losing one's home, she says, is far greater and more ever-present than the level of fear most people experienced due to the Stasi in the GDR.

Reflecting on life in reunited Germany, Peggy explains that she is happy that her children do not have to watch what they say and that they do not have to lie to conform to the state's ideological dictates. Nevertheless she points to many downsides in the capitalist model. Her children, she says, dislike going to the bank with her, because they have to walk past the homeless people begging outside. Peggy, by contrast, first saw a homeless person when she was 14, in Hamburg. She is sorry that her children have to see this. It does not sit well with her that people are left to languish and sleep rough, while others focus on the accumulation of money and goods and foreign travel. 'Things felt more equal in the GDR', Peggy says. She is keen to foster such values in her children. To this end, whenever she gives her children treats in their packed lunches for school, she makes sure that there is enough for every child in the class, so that no one feels left out.

Peggy is conscious that East Germans are often typecast as nostalgic for the GDR, harking back fondly to a time that no longer exists, safe in the knowledge that it is never going to be a viable alternative to the current reality. She knows that West Germans, too, regret that things are no longer as they were. In her eyes, though, their reality has changed far less than hers. When she goes home to Prenzlau, hardly any of her family members are doing the same jobs as when the Wall fell, and none of the shops that were there still exist. Though Peggy believes she was lucky to still be a child at the time of the *Wende*, since she was able to grow used to the changes at a younger age than people of her parents' generation, she still misses the noises and smells of shops like HO, Konsum, and Kaufhalle, and wishes she could go into them just one more time. The past has been blotted out, and, in Peggy's view, this past was not nearly as bad as Western politicians would lead us to believe.

When 10-year-old Peggy learned that the GDR had collapsed, her first reaction was concern that her family would be affected by what she perceived to be Western problems, such as homelessness. Yet while she feared the West in some respects, there were also aspects of it that seemed attractive, such as the tasty-looking biscuits advertised on Western television. Peggy's initial mixed feelings about the West have extended into her adult life. On the one hand, she sees many good aspects of the current set-up, in particular much greater freedom of expression, and she is keen to emphasize that she does not have exclusively positive memories of the GDR, but on the other hand she also believes that the East German system had many advantages—not least feeling fairer. Ultimately though, Peggy concludes, 'I am very pleased to have experienced both living in the GDR and the fall of the Wall, because it means I am familiar with two types of political system. This therefore gives me a differentiated perspective on capitalism.'

Interpreting the End
of East Germany

'People here [in the GDR] saved for half a lifetime for a spluttering Trabant. Then along comes the smooth Mercedes society and makes our whole existence, our dreams, and our identity, laughable.'[1] Less than a year after the Berlin Wall fell, the GDR ceased to exist. And with this development, as East German psychotherapist Hans Joachim Maaz effectively shows, GDR citizens were challenged to make huge adjustments. German reunification on 3 October 1990 may have been marked with celebrations and huge firework displays, however divisions between East and West were far from surmounted. For all that joining a democratic system opened the door to new opportunities that had been unavailable to them under SED rule, GDR citizens lost a specific culture and way of life that many sorely missed. And so, though the incorporation of the East German states into the West German confederation led to wide-reaching practical changes in their daily lives, the period was also marked by notable continuities in the social and mental make-up which had developed under four decades of socialist rule.

Since the GDR has been erased from the map, two extreme characterizations of East Germany have come to dominate popular consciousness. There is the damningly negative Stasi-centred depiction on the one hand, and a rosily positive picture of a socialist utopia on the other. The final chapter of this volume seeks to accomplish two things: first, to offer a general explanation of why the end of East Germany has prompted such contrasting memories of it, and secondly, to review the eight individual accounts of life before, during, and after reunification, with the aim of better understanding these contrasts.

With the end of the GDR, revelations emerged showing just what a difficult time nonconformists had had there: the Stasi had observed and photographed people's movements, secretly searched their homes, listened in to their telephone conversations, and even collected smell samples in jars, the idea being that trained sniffer dogs could tell where a person had been.

Without a doubt, the most sensational details of the Stasi's activities stick in the mind. Mario's story, for example, revealed the various psychological techniques used on political prisoners to get

FIGURE 29 Smell samples collected from political 'enemies' by the Stasi.
© Stasi-Museum Berlin, ASTAK e.V. Foto: John Steer.

them to confess and to divulge the names of other 'political devi-
ants'—be it sleep deprivation for days on end leading to disorientation and confusion, or being locked in a pitch-black van, hunched
with no room to stand and barely room to sit. This is the stuff
newspaper headlines were made of in the aftermath of reunion.

With 91,000 full-time employees and 173,000 informal 'helpers'
in 1989, the Stasi far exceeded the Nazi's 7,000-strong Gestapo in
scale. Even discounting the approximately 10,000 elite troops who
served in the Felix Dzerzhinsky Guards Regiment charged with
protecting the SED, and the 47,000 guards who patrolled the borders of the GDR, it is beyond question that there were large numbers of East Germans who acted as informants for the Stasi.[2] Such
meticulous surveillance meant that in the forty years between the
creation of communist East Germany in 1949 and its collapse,
the Stasi had collected more paper files than had been collected
in the whole of Germany from the Middle Ages to the end of the
Second World War.[3]

Homing in on the Stasi and the dictatorial elements of life in the
GDR served to quash the discussion of anything positive that took
place under SED rule. And it no doubt aided ruling politicians in
reunified Germany in their objective of discrediting the socialist
approach and presenting themselves in a comparably favourable
light. Whatever the motivation for the media focus, it has helped to
establish Stasi-centric memories of the GDR.

If fear and constraint dominated daily life and the GDR was a
dictatorial Stasi-state, it follows logically that the collapse of communism should have been a relief to those who had lived there and
that the transition to the more liberal, Western way of living should
have been relatively easy. However, most East Germans reject this
Stasi-centred characterization of their old homeland.[4] Many claim
that they had no idea of the extent to which the Stasi was inter-
twined with daily life, and therefore they do not remember the
GDR in this way. Furthermore, following reunification many East
Germans mourned the loss of their homeland, suggesting that the

relationship between the GDR and its people was complex and not uniformly antagonistic.

So why might the GDR *not* have felt like a Stasi-state? Focusing on the role of the Stasi in the GDR can lead to the impression that ordinary East Germans had very little control over their lives under SED rule. But rather than being passive victims, many East Germans felt like active citizens, making a positive contribution towards the GDR's collective goals. One of the SED's oft-used slogans was 'work together, plan together, govern together', and citizens were invited to air their views in the GDR, be it in public meetings or through letters of complaint. This contributed to the stability of the system. SED officials did of course have ulterior motives for offering ordinary citizens the chance to voice their grievances, since it gave them insight into the issues affecting ordinary people's lives and allowed them to shape policy in light of what they had heard. Such opportunities for expression may have been conditional on ordinary Germans not challenging the fundamentals of the system such as the basic tenets of communist ideology or the existence of the Wall, but in many ways these conditions were irrelevant to how most East Germans felt about the SED. In their eyes, they had been offered platforms for discussion which led them to trust the regime and made them feel listened to.[5] Contrary to 'top-down' characterizations of the GDR which focus on the Stasi, citizens had some say in how day-to-day life in the GDR developed. This is one of the reasons why many East Germans do not recall the GDR as a dictatorship, but as a country in which they could lead a perfectly ordinary life.[6]

Acceptance rather than hostility characterized the relations between most East Germans and the communist government in the GDR. For though there were no free elections and the people were walled in, once the division was accepted as permanent in the years after the Berlin Wall was built, East Germans pragmatically got on with making the best of a situation they had no expectation of changing.[7] Cooperation, at the very least in the form of passive conformity, was therefore key to SED rule. Driven by a range of motivations, from a desire to improve socialism, to wanting to be promoted at work, to material advantages such as holidays, many East Germans altered their behaviour in a way that helped the state maintain power. Petra, for example, joined the SED, believing it to be the only course of action to help improve the status quo, while Carola's father joined for pragmatic reasons after years of resisting, in the expectation that the socialist system would be the prevailing set-up in the long term. It is therefore rather more helpful to see the state as ruling through society rather than against it.[8] All of this helps to explain why later, after the Wall fell, even East Germans who had felt ambivalent towards the SED regime while living under it, felt more of an attachment to it than they had done at the time. They had lived in a socialist state and grown used to its modus operandi.[9] Only in reunited Germany did the depth of this affiliation to the communist state become apparent. If the relationship between the East German state and its people was characterized more by compromise, bargaining, and shared interests, it is undertandable that so many East Germans later rejected the labelling of the GDR as a Stasi-state, with all of the antagonistic implications inherent in such a term.[10]

However, to an outsider schooled in the virtues of democracy it may well seem counter-intuitive to think that the new opportunities presented to East Germans by reunification could be experienced as anything other than positive. After all, in reunified Germany, East Germans had far greater choice: about what they said, what they did, where they went, and what they ate. Since not all East Germans embraced these changes with open arms, they were unkindly called *Jammerossis* or 'Moaning Easterners' by some of their West German brothers and sisters. If we are seeking to immerse ourselves in their perspective, we should consider what gave rise to their sense of discontentment.[11]

The *Wende* certainly brought many welcome changes for East Germans, such as the democracy that so many of the protestors in

1989 had been clamouring for, as well as greater individual opportunities and freedoms. However there were downsides to the transition that few anticipated.[12] How keenly these were felt relative to the upsides varied from individual to individual. The *Wende* was hard on those who had felt life was satisfactory in the GDR. They had more to lose from the change because they were not unhappy with the status quo and did not feel stifled by the demands of the socialist regime. But the *Wende* was also hard on those who had longed for change, only to find that their high hopes were dashed when united Germany did not live up to expectations.[13]

A number of key factors help to explain why some East Germans have negative feelings about reunification. The first of these is ideological: supporters of the East German government like Petra had believed in the socialist mission that everyone should work together as a society towards a better future. Reunited Germany, they found, was competitive and individualistic, and lacked the solidarity and the sense of joint mission that they had valued in the GDR: this they experienced as a loss.[14] For different reasons, opponents of the GDR, such as Protestant agitators who had made it their mission to preach against the socialist government, also felt a loss of purpose.[15]

Secondly, East Germans who had been reasonably content in the GDR felt let down by reunification due to the widespread unemployment which affected them after 1989: they noticed a loss of stability in their everyday lives as the GDR's uncompetitive command economy was integrated into a competitive market economy. Even two decades later the unemployment rate remains nearly twice as high amongst East Germans as amongst West Germans, with East German women disproportionately affected.[16] When the GDR was absorbed into the Western capitalist model, 98 per cent of its businesses were state-owned. This meant that after reunification around 8,000 state-run enterprises had to be privatized—a move that cost millions of jobs.[17] Alongside these job losses, the difficulties of making East German industries run cleanly and according to new Western environmental standards increased businesses' overheads and resulted in further job cuts. The town of Hoyerswerda is an extreme case in point: its population had swelled tenfold during the communist era due to the vibrant coal industry in the area. After the *Wende*, when West German laws to contain pollution were applied to the former GDR, demand for brown coal (lignite) fell. Consequently, the number of job opportunities in the area shrank dramatically, contributing to rapid depopulation, with the number of inhabitants falling by half in the twenty years following unification.[18] (It was only in 2012 that for the first time in reunited Germany almost as many people moved from West to East as from East to West.[19]) In the former GDR as a whole, the unemployment rate among East Germans rocketed from 0 per cent in 1989 to 7.3 per cent in 1990, a figure that was kept artificially low by reducing the working hours of 20 per cent of the workforce.[20] By 1992 this figure had risen to 15 per cent.[21] And although a government report from November 2013 announced that East German unemployment had hit its lowest rate since reunification, this still amounts to 9.5 per cent of the East German population being out of work, as opposed to 5.8 per cent in the West.[22] Unsurprisingly, a number of the protagonists in this book were affected by the widespread unemployment among East Germans: Robert, Peggy, and Mirko all recounted how their fathers experienced difficulties gaining employment after the *Wende*.

Thirdly, for those East Germans lucky enough to find work, the competitive environment of the West German workplace was also new, requiring different skills and a keener sense of individual responsibility. Employment in united Germany stood in stark contrast with how employment had worked in the GDR: as we saw in the cases of Lisa and Katharina, individuals often had more limited choice about what work they did, but it was guaranteed that everyone would have a job. Employment was both a right and a duty in the GDR, which called on every individual to make an active contribution to the socialist set-up.[23] The long-term gains brought by reunification therefore quickly paled into insignificance for many families who were thrown into crisis by a lack of income and a much-reduced social security net. Indeed, as Mirko and many of the other interviewees remarked, it is all very well to have the freedom to travel or the greater access to consumer goods, but the reality is that these options are only available to those who have the money. These interviewees were not saying that the increased opportunities were negative per se, simply that the extent to which they are really available to all has been exaggerated.[24] In this context it is unsurprising that many East Germans view their past lives in a favourable light.

Fourthly, when they voted for rapid reunification, East Germans understandably assumed that they would gain Western standards of living pretty imminently.[25] That this was not the case has been a further source of disappointment. In reality, many areas of former East Germany suffered very badly economically after 1990. West German Chancellor Helmut Kohl promised East Germans the same standard of living as the West within five years, but what transpired was less rosy. At the time of reunification the average East German salary was less than one-third of the average West German salary. Not only this, but the cost of living for East Germans rose after unification as the unsustainable communist subsidies of basic foodstuffs and rents were lifted.[26] In Leipzig, for example, the cost of rents was between five and ten times greater in 1994 in comparison to 1989. And whereas the average family of four in East Germany spent 5 per cent of their monthly income on rent, the norm in West Germany was 20 per cent.[27] Those who had hoped for a speedy adoption of a Western lifestyle after reunification are frustrated that people living in former East German territory remain consistently poorer than people living in West German territory even though so many years have passed.

Lastly, an apparent failure of understanding and sympathy amongst West Germans for what their Eastern compatriots were going through during the *Wende* was a further source of disappointment for many East Germans, whether supporters or opponents of the socialist regime.[28] Before the Wall fell, West Germans supported East German friends or relatives by sending approximately 25 million parcels per year across the border.[29] They had also shown solidarity with their East German brethren through symbolic actions such as putting a candle in the front windows of their homes to demonstrate that they had not forgotten them.[30] Somewhat counter-intuitively, Germans from opposite sides of the Wall who had kept in touch before November 1989 often found that their relations with those on the other side crumbled once the Iron Curtain had been removed. Was this because the West Germans were no longer the charitable, benevolent givers with the upper hand?[31] Or was it simply that the new unparalleled opportunities for face-to-face interaction revealed just how little they had in common?

After forty years living in societies with very different values, it is hardly surprising that in 1990 both East and West Germans said of each other that 'their clocks tick differently'.[32] As one joke from 1990 had it: the East German says to the West German, '*Wir sind ein Volk*' (We are one people). The West German replies, '*Wir auch*' (Us too).[33] But because East and West Germans shared the same language and long-term history, it was widely expected, as former West German Chancellor Willy Brandt said on 10 November 1989, that the two countries would 'grow together' seamlessly.[34] This has taken much longer than anticipated. Though it was a concrete wall that initially caused the East–West divide, in many ways the impact of division was brought into sharper relief when East and West Germans were standing side by side. The 1980s had seen the highest travel activity between both German states and with few exceptions East as well as West Germans consumed Western television programmes on a daily basis. However neither of these factors counterbalanced the very different outlooks that had developed over forty years of division. Through East German eyes, West Germans with their modern consumer society seemed to look down on every aspect of the GDR as inferior, and to see East Germans as having been infected with an unconvincing ideology.[35] In fact, as one East German wryly observed shortly after the Wall fell, 'Now we'll be the Turks of West Germany', alluding to the high numbers of Turkish immigrants in West Germany.[36] East Germans disliked feeling categorized as second-class citizens and found it hard to accept that nothing from their old lives was worth saving. Looking back on the *Wende* and its impact on his identity, Felix R., who was 9 when the Wall fell, says, 'It is only with reunification that I was made to feel East German.'[37] Therefore, even though reunification gave East Germans significant new freedoms in terms of travel, expression, and purchasing opportunity, it effectively defined and denigrated their identity as East Germans and in so doing revealed ongoing divisions between the East and West of the country.

The way East Germany was incorporated into West Germany upon reunification exacerbated the failure of mutual under-standing, especially from the East German perspective. In contrast to the GDR, where citizens had been encouraged up to a point to share their views with the regime, when it came to unification, the East German citizens (with the exception of a small minority like Petra) felt that they had little say in how the new Germany was shaped.[38] The GDR story, as they remembered it, appeared to have been snuffed out. And instead, the official memory of the GDR seemed to have been established on Western terms through the West German newspapers and television channels that have prevailed over their Eastern counterparts since reunification. This 'Western' version of the GDR past, as East Germans like Robert see it, emphasizes the inferiority of the socialist system both eco-nomically and socially as well as the prevalence of the Stasi in day-to-day life which, as we have seen, many East Germans do not recognize as their experience under socialism. Regarded as the poor relations after unification, East Germans like Robert and Peggy have become keen to defend aspects of their former lives in the GDR, emphasizing some of its material and moral benefits.[39]

Given the way they had been incorporated into the West, many felt nostalgia for the familiarity of life in the GDR, a place that was home, in contrast to the foreign culture that grew up on their native soil after 1990. Social anthropologist Elizabeth Ten Dyke offers useful insights into why East Germans felt such a strong sense of dislocation in the new circumstances:

> We can understand social situations and act in them in ways that are appropriate, and in our best interests, because we have a wealth of learning (memory) on which we can draw as we interpret a wide variety of settings...After the *Wende* East Germans had to function in an almost brand new world. They only slowly acquire the practical experience, and memories, they would need to be successful in this place...The *Wende* rendered a lifetime's worth of memory largely inapplicable to the strange new world of capitalist West Germany.[40]

Daily practices in East Germany that were so routine as to be subconsciously ingrained suddenly appeared both aberrant and bars to success in united Germany. Articulating the sense of uncertainty felt by many East Germans in the wake of the fall of the Wall, one woman noted in her diary entry for December 1989, 'Everywhere is becoming like a foreign land. I have long wished to travel to foreign parts, but I have always wanted to be able to come home...The landscapes will remain the same, the towns and villages will have the same names, but everything here is becoming increasingly unfamiliar.'[41] Above all, East Germans like Petra, Robert, and Peggy feel dissatisfied with the absolute nature of the takeover, which implied that nothing about their former lives was worth preserving. Voicing the resentment of many others, an East German bishop wrote a letter to the former West German Chancellor Helmut Schmidt, saying,

> We are expected merely to listen all the time. It is constantly suggested that we are not capable of anything, and that everything we have done was wrong. We are the only ones who have to learn

something, because, it is said, all of our experiences belong on the
trash pile of history. Apparently it is not worth listening when we are
saying anything. But we can no longer take this permanent know-all
manner and our degrading treatment as disenfranchised failures.[42]

While such sentiments were wholly understandable to other East
Germans who had lived through the massive upheaval of reunification, it was nonetheless with these kinds of remarks that East
Germans consolidated their reputation amongst some West Germans as moaning Easterners in the newly reunited Germany. They
were also seen as ungrateful, not least because the financial burden
of the union fell on West German taxpayers, to the tune of 140
billion Deutsche Marks per year during the 1990s.[43] Conversely, as
we saw in Katharina's story, West Germans, who seemed overly
confident, quick to criticize the GDR, or to lord over East Germans the superiority of Western ways, were often regarded as
'Know-it-all West Germans' by their East German compatriots.
Fundamentally, though, for East Germans, 'under the wreckage of
the old [SED] regime lay most of the certainties of life that [they]
had long taken for granted'.[44]

It is little wonder in this context that many East Germans in the
mid-1990s stated that they preferred living in divided Germany.
Marked social differences and uncomfortable economic realities
are critical factors in explaining the far from seamless transition to
a united Germany in the decades that followed unification. The
same reasons account for the other prevailing memory of the
GDR, based on nostalgia for the former East.

Though many East Germans in the years following reunification
did express fond memories of life behind the Iron Curtain, *Ostalgie*
is often misunderstood.[45] The East Germans I spoke to did not
describe their *Ostalgie* as nostalgia for the apparatus of the socialist
state. Nor was their *Ostalgie* really captured by East German products like the Trabant and the distinctive *Ampelmänner* (East German
traffic light men in red and green with unique hats) which have

FIGURE 30 Traffic light men (*Ampelmänner*) in East Berlin.
© Getty Images.

since assumed cult status—these are merely symptomatic of a resurgent fashion for vintage items, and a focus on such items is in fact damaging as it belittles a very real and understandable desire to retain a connection with where they have come from.

With the fall of the Wall, a whole way of life evaporated. The certainties on which day-to-day routines had been built ceased to exist.[46] The old and familiar life in the GDR was replaced with unknowns, and unknowns provoked fears: 'Fears about change that we didn't really want; fears about rules that we don't know; fears about unemployment...and fears about drugs.'[47] After the *Wende*, East Germans read uncensored newspapers for the first time—newspapers reporting horrible crimes that had not been covered in the controlled East German press even when such things happened. And with this, a naive feeling of safety was swept away for good. Whether or not the crime rates really were lower in East Germany, many interviewees expressed that they felt it was safer growing up in the GDR than it is in united Germany.[48] Discomfort

FIGURE 31 A Trabant outside the Brandenberg Gate, Berlin, 1984.
© Getty Images.

at unfamiliar cultural norms in reunited Germany and also the absence of their usual way of life combined to intensify fond memories of life in the GDR. Indeed, as one East German put it, 'Even a topsy-turvy world is home when everyone lives there.'[49] That home simply disappeared with the *Wende*. What emerges almost unanimously from the interview testimony, is that former GDR citizens draw a clear distinction between the regime (of which none of those interviewed harboured positive memories) and what people experienced as a specific culture. The nostalgia then is not chiefly political, but is instead nostalgia for the shared understanding stemming from joint memories and similar experiences. In many ways, then, it is no different from West Germans who remember aspects of their past in a positive light. Crucially, though, the FRG still exists but the GDR does not.

Having considered some general reasons why East Germans have such contrasting abiding memories of the GDR, what can we learn from the eight stories we have heard? Since historians are ill-equipped to peer into the inner workings of the human brain to understand why it retains some pieces of information while discarding others, accounting for the different versions of the transition of 1989 will be more achievable by reaching back into the protagonists' individual histories in the GDR. What were their lives like as they faced a new reality in united Germany?[50]

Interviewing people for this project has confounded my expectations at every turn. People resist categorization. It might seem reasonable to think that a person would react in a certain way because of what age they are, where they are from, what religion they are, or how they interacted with the state—and then they surprise you. People do not always remain consistent in their views and opinions, and it is a mistake to expect them to be wholly logical or rational.[51]

Thinking about it rationally, Mario had every reason to be delighted by the demise of the GDR. It was the country that had denied him his freedom, imprisoned him for exercising the internationally recognized human right to leave his country of origin, and left him with fragile mental health. Katharina also had good reason to be pleased to see the back of the socialist state: as a Christian she had been bullied and mocked for her beliefs at school, and made to feel like an outsider among the atheist masses; her opportunities for further education were restricted to theology, and in the years after her dissident husband was released from prison, she was acutely aware that their behaviour had to appear impeccable to the regime if he was to avoid being rearrested. And yet neither Mario nor Katharina had the reactions we might expect to the new status quo. Mario was initially anxious and frightened, scared that the Wall that had kept his persecutors at bay (once he had been allowed to move to the West) would no longer protect him.[52] And Katharina, although she firmly characterizes herself amongst the winners of the changes of 1989 and has achieved more genuine freedom to exercise her beliefs, still believes that day-to-day life in the GDR was nowhere near as bad as outsiders seem to think.

Significantly, it was when the interviewees reached their teenage years that they generally began to knock up against the state's boundaries. The stories told here show how disparate the responses to these restrictions were—from risking life and limb to escape, to lobbying the government for change, to accepting the circumstances pragmatically. For people like Petra, Lisa, and Peggy, whose behaviour provoked very little trouble with the authorities, the socialist system felt much less restrictive than for those like Carola, Mario, and Mirko, who found it more of a struggle to conform to the state's rules. While Mario genuinely feared encountering his Stasi interrogators, Petra or Lisa by contrast had no reason to have a strong aversion to supporters of the socialist government. For people like Robert, who came from a humble background, the regime's active promotion of the working classes gave him and his family greater opportunities than they would have had in a Western capitalist country. At the same time, for Katharina, her family experienced many more difficulties than they would have encountered in the West, because of their Christianity. And while some interviewees like Robert and Peggy describe the sense of loss following the eradication of their socialist milieu, all the protagonists explain that the *Wende* brought hugely positive opportunities.

As we have seen, German reunification represented a major transformation in the lives of ordinary East Germans. Superficially at least, everything changed. But the changes also brought a clash between the values and practices established in the socialist system and the values and practices in the new status quo. Whilst East Germans were forced to adjust to the situational differences at once, their habits, behaviour, and values were not so easily altered. Internal change did not mirror the external transformation, or at least not as quickly. It was not possible to snuff out years of socialization.[53] The country they had grown up in no longer existed in fact, but it continued to exist in their minds.[54] No matter what they thought about that country, their individual day-to-day lives were bound up with it. As one East German explained, 'We belonged to it, it belonged to us.'[55]

The stories told here show the long-lasting impact of socialist socialization on East Germans. We see this in Peggy's critical attitude to capitalism, in Mirko's dislike of the fact that the state still holds a great deal of personal information about individuals, be it through CCTV or as a condition of receiving state benefits. We can also observe the long-term effects of living under socialism in Robert's heightened appreciation of literature that he previously could not get hold of, and in Mario's dislike of cashiers behind desks in banks, which remind him of being interrogated at Hohenschönhausen. In addition to this, Mario, Robert, Peggy, and Mirko are all engaged in work which relates to their experiences of living in the SED system. As we have seen, Mario does tours of Hohenschönhausen Stasi prison, with the aim of educating visitors about the brutal side of life in the GDR; Robert and Peggy conduct tours in Berlin's GDR museum, both in part motivated by a desire to correct visitors' often negative misapprehensions about daily life under socialism; and Mirko runs a cultural institute arranging exchanges between Eastern European and German youths, in the hope that participants will learn about different cultures and types of government through their trips. The collection also illustrates how foreign West German ways continue to seem to former citizens of the GDR. Indeed, Carola, Lisa, Robert, and Peggy all explained that, more than two decades later, they still generally find common ground more easily with East Germans than with West Germans.

The stories furthermore reveal that the protagonists were often disappointed in West Germans. Robert, for example, is disappointed that Westerners often seem so ignorant about life in the GDR, and appear to base their views on the false impression that East Germans did not have enough to eat and were constantly trailed by the Stasi. Katharina is disappointed at the lack of humanity among ruthless West German capitalists, many of whom traded on East German naivety to make a profit after 1989. Peggy feels disappointed that West Germans often seem unable to understand the magnitude of the upheaval for East Germans following reunification. Petra laments the fact that reunification was not based on more of a mix of the two political systems, and feels disillusioned that Westerners were not open to learning anything from the East German set-up. And Mario feels it is wrong that the West German justice system that operated after unification did not do more to prosecute those who had worked for the Stasi. Generally too, among the interviewees, there was a feeling that the ongoing difficulties facing East Germans since the transition have been sidelined and that the government believes these difficulties will self-correct with time.

Despite the personal tumult and uncertainty that the *Wende* brought for East Germans, none of the interviewees would wish to return to the GDR, even if it were possible. There are a number of reasons for this. In the eyes of many East Germans the old system has been discredited. The socialist leadership promised a classless society with social equality and easy access to food, shelter, and employment. And many of those I interviewed grew up firm in the belief that 'what we're doing here [in the GDR] is the right thing', with fair and equal opportunities for all.[56] After 1989, however, it gradually became apparent that some were more equal than others in the GDR: Party bigwigs lived in relative luxury in the forested area of Wandlitz outside Berlin, and their lives were free from the worries that concerned ordinary citizens in the GDR since they had ready access to Western goods. This hypocrisy, that these politicians claimed to be striving for equality while hoarding privileges for themselves, has made it easier for many East Germans to leave their GDR past behind them.[57] For some, like Mario or Carola, who had hated many aspects of life in the GDR, there were overwhelming upsides to be had from living within the Western model. For the majority, who had grown used to the terms and conditions of living under socialist rule, German reunification was still a positive development when viewed over the longer term. It was a facilitator. Now, from the comfort of what they see as an improved situation, East Germans like Robert and Peggy can point to elements of the old system that were good.[58] Critics of the old system like Mario understandably fear that any positive recollections may overshadow the very real suffering that the regime caused. Can there really be anything to learn, they ask, from a country that used barbed wire to keep its people locked in?[59] On the other hand, it is equally understandable that other East Germans wish West Germans would acknowledge that the West could in fact learn from some of the GDR's ideals, policies, and approaches, even if they were not perfectly executed at the time.

Writing on the day Germany was formally reunited, an anonymous East German diarist declared, 'A country is erased, just like that, struck out, finished, over, full stop.'[60] For those individuals born in the GDR, the Berlin Wall and all it symbolized continued to cast a shadow long after it fell. The collapse of communism was certainly not the end of the story, but rather the start of a new chapter. A quarter of a century later, opinion is still divided about the extent to which East and West have truly merged.[61] This collection of contrasting stories shows how one central event affects everyone but is felt differently in each life. There is no one-size-fits-all account for how young East Germans experienced the transition to living in a Western consumer society. However, in hearing from eight of the people caught up in the historic events of November 1989, *Born in the GDR* both deepens our understanding of why such different memories of the GDR exist and sheds light on the ongoing and complex legacies of communist rule on East German soil.

Notes

Introduction

1. Cf. Hans-Joachim D. interview, February 2013; Matthias S. interview, February 2012; Angelique L. questionnaire, February 2012; Robert Ide, *Geteilte Träume: Meine Eltern, die Wende und ich* (Munich, 2009), 72.

2. Peter Schneider, *Wall Jumper* (Chicago, 1983), 119. In his novel, Schneider coined the phrase 'the Wall in our heads' predicting that 'it will take us longer to tear down the Wall in our heads than any wrecking company will need for the Wall we can see'.

3. Juliane Cieslak and Paula Hannaske, 'Vergangenheit heute: Einblicke in die Arbeit einer ostdeutschen Biografiegruppe', in Michael Hacker, et al. (eds.), *Dritte Generation Ost: Wer wir sind, was wir wollen* (Berlin, 2012), 57; Katja Warchold ' "So etwas ist in meiner DDR nicht vorgekommen": Erinnerungen an ein Aufwachsen in der DDR und im vereinten Deutschland', in Hacker et al. (eds.), *Dritte Generation Ost*, 69.

4. Peter Erler and Hubertus Knabe, *The Prohibited District: The Stasi Restricted Area Berlin Hohenschoenhausen* (Berlin, 2008), 9–12; Ruth Hoffman, *Stasi-Kinder: Aufwachsen im Ueberwachungsstaat* (Berlin, 2012), 33–4; Mary Fulbrook, *Dissonant Lives* (Oxford, 2011), 378; Ines Veith, *Leben und Alltag...der DDR-Flüchtlinge* (Kempen, 2010), 34; Anne McElvoy, *The Saddled Cow: East Germany's Life and Legacy* (London, 1992), 102–3.

5. The term 'Stasiland', famously used by Anna Funder in her book of that name, focuses on the dictatorial elements of life in the GDR, and suggests that the East German secret police, the Stasi, were all-pervasive.

6. Alf Lüdtke, 'What Is the History of Everyday Life and Who Are Its Practitioners?', in Lüdtke (ed.), *The History of Everyday Life: Reconstructing Historical Experiences and Ways of Life*, trans. William Templer (Princeton, 1995), 3–4.

7. Martin Diewald, Anne Goedicke, and Karl Ulrich Mayer, *After the Fall of the Wall: Life Courses in the Transformation of East Germany* (Stanford, Calif., 2006), 8.

8. This amounted to approximately 1,600 people leaving East Germany every month. For details see Christopher Hilton, *The Wall: The People's Story* (Stroud, 2001), 12.

9. Edith Sheffer, *Burned Bridge: How East and West Germans Made the Iron Curtain* (Oxford, 2011), 10.

10. The states in the communist Eastern bloc were the USSR, GDR, Poland, Czechoslovakia, Hungary, Romania, Romania, Bulgaria, Yugoslavia until the Tito–Stalin split in 1948, and Albania until 1960.

11. As seen in Peter Dittrich's cartoon, featured in the DDR Museum, Berlin.

12. Cf. Anne Marie B. interview, June 2012.

13. Jürgen Weber, *Germany 1945–1990: A Parallel History* (New York, 2004), 148; Jonathan Grix, *The Role of the Masses in the Collapse of the GDR* (London, 2000), 25–6.

14. Mark Pittaway, *Eastern Europe 1939–2000* (New York, 2004), 189; George Schöpflin, *Politics in Eastern Europe* (Oxford, 1993), 233–4.

15. Peter Grieder, ' "To Learn from the Soviet Union is to Learn How to Win": The East German Revolution, 1989–1990', in Kevin McDermott and Matthew Stibbe (eds.), *Revolution and Resistance in Eastern Europe: Challenges to Communist Rule* (Oxford, 2006), 164–6.

16. Bartosz Kaliski, 'Solidarity, 1980–1981: The Second Vistula Miracle?', in McDermott and Stibbe (eds.), *Revolution and Resistance in Eastern Europe*, 134.

17. Mark Pittaway, *Eastern Europe 1939–2000* (New York, 2004), 175–6, 193–4; Schöpflin, *Politics in Eastern Europe*, 236–7.

18. Pittaway, *Eastern Europe 1939–2000*, 184.

19. Pittaway, *Eastern Europe 1939–2000*, 189–91; Schöpflin, *Politics in Eastern Europe*, 237.

20. DTA 1071/1, Anonymous diary, 1988–1989, p. 129; Cornelia Heins, *The Wall Falls: An Oral History of the Reunification of the Two Germanies* (London, 1994), 198.

21. Grieder, ' "To Learn from the Soviet Union is to Learn How to Win" ', 167, 171; Michael Gehler, *Three Germanies: West Germany, East Germany and the Berlin Republic* (London, 2011), 202.

22. Heins, *The Wall Falls*, 183–5, 195, 223; Eva Kolinsky (ed.), *Between Hope and Fear* (Keele, 1995), 229.

23. Charles Krauthammer, 'Bless Our Pax Americana', *Washington Post*, 22 March 1991.

24. Konrad H. Jarausch (ed.), *After Unity: Reconfiguring German Identities* (Berghahn, 1997), 16; David Childs, *The Fall of the GDR: Germany's Road to Unity* (Edinburgh, 2001), 22; Chris Flockton and Eva Kolinsky (eds.), *Recasting East Germany: Social Transformation after the GDR* (London, 1999), 1; Diewald, Goedicke, and Mayer, *After the Fall of the Wall*, 316.

25. Konrad Jarausch, *The Rush to German Unity* (Oxford, 1994), 160.

26. Roger Willemsen, 'Ein kleines Winken', in Julia Franck (ed.), *Grenzübergänge: Autoren aus Ost und West erinnern sich* (Frankfurt am Main, 2009), 154; Ernest D. Plock, *East German–West German Relations and the Fall of the GDR* (Oxford, 1993), 173; Claudia Rusch, *Meine Freie Deutsche Jugend* (Frankfurt am Main, 2003), 75.

27. Mary Fulbrook, *The Divided Nation* (Oxford, 1991), 223.

28. Fulbrook, *The Divided Nation*, 245; Paul Kubicek, 'The Diminishing Relevance of Ostalgie 20 Years after Reunification', in Katharina Gerstenberger and Jana Evans Braziel, *After the Berlin Wall: Germany and Beyond* (London, 2011), 87; Ulrich K. Preuss, 'Political Institutions and German Unification', in Peter C. Caldwell and Robert R. Shandley (eds.), *German Unification: Expectations and Outcomes* (London, 2011), 150.

29. Kristina Matschat quoted in Heins, *The Wall Falls*, 321.

30. Walter Momper quoted in Heins, *The Wall Falls*, 320; cf. Angelique L. questionnaire, February 2012.

31. Ide, *Geteilte Träume*, 13.

32. Jonathan Grix and Paul Cooke (eds.), *East German Distinctiveness in a Unified Germany* (Birmingham, 2002), 1, 5, 11.

33. Corey Ross, *The East German Dictatorship: Problems and Perspectives in the Interpretation of the GDR* (London, 2002), 3.

34. 'Spiegel Spezial, Vereint aber Fremd', *Der Spiegel*, 1 (1991), 32–48; Elizabeth A. Ten Dyke, *Dresden: Paradoxes of Memory in History* (New York, 2001), 114–15; Andreas Glaeser, *Divided in Unity: Identity, Germany and the Berlin Police* (Chicago, 2000), 332–3.

35. Hans-Joachim D. interview, February 2013.

36. Dirk M. interview, December 2011.

37. Dirk Philipsen, *We Were the People: Voices From East Germany's Revolutionary Autumn of 1989* (London, 1993), 333.

38. Charles S. Maier, *Dissolution: The Crisis of Communism and the End of East Germany* (Princeton, 1997), 286.

39. Fulbrook, *Dissonant Lives*, 449.

40. Hans-Joachim D. interview, February 2013; Heike K. interview, February 2013; Claudia S. interview, June 2012; Anna-Maria G. questionnaire, February 2012; Thomas S. questionnaire, February 2012; Diewald, Goedicke, and Mayer, *After the Fall of the Wall*, 313; Thomas Scharf, 'Older People: Coping with the Challenges of Everyday Life', in Kolinsky (ed.), *Between Hope and Fear*, 211; Juliane Cieslak and Paula Hannaske, 'Vergangenheit heute: Einblicke in die Arbeit einer ostdeutschen Biografiegruppe', in Hacker et al. (eds.), *Dritte Generation Ost*, 54; Ide, *Geteilte Träume*, 13.

41. Matthias S. interview, February 2012.

42. Fulbrook, *Dissonant Lives*, 348, 359, 464; Sheffer, *Burned Bridge*, 167; Jeannette Z. Madarasz, *Conflict and Compromise in East Germany, 1971–1989* (Basingstoke, 2003), 15.

43. Hans-Jürgen van der Gieth, *Leben und Alltag im geteilten Deutschland* (Kempen, 2001), 33, 44.

44. Claudia Rusch, *Meine Freie Deutsche Jugend* (Frankfurt am Main, 2003), 47; Joanna McKay, 'East German Identity in the GDR', in Grix and Cooke (eds.), *East German Distinctiveness in a Unified Germany*, 15–16.

45. Thomas J. interview, June 2012; Mirko Sennewald interview, April 2012.

46. Mark Fenemore, *Sex, Thugs and Rock 'n' Roll: Teenage Rebels in Cold-War East Germany* (London, 2007), 63, 70, 78, 102, 239.

47. Ide, *Geteilte Träume*, 102.

48. Jana Hensel, *After the Wall: Confessions from an East German Childhood and the Life that Came Next*, trans. Jefferson Chase (New York, 2004), 5–11; cf. Angelique L. questionnaire, February 2012.

49. Grix and Cooke (eds.), *East German Distinctiveness in a Unified Germany*, 11.

50. Günter Gaus, *Wo Deutschland liegt: Eine Ortsbestimmung* (Hamburg, 1983), 156–7.

51. Geoff Eley, 'Forward', in Lüdtke (ed.), *The History of Everyday Life*, viii.

52. Anna Saunders, *Honecker's Children: Youth and Patriotism in East(ern) Germany, 1979–2002* (Manchester, 2007), 136.

53. Hensel, *After the Wall*, 175.
54. Three of the thirty participants in this project answered the same questions as a questionnaire rather than in person: Thomas S., Anna-Maria G., and Angelique L.
55. Lüdtke, 'What Is the History of Everyday Life and Who Are Its Practitioners?', 5–6.
56. Lüdtke, 'What Is the History of Everyday Life and Who Are Its Practitioners?', 174.
57. Fenemore, *Sex, Thugs and Rock 'n' Roll*, 8; Dyke, *Dresden*, 252, 256.
58. Paul Cooke, 'Literature and the Question of East German Cultural Identity since the Wende', in Grix and Cooke (eds.), *East German Distinctiveness in a Unified Germany*, 164.
59. Lynn Abrams, *Oral History Theory* (Oxford, 2010), 103, 105.
60. Abrams, *Oral History Theory*, 53, 97; Cooke, 'Literature and the Question of East German Cultural Identity since the Wende', 164.
61. Paul Thompson, *The Voice of the Past* (Oxford, 1988), 122, 148; Mary Fulbrook, 'Re-presenting the Nation: History and Identity in East and West Germany', in Fulbrook and Martin Swales (eds.), *Representing the German Nation: History and Identity in Twentieth-Century Germany* (Manchester, 2000), 186; Ross, *The East German Dictatorship*, 109–10.
62. Fulbrook, *Dissonant Lives*, 462, 479.
63. Pavel Seifter, 'Foreword', in McDermott and Stibbe (eds.), *Revolution and Resistance in Eastern Europe*, xiii.
64. Full names are used in the case of Petra Bläss, Mario Röllig, Katharina Furian, Carola Koehler, and Mirko Sennewald. All the other interviewees have been anonymized.
65. Francis Meehan quoted in Heins, *The Wall Falls*, 320.

Chapter 1

1. For other recollections of the night of 9 November 1989 see Claudia Rusch, *Meine Freie Deutsche Jugend* (Frankfurt am Main, 2003), 75.
2. David Childs, *The Fall of the GDR: Germany's Road to Unity* (Edinburgh, 2001), 84; Jonathan Grix, *The Role of the Masses in the Collapse of the GDR* (London, 2000), 136.
3. Andreas Glaeser, *Divided in Unity: Identity, Germany and the Berlin Police* (Chicago, 2000), 110.

4. Jürgen Weber, *Germany 1945–1990: A Parallel History* (New York, 2004), 211; Childs, *The Fall of the GDR*, 86–8; Anne McElvoy, *The Saddled Cow: East Germany's Life and Legacy* (London, 1992), 206.

5. McElvoy, *The Saddled Cow*, 207–8.

6. There were several other political parties in the GDR but they were all collected under the SED-dominated National Front for Democratic Germany. These other parties included the East German branch of the Christian Democratic Union, the Liberal Democratic Party, and the National Democratic Party.

7. Throughout the book, where the protagonist's opinions or experiences have been shared by other interviewees, this will be indicated by 'cf.' in the notes. Cf. Silvio G. interview, January 2013.

8. Mike Dennis, 'The East German Family: Change and Continuity', in Chris Flockton and Eva Kolinsky (eds.), *Recasting East Germany: Social Transformation after the GDR* (London, 1999), 85.

9. Isabel Hempel, 'Zukunft ist kein Schicksalsschlag: Frauen machen Neue Länder', in Michael Hacker et al. (eds.), *Dritte Generation Ost: Wer wir sind, was wir wollen* (Berlin, 2012), 172.

10. Cf. Thomas J. interview, June 2012; Anne Marie B. interview, June 2012.

11. Cf. Claudia S. interview, June 2012.

12. Childs, *The Fall of the GDR*, 105; Glaeser, *Divided in Unity*, 110; Weber, *Germany 1945–1990*, 224–5.

13. Ernest D. Plock, *East German–West German Relations and the Fall of the GDR* (Oxford, 1993), 174–5; Timothy Garton Ash, *In Europe's Name: Germany and the Divided Continent* (New York, 1993), 346; Childs, *The Fall of the GDR*, 77; Michael Gehler, *Three Germanies: West Germany, East Germany and the Berlin Republic* (London, 2011), 211.

14. Glaeser, *Divided in Unity*, 110; McElvoy, *The Saddled Cow*, 210.

15. Peter Grieder, ' "To Learn from the Soviet Union is to Learn How to Win": The East German Revolution, 1989–1990', in Kevin McDermott and Matthew Stibbe (eds.), *Revolution and Resistance in Eastern Europe: Challenges to Communist Rule* (Oxford, 2006), 168–9; Edith Sheffer, *Burned Bridge: How East and West Germans Made the Iron Curtain* (Oxford, 2011), 246; McElvoy, *The Saddled Cow*, 1992, 212.

16. For further description of this period of hiatus see Rusch, *Meine Freie Deutsche Jugend*, 90.

17. Juergen A. K. Thomaneck, 'From Euphoria to Reality: Social Problems of Post-Unification', in Derek Lewis and John R. P. McKenzie (eds.), *The New Germany: Social, Political and Cultural Challenges of Unification* (Exeter, 1995), 23.

18. Cf. Anne Marie B. interview, June 2012; Robert S. interview, December 2011.

19. Weber, *Germany 1945–1990*, 252.

20. Cf. Mario Röllig interview, December 2011; Carola Koehler interview, June 2012. Grix and Cooke (eds.), *East German Distinctiveness in a Unified Germany*, 10.

21. Daniel Hough, 'East German Identity and Party Politics', in Jonathan Grix and Paul Cooke (eds.), *East German Distinctiveness in a Unified Germany* (Birmingham, 2002), 101, 109, 113; cf. Felix R. interview, April 2013.

22. Daphne Berdahl, *Where the World Ended: Re-Unification and Identity in the German Borderland* (Berkeley and Los Angeles, 1999), 169.

23. DTA 1071/1, Anonymous diary, 1988–1989, p. 136; Berdahl, *Where the World Ended*, 158.

24. Berdahl, *Where the World Ended*, 164; Robert Ide, *Geteilte Träume: Meine Eltern, die Wende und ich* (Munich, 2009), 38, 45.

25. Rusch, *Meine Freie Deutsche Jugend*, 75.

26. DTA 1071/1, Anonymous diary, 1988–1989, p. 154; Cf. Heike K. interview, February 2013; Katharina Furian interview, June 2012; Thomas J., interview June 2012; Sheffer, *Burned Bridge*, 243–4.

27. Glaeser, *Divided in Unity*, 110.

Chapter 2

1. Christopher Hilton, *The Wall: The People's Story* (Stroud, 2001), 114, 252, 260, 305; Edith Sheffer, *Burned Bridge: How East and West Germans Made the Iron Curtain* (Oxford, 2011), 197; Ines Veith, *Leben und Alltag…der DDR-Flüchtlinge* (Kempen, 2010), 22, 40; Dr Wulf Rothenbächer quoted in Cornelia Heins, *The Wall Falls: An Oral History of the Reunification of the Two Germanies* (London, 1994), 123; Robert Ide, *Geteilte Träume: Meine Eltern, die Wende und ich* (Munich, 2009), 82.

2. Werner Filmer and Heribert Schwann (eds.), *Alltag im anderen Deutschland* (Düsseldorf, 1985).

3. Cf. Thomas J. interview, June 2012; DTA 1071/1, Anonymous diary, 1988–1989, p. 126; DTA, Reg. Nr. 2166,1, Anonymous diary entry from 1989; Elizabeth A. Ten Dyke, *Dresden: Paradoxes of Memory in History* (New York, 2001), 172; Ruth Hoffman, *Stasi-Kinder: Aufwachsen im Überwachungsstaat* (Berlin, 2012), 57, 269, 284; Veith, *Leben und Alltag... der DDR-Flüchtlinge*, 16; Arbeitsgemeinschaft Jugend und Bildung e.V. (ed.), *Wir in Ost und West—Jugend, Alltag, Freizeit* (Wiesbaden, 1986), 21.

4. Cf. DTA 1071/1, Anonymous diary, 1988–1989, p. 128.

5. Daphne Berdahl, *Where the World Ended: Re-Unification and Identity in the German Borderland* (Berkeley and Los Angeles, 1999), 154.

6. Hoffman, *Stasi-Kinder*, 268.

7. David Childs, *The Fall of the GDR: Germany's Road to Unity* (Edinburgh, 2001), 17, 31–2; cf. Hans-Michael S. interview, April 2012.

8. Ralph H. interview, June 2012.

9. Claudia Rusch, *Meine Freie Deutsche Jugend* (Frankfurt am Main, 2003), 129, 133.

10. Cf. Matthias S. interview, February 2012; Ide, *Geteilte Träume*, 81.

11. Cf. Thomas J. interview, June 2012.

12. Berdahl, *Where the World Ended*, 78; Hubertus Knabe, *Umweltkonflikte im Sozialismus: Möglichkeiten und Grenzen gesellschaftlicher Problemartikulation in sozialistischen Systemen: Eine vergleichende Analyse der Umweltdiskussion in der DDR und Ungarn* (Cologne, 1994), 312.

13. Knabe, *Umweltkonflikte im Sozialismus*, 121.

14. Knabe, *Umweltkonflikte im Sozialismus*, 128–9, 143.

15. 'Es geht um mehr als Bäumepflanzen: Interview mit einer Schweriner Umweltinitiative', *Kirche im Sozialismus*, 5–6 (1980); cf. Felix R. interview, April 2013; Hubertus Knabe, *Umweltkonflikte im Sozialismus*, 315–16, 318, 346.

16. Exhibition at the Tränenpalast in Berlin.

17. Knabe, *Umweltkonflikte im Sozialismus*, 325.

18. Cf. Katharina Furian interview, June 2012; Anne Marie B. interview, June 2012; Hans-Michael S. interview, April 2012.

19. Rusch, *Meine Freie Deutsche Jugend*, 129.

20. Uwe Wunderlich quoted in Heins, *The Wall Falls*, 109.

21. Sheffer, *Burned Bridge*, 167.

22. Cf. Heike K. interview, February 2013; Hanno H. interview, January 2013.

23. Kurt Hager interview with *Der Stern* (10 April 1987); Andreas Glaeser, *Divided in Unity: Identity, Germany and the Berlin Police* (Chicago, 2000), 109.

24. Cf. Katharina Furian, interview June 2012; DTA 1071/1, Anonymous diary, 1988–1989, pp. 97, 140.

25. Peter Grieder, ' "To Learn from the Soviet Union is to Learn How to Win": The East German Revolution, 1989–1990', in Kevin McDermott and Matthew Stibbe (eds.), *Revolution and Resistance in Eastern Europe: Challenges to Communist Rule* (Oxford, 2006), 157.

26. Glaeser, *Divided in Unity*, 110.

27. Roland Jahn, 'Wissen, wie es war', in Michael Hacker et al. (eds.), *Dritte Generation Ost: Wer wir sind, was wir wollen* (Berlin, 2012), 75.

28. Cf. Heike K. interview, February 2013; Hans-Joachim D. interview, February 2013; Jonathan Grix and Paul Cooke (eds.), *East German Distinctiveness in a Unified Germany* (Birmingham, 2002), 10.

Chapter 3

1. Christine Leuenberger, 'From the Berlin Wall to the West Bank Barrier: How Material Objects and Psychological Theories Can Be Used to Construct Individual and Cultural Traits', in Katharina Gerstenberger and Jana Evans Braziel (eds.), *After the Berlin Wall: Germany and Beyond* (London, 2011), 60.

2. Cf. Hanno H. interview, January 2013.

3. Cf. Claudia S. interview, June 2012; Katharina Furian interview, June 2012; Heike K. interview, February 2013; DTA 1071/1, Anonymous diary, 1988–1989, p. 125.

4. Cf. Dirk L. interview, March 2013.

5. Cf. Anne Marie B. interview, June 2012.

6. Robert Ide, *Geteilte Träume: Meine Eltern, die Wende und ich* (Munich, 2009), 79; Jonathan Grix, *The Role of the Masses in the Collapse of the GDR* (London, 2000), 23–4.

7. Derek Lewis, 'The GDR: Wende and Legacy', in Lewis and John R. P. McKenzie (eds.), *The New Germany: Social, Political and Cultural Challenges of Unification* (Exeter, 1995), 58; Elizabeth A. Ten Dyke, *Dresden: Paradoxes of Memory in History* (New York, 2001), 209.

8. Ruth Hoffman, *Stasi-Kinder: Aufwachsen im Ueberwachungsstaat* (Berlin, 2012), 256.

9. Roger Willemsen, 'Ein kleines Winken', in Julia Franck (ed.), *Grenzübergänge: Autoren aus Ost und West erinnern sich* (Frankfurt am Main, 2009), 157; Ide, *Geteilte Träume*, 62.

10. Jürgen A. K. Thomaneck, 'From Euphoria to Reality: Social Problems of Post-Unification' in Lewis and McKenzie (eds.), *The New Germany*, 27–8.

11. Eva Windmöller and Thomas Höpker, *Leben in der DDR* (Hamburg, 1980), 88; Hans-Jürgen van der Gieth, *Leben und Alltag im geteilten Deutschland* (Kempen, 2001), 26.

12. Daphne Berdahl, *Where the World Ended: Re-Unification and Identity in the German Borderland* (Berkeley and Los Angeles, 1999), 120.

13. Berdahl, *When the World Ended*, 118–21.

14. Björn Held, 'Bei der tiefen Stimme der "Gloriosa"', in Werner Filmer and Heribert Schwann (eds.), *Alltag im anderen Deutschland* (Düsseldorf, 1985), 121–2; Anne Marie B. interview, June 2012; Matthias S. interview, February 2012; Judd Stitziel, 'Shopping, Sewing, Networking, Complaining: Consumer Culture and the Relationship between State and Society in the GDR', in Katherine Pence and Paul Betts (eds.), *Socialist Modern: East German Everyday Culture and Politics* (Ann Arbor, 2008), 253; Eva Kolinsky (ed.), *Between Hope and Fear: Everyday Life in Post-Unification East Germany* (Keele, 1995), 30; Anne McElvoy, *The Saddled Cow: East Germany's Life and Legacy* (London, 1992), 233; Berdahl, *Where the World Ended*, 15.

15. Cf. Dirk L. interview, March 2013.

16. Cf. Anne Marie B. interview, June 2012.

17. Cf. Anna-Maria G. questionnaire, February 2012; Angela H. interview, October 2011.

18. Cf. Heike K. interview, February 2013.

19. Cf. Andreas S. interview, April 2012; cf. Ide, *Geteilte Träume*, 62.

20. The name of Lisa's boyfriend has been changed.

21. Hoffman, *Stasi-Kinder*, 26, 84.

22. Cf. Ralph Hoppe interview, June 2012; Katharina Furian interview June 2012.

23. Cf. Christian Luchmann interview, April 2012; Jürgen Weber, *Germany 1945–1990: A Parallel History* (New York, 2004), 212; Andreas Glaeser, *Divided in Unity: Identity, Germany and the Berlin Police* (Chicago, 2000), 2.

24. Cf. Thomas J. interview, June 2012; Claudia S. interview, June 2012; Anne Marie B. interview, June 2012.

25. Cf. Thomas J. interview, June 2012.

26. SED rule was most notably challenged in the uprising of June 1953.

27. DTA 1071/1, Anonymous diary, 1988–1989, pp. 12, 34.

28. Cf. Dirk L. interview, March 2013.

29. Cf. Claudia S. interview, June 2012.

Chapter 4

1. Dagmar Herzog, 'East Germany's Sexual Evolution', in Katherine Pence and Paul Betts (eds.), *Socialist Modern* (Ann Arbor, 2008), 37; see also Josie McLellan, *Love in the Time of Communism* (Cambridge, 2011).

2. Cf. Angelique L.'s questionnaire from February 2012; Felix R.'s interview, April 2013.

3. Gottfried's name has been changed to protect his anonymity.

4. Exhibition at the Tränenpalast in Berlin.

5. Uwe Kolbe, 'Tabu', in Julia Franck (ed.), *Grenzübergänge: Autoren aus Ost und West erinnern sich* (Frankfurt am Main, 2009), 39.

6. Claudia Rusch, *Meine Freie Deutsche Jugend* (Frankfurt am Main, 2003), 16; Anne McElvoy, *The Saddled Cow: East Germany's Life and Legacy* (London, 1992), 102–3. See also Paul Betts, *Within Walls: Private Life in the German Democratic Republic* (Oxford, 2010).

7. Werner Filmer and Heribert Schwann (eds.), *Alltag im anderen Deutschland* (Düsseldorf, 1985); Ernest D. Plock, *East German–West German Relations and the Fall of the GDR* (Oxford, 1993), 69–70.

8. Jürgen Weber, *Germany 1945–1990: A Parallel History* (New York, 2004), 150–1.

9. Mario later discovered that the GDR falsified the maps they sold, distorting distances. For further details see Edith Sheffer, *Burned Bridge: How East and West Germans Made the Iron Curtain* (Oxford, 2011), 197.

10. Peter Erler and Hubertus Knabe, *The Prohibited District: The Stasi Restricted Area Berlin Hohenschönhausen* (Berlin, 2008), 18; Thassilo Borchart quoted in Cornelia Heins, *The Wall Falls: An Oral History of the Reunification of the Two Germanies* (London, 1994), 156; Ines Veith, *Die Frau vom Checkpoint Charlie* (Munich, 2006), 22.

11. Erler and Knabe, *The Prohibited District*, 46; Anthony Glees, 'Social Transformation Studies and Human Rights Abuses in East Germany

after 1945', in Chris Flockton and Eva Kolinsky (eds.), *Recasting East Germany: Social Transformation after the GDR* (London, 1999), 173.

12. Erler and Knabe, *The Prohibited District*, 62.

13. Ekkehard Kaul quoted in Gilbert Furian (ed.), *Mehl aus Mielkes Mühlen: Politische Häftlinge und ihre Verfolger* (Berlin, 2008), 222–3.

14. DTA 1071/1, Anonymous diary, 1988–1989, p. 97.

15. Klaus Freymuth quoted in Furian (ed.), *Mehl aus Mielkes Mühlen*, 69–70; DTA 1511,2, Angela Kowalczyk, March 1982.

16. Bärbel Schleim quoted in Furian (ed.), *Mehl aus Mielkes Mühlen*, 76; Gilbert Furian quoted in Furian (ed.), *Mehl aus Mielkes Mühlen*, 167.

17. Ruth Hoffman, *Stasi-Kinder: Aufwachsen im Ueberwachungsstaat* (Berlin, 2012), 100–1.

18. Ines Veith, *Leben und Alltag...der DDR-Flüchtlinge* (Kempen, 2010), 21.

19. Veith, *Leben und Alltag...der DDR-Flüchtlinge*, 37.

20. Ulrike Poppe quoted in Heins, *The Wall Falls*, 335–6; Martin Bernhardt quoted in Furian (ed.), *Mehl aus Mielkes Mühlen*, 134; Ulrike Poppe quoted in Heins, *The Wall Falls*, 335–6; David Gill quoted in Heins, *The Wall Falls*, 333; Veith, *Leben und Alltag...der DDR-Flüchtlinge*, 34.

21. Sheffer, *Burned Bridge*, 201; Klaus Freymuth quoted in Furian (ed.), *Mehl aus Mielkes Mühlen*, 67.

22. Hoffman, *Stasi-Kinder*, 176.

23. Erler and Knabe, *The Prohibited District*, 11, 42; Dr Wulf Rothenbaecher quoted in Heins, *The Wall Falls*, 118, 123; Veith, *Leben und Alltag...der DDR-Flüchtlinge*, 44–5; David Childs, *The Fall of the GDR: Germany's Road to Unity* (Edinburgh, 2001), 27; McElvoy, *The Saddled Cow*, 190.

24. Ludwig A. Rehlinger, *Freikauf: Die Geschäfte der DDR mit politisch Verfolgten 1963–1989* (Berlin, 1991).

25. Heinz Loesner quoted in Furian (ed.), *Mehl aus Mielkes Mühlen*, 106.

26. Jutta Zschau quoted in Furian (ed.), *Mehl aus Mielkes Mühlen*, 132.

27. Cf. Peggy M., interview January 2013; Carola Koehler, interview June 2012; Hanna K., interview December 2011.

28. DTA, Reg. Nr. 2166,1, 13 November 1989.

29. Derek Lewis, 'The GDR: Wende and Legacy', in Lewis and John R. P. McKenzie (eds.), *The New Germany: Social, Political and Cultural Challenges of Unification* (Exeter, 1995), 68.

30. Cf. Claudia S. interview, June 2012; Rusch, *Meine Freie Deutsche Jugend*, 115; Mike Dennis, 'The East German Family: Change and Continuity', in Flockton and Kolinsky (eds.), *Recasting East Germany*, 88–9.

31. Hans-Joachim Maaz, *Behind the Wall: The Inner Life of Communist Germany* (New York, 1995), 79.

32. DTA 1071/1, Anonymous diary, 1988–1989, p. 148.

33. Cf. Anne Marie B. interview, June 2012; Rusch, *Meine Freie Deutsche Jugend*, 148.

34. Amongst other places, the prison at Hohenschönhausen had lino flooring.

35. Erler and Knabe, *The Prohibited District*, 21; Heins, *The Wall Falls*, 340.

36. McElvoy, *The Saddled Cow*, 73–6; Heins, *The Wall Falls*, 98.

37. Cf. Matthias S. interview, February 2012; A. James McAdams, *Judging the Past in Unified Germany* (Cambridge, 2001), 15, 66.

38. Konrad Jarausch, Hinrich C. Seeba, and David P. Conradt, 'The Presence of the Past', in Jarausch (ed.), *After Unity* (Berghahn, 1997), 53; Marianne Birthler, 'Epilogue: The End of Dictatorship and Its Aftermath: Personal Reflections of the Federal Commissioner for the Records of the State Security Agency of the German Democratic Republic', in Peter C. Caldwell and Robert R. Shandley, *German Unification: Expectations and Outcomes* (London, 2011), 178; McElvoy, *The Saddled Cow*, 134.

39. Wolfgang Schäuble quoted in Heins, *The Wall Falls*, 257.

40. Heins, *The Wall Falls*, 331.

Chapter 5

1. Mario Röllig interview, December 2011.

2. Victor Sebetsyen, *Revolution 1989: The Fall of the Soviet Empire* (New York, 2009).

3. Angela H. interview, October 2011.

4. Cf. Angela H. interview October 2011; Christoph Klessmann, *Kinder der Opposition: Berichte aus Pfarrhäusern in der DDR* (Gütersloh, 1993), 68; Michael Hacker et al. (eds.), *Dritte Generation Ost: Wer wir sind, was wir wollen* (Berlin, 2012), 51.

5. John Sandford, 'The Peace Movement and the Church', in Gert-Joachim Gaessner and Ian Wallace (eds.), *The German Revolution of 1989:*

Causes and Consequences (Oxford, 1993), 127; Hans-Jürgen van der Gieth, *Leben und Alltag im geteilten Deutschland* (Kempen, 2001), 44; Daphne Berdahl, *Where the World Ended: Re-Unification and Identity in the German Borderland* (Berkeley and Los Angeles, 1999), 91.

6. Klessmann, *Kinder der Opposition*, 41–2, 131.

7. Cf. Angela H. interview June 2012; Anne Marie B. interview, June 2012; Friedrich Schorlemmer quoted in Cornelia Heins, *The Wall Falls: An Oral History of the Reunification of the Two Germanies* (London, 1994), 218.

8. Cf. Anne Marie B. interview, June 2012.

9. Mary Fulbrook, *Anatomy of a Dictatorship: Inside the GDR, 1949–1989* (Oxford, 1995), 50.

10. Angela H. interview, October 2011; see also Anna-Maria G. questionnaire, February 2012.

11. Klessmann, *Kinder der Opposition*, 98.

12. Anne-Marie B. interview, June 2012; Angela H. interview, October 2011; Claudia Rusch, *Meine Freie Deutsche Jugend* (Frankfurt am Main, 2003), 35.

13. Rusch, *Meine Freie Deutsche Jugend*, 27.

14. Cf. Hans-Michael S. interview, April 2012; Matthias S. interview, February 2012; Angela H. interview, October 2011; DTA 1071/1, Anonymous diary, 1988–1989, pp. 91, 123; Klessmann, *Kinder der Opposition*, 7; Andrea Backhaus in Hacker et al. (eds.), *Dritte Generation Ost*, 18.

15. DTA 1071/1, Anonymous diary, 1988–1989, p. 136; Peter Grieder, ' "To Learn from the Soviet Union is to Learn How to Win": The East German Revolution, 1989–1990', in Kevin McDermott and Matthew Stibbe (eds.), *Revolution and Resistance in Eastern Europe: Challenges to Communist Rule* (Oxford, 2006), 162.

16. David Childs, *The Fall of the GDR: Germany's Road to Unity* (Edinburgh, 2001), 43.

17. Karl Cordell, 'The Church: Coming to Terms with Change', in Kolinsky (ed.), *Between Hope and Fear* (Keele, 1995), 123–7.

18. Konrad Jarausch, Hinrich C. Seeba, and David P. Conradt, 'The Presence of the Past' in Jarausch (ed.), *After Unity* (Berghahn, 1997), 41.

19. Cf. Angela H. interview, October 2011.

20. Geoffrey Pridham, *The Democratization of Eastern Europe* (London, 1994), 52; DTA 1071/1, Anonymous diary, 1988–1989, p. 82; Rusch, *Meine Freie Deutsche Jugend*, 124.

21. Heins, *The Wall Falls*, 212.

22. Cf. Matthias S. interview, February 2012.

23. Ann Taylor Allen, *Women in Twentieth Century Europe* (London, 2008), 132–49.

24. Cf. Angela H. interview, October 2011; Klessmann, *Kinder der Opposition*, 94, 103–4.

25. Cf. Thomas S. questionnaire, February 2012; Edith Sheffer, *Burned Bridge: How East and West Germans Made the Iron Curtain* (Oxford, 2011), 227.

26. Elizabeth A. Ten Dyke, *Dresden: Paradoxes of Memory in History* (New York, 2001), xxi; cf. Heike K. interview, February 2013.

27. DTA 1071/1, Anonymous diary, 1988–1989, p. 127.

28. Cf. Matthias S. interview, February 2012; Anne Marie B. interview, June 2012; Thomas J. interview, June 2012; Romy Koehler and Susanne Herrmann-Sinai, 'Denken in Grenzen', in Hacker et al. (eds.), *Dritte Generation Ost*, 182.

29. Exhibition notes at the DDR Museum, Berlin.

30. Cf. Anna-Maria G. questionnaire, February 2012; Hans-Michael S., interview April 2012; Thassilo Borchart quoted in Heins, *The Wall Falls*, 102; Judd Stitziel, 'Shopping, Sewing, Networking, Complaining: Consumer Culture and the Relationship between State and Society in the GDR', in Katherine Pence and Paul Betts (eds.), *Socialist Modern* (Ann Arbor, 2008), 253.

31. Cf. Anna-Maria G. questionnaire, February 2012; Thomas J., interview June 2012.

32. Juliane Koehler, 'Wie in einem alten Film: Eindrücke einer Klassenfahrt in die DDR', *Die Zeit*, Nr.3 v.15.1. 1982, p. 41, quoted in Gieth, *Leben und Alltag im geteilten Deutschland*, 37–8.

33. Cf. Hanno H. interview, January 2013; Dyke, *Dresden*, 177.

34. Wille Bremkes, 'Wenn DDR-Bürger Urlaub machen' [When GDR Citizens Go on Vacation], *Frankfurter Rundschau*, 30 August 1980.

35. Gilbert Furian (ed.), *Mehl aus Mielkes Mühlen: Politische Häftlinge und ihre Verfolger* (Berlin, 2008).

36. Paul Betts, *Within Walls: Private Life in the German Democratic Republic* (Oxford, 2010).

37. Angela H. interview, October 2011.

38. Andreas Glaeser, *Divided in Unity: Identity, Germany and the Berlin Police* (Chicago, 2000), 44.

39. Sheffer, *Burned Bridge*, 234.

40. Kristina Matschat quoted in Heins, The Wall Falls, 321.

41. Angela H. interview, October 2011; Rusch, *Meine Freie Deutsche Jugend*,64; Hacker et al. (eds.), *Dritte Generation Ost*, 44, 80, 83; 'Bin ich ostdeutsch? Vom Umgang mit den kleinen Unterschieden', *SUPERIllu*, 30 (2012), 13.

42. Berdahl, Where the World Ended, 157–8; Anne McElvoy, *The Saddled Cow: East Germany's Life and Legacy* (London, 1992), 209.

43. Rusch, *Meine Freie Deutsche Jugend*, 86; Childs, *The Fall of the GDR*, 28.

44. Cf. Thomas S. questionnaire, February 2012.

45. Cf. Heike K. interview, February 2013; Robert Ide, *Geteilte Träume: Meine Eltern, die Wende und ich* (Munich, 2009), 121.

46. Berdahl, *Where the World Ended*, 167, 173.

47. Cf. Dirk L. interview, March 2013; Hans-Joachim D. interview, February 2013; Ruth Hoffman, *Stasi-Kinder: Aufwachsen im Ueberwachungsstaat* (Berlin, 2012), 144.

48. Cf. Angela H. interview, October 2011.

Chapter 6

1. Armin Mitter and Stefan Wolle, *Untergang auf Raten* (Munich, 1993), 7.

2. Katharina Furian interview, June 2012.

3. Jonathan Grix, *The Role of the Masses in the Collapse of the GDR* (London, 2000), 23–4.

4. Cf. Hanno H. interview, January 2013.

5. Cf. Ralph Hoppe interview, June 2012; Thomas J. interview, June 2012; DTA 1071/1, Anonymous diary, 1988–1989, p. 106. See also Claudia Rusch, *Meine Freie Deutsche Jugend* (Frankfurt am Main, 2003), 28.

6. Mary Fulbrook, *Dissonant Lives* (Oxford, 2011), 384; Matthias S. interview, February 2012; Ralf Matschat quoted in Cornelia Heins, *The Wall Falls: An Oral History of the Reunification of the Two Germanies* (London, 1994), 154; Stuart Parkes, *Understanding Contemporary Germany* (London, 1997), 7; Ruth Hoffman, *Stasi-Kinder: Aufwachsen im Ueberwachungsstaat* (Berlin, 2012), 74.

7. Cf. Ralph Hoppe interview, June 2012.

8. Jorge Seidel quoted in Heins, *The Wall Falls*, 336.

9. Peter Erler and Hubertus Knabe, *The Prohibited District: The Stasi Restricted Area Berlin Hohenschoenhausen* (Berlin, 2008), 18.

10. Fulbrook, *Dissonant Lives*, 470–5.

11. For a more detailed explanation of the opening of the Stasi files, please see Chapter 5.

12. Cf. Anna-Maria G. questionnaire, February 2012.

13. Cf. Heike K. interview, February 2013.

14. Cf. Thomas J. interview June 2012; Julia Franck, 'Die Überwindung der Grenze liegt im Erzählen', in Franck (ed.), *Grenzübergänge: Autoren aus Ost und West erinnern sich* (Frankfurt am Main, 2009), 20.

15. Cf. Dirk M. interview, December 2011; Matthias S. interview, February 2012; Anna-Maria G. questionnaire, February 2012; Thomas S. questionnaire, November 2011; Thomas J. interview, June 2012; Rusch, *Meine Freie Deutsche Jugend*, 86.

16. Joanna McKay, 'East German Identity in the GDR', in Jonathan Grix and Paul Cooke (eds.), *East German Distinctiveness in a Unified Germany* (Birmingham, 2002), 24.

17. Cf. Felix R. interview, April 2013.

18. Cf. Thomas S. questionnaire, November 2011.

19. Fulbrook, *Dissonant Lives*, 487.

20. Rusch, *Meine Freie Deutsche Jugend*, 124; Cf. Dirk S. interview, December 2011; Angela Kowalczyk, *Negativ und Dekaden: Ostberliner Punk Erinnerungen* (Berlin, 2003); Mark Fenemore, *Sex, Thugs and Rock 'n' Roll: Teenage Rebels in Cold-War East Germany* (New York, 2007), 74–5, 91–2, 132, 151, 170.

21. DTA 1071/1, Anonymous diary, 1988–1989, pp. 31, 82, 86, 103–4, 118; Rusch, *Meine Freie Deutsche Jugend*, 124; Hans-Jürgen van der Gieth, *Leben und Alltag im geteilten Deutschland* (Kempen, 2001), 40.

22. Cf. Dirk M. interview, December 2011.

23. Cf. Anne Marie B. interview, June 2012.

24. Cf. Dirk M. interview, December 2011; Thomas S. questionnaire, November 2011; Matthias S. interview, February 2012; Anne Marie B. interview, June 2012; Katharina Furian interview, June 2012; DTA 1071/1, Anonymous diary, 1988–1989, pp. 31, 97, 128, 137; Rusch, *Meine Freie Deutsche Jugend*, 75.

25. Cf. Anne Marie B. interview, June 2012; Kurt Masur quoted in Heins, *The Wall Falls*, 229; Roger Willemsen, 'Ein kleines Winken', in Franck

(ed.), *Grenzübergänge*, 154; Ernest D. Plock, *East German–West German Relations and the Fall of the GDR* (Oxford, 1993), 173.

26. Ulrike Poppe quoted in Heins, *The Wall Falls*, 264; Robert Ide, *Geteilte Träume: Meine Eltern, die Wende und ich* (Munich, 2009), 28; Timothy Garton Ash, *In Europe's Name: Germany and the Divided Continent* (New York, 1993), 343.

27. Cf. Silvio G. interview, January 2013; Hans-Joachim D. interview, February 2013; Heike K. interview, February 2013; Edith Sheffer, *Burned Bridge: How East and West Germans Made the Iron Curtain* (Oxford, 2011), 244.

28. Cf. Katharina Furian interview, June 2012; Anne Marie B. interview, June 2012; Heins, *The Wall Falls*, 353; Paul Kubicek, 'The Diminishing Relevance of Ostalgie 20 Years after Reunification', in Katharina Gerstenberger and Jana Evans Braziel (eds.), *After the Berlin Wall: Germany and Beyond* (London, 2011), 88; Elizabeth A. Ten Dyke, *Dresden: Paradoxes of Memory in History* (New York, 2001), 138–46; Daphne Berdahl, *Where the World Ended: Re-Unification and Identity in the German Borderland* (Berkeley and Los Angeles, 1999), 169; Anne McElvoy, *The Saddled Cow: East Germany's Life and Legacy* (London, 1992), 216.

29. Cf. Hans-Michael S. interview, April 2012.

30. Stefan Wolle, *Die heile Welt der Diktatur* (Berlin, 2001), 344.

31. The East German population was approximately 17 million when the GDR formed, but this had shrunk to nearer 16 million by the 1980s.

32. Cf. Hans-Michael S. interview, April 2012; Paul Cook, *Representing East Germany: From Colonization to Nostalgia* (Oxford, 2005); Linda Bunckenburg and Susan Muecke, 'Jugend im Aufbruch: Wendejugendliche erinnern sich an ihren Herbst 1989', in Michael Hacker et al. (eds.), *Dritte Generation Ost: Wer wir sind, was wir wollen* (Berlin, 2012), 44.

33. Jana Wessendorf and Anne Wessendorf, 'Wendekinder: Zwei Schwestern im Gespräch', in Hacker et al. (eds.), *Dritte Generation Ost*, 88.

34. Berdahl, *Where the World Ended*, 198; Dyke, *Dresden*, 251.

35. Cf. Mike M. interview, April 2013; Felix R. interview, April 2013.

36. Ide, *Geteilte Träume*, 88; Wessendorf and Wessendorf, 'Wendekinder', 81; Esther von Richthofen, *Bringing Culture to the Masses: Control, Compromise and Participation in the GDR* (New York, 2009), 1; Fenemore, *Sex, Thugs and Rock 'n' Roll*, xiii; Andreas Glaeser, 'Why Germany Remains Divided', in Todd Herzog and Sander L. Gilman (eds.), *A New Germany in a New Europe* (New York, 2001), 179–80.

37. DTA 1071/2, March 2002, p. 50.

38. Cf. Anna-Maria G. questionnaire, February 2012; Andreas S. interview, April 2012; Claudia S. interview, June 2012; Hacker et al. (eds.), *Dritte Generation Ost*, 12; Adriana Letrari, 'Potenziale der Dritten Generation Ostdeutschland: Nicht entweder oder, sondern sowohl als auch', in Hacker et al. (eds.), *Dritte Generation Ost*, 178; Johannes Stämmler, 'Wir, die stumme Generation Ost', in Hacker et al. (eds.), *Dritte Generation Ost*, 213.

39. Eva Kolinsky (ed.), *Between Hope and Fear: Everyday Life in Post-Unification East Germany* (Keele, 1995), 33, 231, 234; Uta Starke, 'Young People: Lifestyles, Expectations and Value Orientations since the Wende', in Kolinsky (ed.), *Between Hope and Fear*, 155–75, at 162; Andreas Glaeser, *Divided in Unity: Identity, Germany and the Berlin Police* (Chicago, 2000), 350.

40. Heins, *The Wall Falls*, 319–20.

Chapter 7

1. Michael Gehler, *Three Germanies: West Germany, East Germany and the Berlin Republic* (London, 2011), 200.

2. After December 1991, when East Germans were granted access to their individual Stasi files, the man in the mining society discovered that Mirko's father had informed on him. Mirko's father said that he had agreed to do so because he regarded him as a friend and wanted to protect him from further problems with the regime. Accepting this version of events, the friend did not reject Mirko's father and they have been close friends ever since.

3. Many East Germans cut off contact with their Western relatives either because they knew the SED frowned upon it or because it was a condition of their job that they sign a document agreeing to do so.

4. Cf. Hans-Joachim D. interview, February 2013; Silvio G. interview, January 2013.

5. Cf. Hans-Michael S. interview, April 2012.

6. Ruth Hoffman, *Stasi-Kinder: Aufwachsen im Überwachungsstaat* (Berlin, 2012), 8, 9, 26, 61.

7. Cf. Claudia S. interview, June 2012.

8. Cf. Lisa E. interview, June 2012.

9. Cf. Anne-Marie B. interview, June 2012; Thomas J. interview, June 2012; Hoffman, *Stasi-Kinder*, 58; Edith Sheffer, *Burned Bridge: How East and West Germans Made the Iron Curtain* (Oxford, 2011), 169.

10. Anne McElvoy, *The Saddled Cow: East Germany's Life and Legacy* (London, 1992), 156.

11. Cf. Dirk L. interview, March 2013; Hans-Joachim D. interview, February 2013; Heike K. interview, February 2013.

12. Robert Ide, *Geteilte Träume: Meine Eltern, die Wende und ich* (Munich, 2009), 83–4.

13. Cf. Ide, *Geteilte Träume*, 104; Elizabeth A. Ten Dyke, *Dresden: Paradoxes of Memory in History* (New York, 2001), 169–70.

14. Hoffman, *Stasi-Kinder*, 56.

15. Cf. Ide, *Geteilte Träume*, 104.

16. Cf. Felix R. interview, April 2013.

17. See the permanent exhibition at the GDR Museum, Berlin and <www.ironcurtainkid.com>.

18. Cf. Hanno H. interview, January 2013; Felix R. interview, April 2013.

19. Ide, *Geteilte Träume*, 16; Johannes Stämmler, 'Ich entdecke den Osten neu: Ein Interview mit dem Chefredaktuer der SUPERillu, Robert Schneider', in Michael Hacker et al. (eds.), *Dritte Generation Ost: Wer wir sind, was wir wollen* (Berlin, 2012), 167.

20. DTA 1071/2, Anonymous diary, 28 February 2006, p. 162.

21. Cf. Silvio G. interview, January 2013; Linda Bunckenburg and Susan Mücke, 'Jugend im Aufbruch: Wendejugendliche erinnern sich an ihren Herbst 1989', in Hacker et al. (eds.), *Dritte Generation Ost*, 40.

22. Anja Görnitz in Hacker et al. (eds.), *Dritte Generation Ost*, 25–6.

Chapter 8

1. Cf. Mike M. interview, April 2013.

2. Cf. Thomas J. interview, June 2012.

3. Cf. Claudia S. interview, June 2012; DTA 1071/1, Anonymous diary, 1988–1989, pp. 44, 96.

4. Cf. Anna-Maria G. questionnaire, February 2012; Felix R. interview, April 2013; Kristina Matschat quoted in Cornelia Heins, *The Wall Falls: An Oral History of the Reunification of the Two Germanies* (London, 1994), 233; DTA 1071/1, Anonymous diary, 1988–1989, p. 147.

5. Michael Gehler, *Three Germanies: West Germany, East Germany and the Berlin Republic* (London, 2011), 200.

6. Cf. Robert Ide, *Geteilte Träume: Meine Eltern, die Wende und ich* (Munich, 2009), 62.

7. Cf. Dirk L. interview, March 2013.

8. Cf. Petra Bläss interview, June 2012.

9. Felix R. interview, April 2013.

10. Silvio G. interview, January 2013; Andreas Glaeser, *Divided in Unity: Identity, Germany and the Berlin Police* (Chicago, 2000), 44.

11. Ide, *Geteilte Träume*, 121.

12. Romy Koehler and Susanne Herrmann-Sinai, 'Denken in Grenzen', in Michael Hacker et al. (eds.), *Dritte Generation Ost: Wer wir sind, was wir wollen* (Berlin, 2012), 185.

13. Cf. Hanna K. interview, December 2011; Angela H. interview, October 2011; Nina Benedict, *Böse Briefe über Deutschland* (Schkeuditz, 1993), 62.

14. Benedict, *Böse Briefe über Deutschland*, 62.

15. Daphne Berdahl, *Where the World Ended: Re-Unification and Identity in the German Borderland* (Berkeley and Los Angeles, 1999), 58.

16. 'High German' is a term used for formal German, most often used in written German, and frequently associated with the Hanover region in Western Germany.

17. Cf. Dirk L. interview, March 2013.

18. Cf. Felix R. interview, April 2013.

19. Franz Kafka quoted in Heins, *The Wall Falls*, 102.

20. Claudia Rusch, *Meine Freie Deutsche Jugend* (Frankfurt am Main, 2003), 76.

21. Hans-Michael S. interview, April 2012; DTA 1071/2, Anonymous, June 2002, p. 58; Anne Schreiter, 'Bin ich ostdeutsch? Vom Umgang mit den kleinen Unterschieden', in Hacker et al. (eds.), *Dritte Generation Ost*, 79; Juliane Cieslak and Paula Hannaske, 'Vergangenheit heute: Einblicke in die Arbeit einer ostdeutschen Biografiegruppe', in Hacker et al. (eds.), *Dritte Generation Ost*, 49.

22. Erich Honecker speaking at the IXth SED Party Congress, 17–21 November 1986.

23. Cf. Mike M. interview, April 2013; 'Alle wollen an die Ostsee reisen' [Everyone Wants to Travel to the Baltic Sea], *Der Tagesspiegel*, 23 May 1963.

24. Cf. Mike M. interview, April 2013.

25. Cf. Felix R. interview, April 2013.

26. Walther Ulbricht quoted in Molly Wilkinson Johnson, *Training Socialist Citizens: Sports and the State in East Germany* (Brill, 2008), 2.

27. Joanna McKay, 'East German Identity in the GDR', in Jonathan Grix and Paul Cooke (eds.), *East German Distinctiveness in a Unified Germany*

(Birmingham, 2002), 18; Wilkinson Johnson, *Training Socialist Citizens*, 64, 203.

28. Cf. Angela H. interview, October 2011; Anna-Maria G. questionnaire, February 2012; Stuart Parkes, *Understanding Contemporary Germany* (London, 1997), 95.

29. Cf. Lisa E. interview, June 2012; Jürgen A. K. Thomaneck, 'From Euphoria to Reality: Social Problems of Post-Unification', in Derek Lewis and John R. P. McKenzie (eds.), *The New Germany: Social, Political and Cultural Challenges of Unification* (Exeter, 1995), 27–8.

30. Cf. Angela H. interview, October 2011.

31. Cf. Angelique L. questionnaire, February 2012; 'Bin ich ostdeutsch? Vom Umgang mit den kleinen Unterschieden', *SUPERillu*, 30 (2012), 13; Edith Sheffer, *Burned Bridge: How East and West Germans Made the Iron Curtain* (Oxford, 2011), 227; Anne McElvoy, *The Saddled Cow: East Germany's Life and Legacy* (London, 1992), 221.

32. Thomaneck, 'From Euphoria to Reality', 27–8.

Chapter 9

1. Hans-Joachim Maaz quoted in Anne McElvoy, *The Saddled Cow: East Germany's Life and Legacy* (London, 1992), 219.

2. Hans-Hermann Hertle, Konrad Jarausch, and Christoph Kleßmann, *Mauerbau und Mauerfall* (Berlin 2002), 299; Hagen Koch and Peter Joachim Lapp, *Die Garde des Erich Mielke—Der militärisch-operative Arm des MfS—Das Berliner Wachregiment 'Feliks Dzierzynski'* (Aachen 2008).

3. Peter Erler and Hubertus Knabe, *The Prohibited District: The Stasi Restricted Area Berlin Hohenschoenhausen* (Berlin, 2008), 9–12; Ruth Hoffman, *Stasi-Kinder: Aufwachsen im Ueberwachungsstaat* (Berlin, 2012), 33–4; Mary Fulbrook, *Dissonant Lives* (Oxford, 2011), 378; Ines Veith, *Leben und Alltag…der DDR-Flüchtlinge* (Kempen, 2010), 34; McElvoy, *The Saddled Cow*, 102–3.

4. Cf. Robert S. interview, December 2011; Lisa E. interview, April 2012; Petra Bläss interview, April 2012; Peggy M. interview, January 2013.

5. Katherine Pence and Paul Betts (eds.), *Socialist Modern: East German Everyday Culture and Politics*, (Michigan, 2008), 9; Jonathan Grix, *The Role of the Masses in the Collapse of the GDR* (London, 2000), 23–4, 38, 62; Daphne Berdahl, *Where the World Ended: Re-Unification and Identity in the German Borderland* (Berkeley and Los Angeles, 1999), 60–1.

6. Jeannette Z. Madarasz, *Conflict and Compromise in East Germany, 1971–1989* (Basingstoke, 2003), 7.

7. Mary Fulbrook, *Anatomy of a Dictatorship: Inside the GDR, 1949–1989* (Oxford, 1995), 143.

8. Mary Fulbrook, *The People's State: East German Society from Hitler to Honecker* (Oxford, 2008), 292.

9. Pence and Betts (eds.), *Socialist Modern*, 5, 9; Stuart Parkes, *Understanding Contemporary Germany* (London, 1997), 7.

10. Konrad Jarausch, *The Rush to Germany Unity* (Oxford, 1994).

11. Jonathan Grix and Paul Cooke (eds.), *East German Distinctiveness in a Unified Germany* (Birmingham, 2002), 1.

12. Matthias S. interview, February 2012; Andreas Glaeser, *Divided in Unity: Identity, Germany and the Berlin Police* (Chicago, 2000), 117, 176; Wolfgang Seibel, 'The Quest for Freedom and Stability: Political Choices and the Economic Transformation of East Germany, 1989–1991', in Peter C. Caldwell and Robert R. Shandley (eds.), *German Unification: Expectations and Outcomes* (London, 2011), 99; Emine Sevgi Oezdamar, 'Lieber Besson', in Julia Franck (ed.), *Grenzübergänge: Autoren aus Ost und West erinnern sich* (Frankfurt am Main, 2009), 138.

13. Marianne Birthler, 'Epilogue: The End of Dictatorship and Its Aftermath: Personal Reflections of the Federal Commissioner for the Records of the State Security Agency of the German Democratic Republic', in Caldwell and Shandley (eds.), *German Unification*, 175; Kristen Ghodsee, *Lost in Transition: Ethnographies of Everyday Life after Communism* (Durham, NC, 2011), 186–7.

14. Cf. Petra Bläss interview, June 2012; Hanna K. interview, December 2011.

15. Elviera Thiedemann, *Es kame in langer lichter Herbst: Tagebuch der Wendezeit 1989/90* (Berlin, 2000), 46–7; Berdahl, *Where the World Ended*, 2–3.

16. Paul Kubicek, 'The Diminishing Relevance of Ostalgie 20 Years after Reunification', in Katharina Gerstenberger and Jana Evans Braziel (eds.), *After the Berlin Wall: Germany and Beyond* (London, 2011), 86.

17. Derek Lewis, 'The GDR: Wende and Legacy', in Lewis and John R. P. McKenzie (eds.), *The New Germany: Social, Political and Cultural Challenges of Unification* (Exeter, 1995), 55; Caldwell and Shandley, *German Unification*, 6.

18. Cf. Dirk L. interview, March 2013; Hans-Joachim D. interview, February 2013; Heike K. interview, February 2013.

19. 'Jahresbericht des Bundesregierung zum Stand der Deutschen Einheit 2013', published on 20 November 2013: <www.beauftragter-neue-laender.de>.

20. Jarausch, *The Rush to German Unity*, 153; Fulbrook, *Dissonant Lives*, 461; Mike Dennis, 'The East German Family: Change and Continuity', in Chris Flockton and Eva Kolinsky (eds.), *Recasting East Germany: Social Transformation after the GDR* (London, 1999), 89; Jürgen Weber, *Germany 1945–1990: A Parallel History* (New York, 2004), 237; Frithjof H. Knabe, 'Unemployment: Developments and Experiences', in Eva Kolinsky (ed.), *Between Hope and Fear* (Keele, 1995), 74, 84.

21. Werner Smolny, 'Wage Adjustment, Competitiveness and Unemployment: East Germany After unification', *Jahrbücher für Nationalökonomie und Stastistik*, 229/2–3 (2009), 130–45, at 133.

22. 'Jahresbericht des Bundesregierung zum Stand der Deutschen Einheit 2013', published on 20 November 2013: <www.beauftragter-neue-laender.de>; Philip Oltermann, 'Divided Germany Appears as Year of War and Wall Anniversaries Begin', *The Guardian*, 2 January 2014.

23. Frithjof H. Knabe, 'Unemployment: Developments and Experiences', in Kolinsky (ed.), *Between Hope and Fear*, 74, 84.

24. Cf. Mirko Sennewald interview, April 2012; Carola Koehler interview, June 2012; Robert S. interview, December 2011; Anne-Marie B. interview, April 2012; Peggy M. interview, January 2013.

25. Wolf von Holleben quoted in Cornelia Heins, *The Wall Falls: An Oral History of the Reunification of the Two Germanies* (London, 1994), 166; Dr Kristina Matschat quoted in Heins, *The Wall Falls*, 267; cf. Matthias S. interview, February 2012.

26. Peter Grieder, '"To Learn from the Soviet Union is to Learn How to Win": The East German Revolution, 1989–1990', in Kevin McDermott and Matthew Stibbe (eds.), *Revolution and Resistance in Eastern Europe: Challenges to Communist Rule* (Oxford, 2006), 160; Martin Diewald, Anne Goedicke, and Karl Ulrich Mayer, *After the Fall of the Wall: Life Courses in the Transformation of East Germany* (Stanford, Calif., 2006), 32.

27. Alice Kahl, 'Housing and the Quality of Urban Living', in Kolinsky (ed.), *Between Hope and Fear*, 140; Hans-Jürgen van der Gieth, *Leben und Alltag im geteilten Deutschland* (Kempen, 2001), 20–2.

28. Berdahl, *Where the World Ended*, 2–3.

29. Judd Stitziel, 'Shopping, Sewing, Networking, Complaining: Consumer Culture and the Relationship between State and Society in the GDR', in Pence and Betts (eds.), *Socialist Modern*, 253.

30. Exhibition at the Tränenpalast in Berlin.

31. Katharina Furian interview, June 2012; Edith Sheffer, *Burned Bridge: How East and West Germans Made the Iron Curtain* (Oxford, 2011), 11, 213, 249.

32. Andreas Glaeser, *Divided in Unity: Identity, Germany and the Berlin Police* (Chicago, 2000), 143.

33. Kubicek, 'The Diminishing Relevance of Ostalgie 20 Years after Reunification', 86.

34. Glaeser, *Divided in Unity*, 344; Timothy Garton Ash, *In Europe's Name: Germany and the Divided Continent* (New York, 1993), 343.

35. Cf. Peggy M. interview, January 2013; Angela H. interview, October 2011; Hanna K. interview, December 2011; Diewald, Goedicke, and Mayer, *After the Fall of the Wall*, 312.

36. Dirk L. interview, March 2013.

37. Felix R. interview, April 2013; Sheffer, *Burned Bridge*, 246.

38. Robert S. interview, December 2011; Paul Betts, *Within Walls: Private Life in the German Democratic Republic* (Oxford, 2010), 229; DTA 1071/1, Anonymous diary, 1988–1989, December 1989–March 1990, pp. 153–4.

39. Cf. Robert S. interview, December 2011; Peggy M. interview, January 2013; Heike K. interview, February 2013; Grix and Cooke (eds.), *East German Distinctiveness in a Unified Germany*, 1.

40. Elizabeth A. Ten Dyke, *Dresden: Paradoxes of Memory in History* (New York, 2001), 136–7.

41. DTA 1071/1, Anonymous diary, 1988–1989, December 1989–March 1990, pp. 153–4; Robert Ide, *Geteilte Träume: Meine Eltern, die Wende und ich* (Munich, 2009), 58; Michael Gehler, *Three Germanies: West Germany, East Germany and the Berlin Republic* (London, 2011), 237.

42. Dirk Philipsen, *We Were the People: Voices From East Germany's Revolutionary Autumn of 1989* (London, 1993), 329, 330; Ide, *Geteilte Träume*, 14; Mark Fenemore, *Sex, Thugs and Rock 'n' Roll: Teenage Rebels in Cold-War East Germany* (New York, 2007), xiii.

43. Cf. Katharina Furian interview, June 2012; Thomas J. interview, June 2012; Grix and Cooke (eds.), *East German Distinctiveness in a Unified Germany*, 2. Both before and after the collapse of communism in Europe,

the GDR occupied a unique position in comparison to other countries in the Eastern bloc. It was subsidized by the FRG during the period of division and it was incorporated into the West German system after the Wall fell. Other Eastern bloc countries, by contrast, had not had the benefit of such subsidies and had to rebuild their countries' governing structures entirely from scratch after 1989.

44. Philipsen, *We Were the People*, 332.
45. Konrad H. Jarausch (ed.), *After Unity: Reconfiguring German Identities* (Berghahn, 1997), 19.
46. Cf. Anne-Marie B. interview, June 2012; Hans-Joachim D. interview, February 2012; Fulbrook, *Dissonant Lives*, 455.
47. Ide, *Geteilte Träume*, 37.
48. Cf. Claudia S. interview, June 2012; Ralph Hoppe interview, June 2012; David Childs, *The Fall of the GDR: Germany's Road to Unity* (Edinburgh, 2001), 31–2; McElvoy, *The Saddled Cow*, 226.
49. McElvoy, *The Saddled Cow*, 234; Anne-Marie B. interview, June 2012; DTA 1071/2, 11 March 2001, pp. 9–10.
50. Diewald, Goedicke, and Mayer, *After the Fall of the Wall*, 29.
51. Fulbrook, *Dissonant Lives*, 449.
52. Johannes Stämmler, 'Wir, die stumme Generation Ost', in Michael Hacker et al.. (eds.), *Dritte Generation Ost: Wer wir sind, was wir wollen* (Berlin, 2012), 212.
53. Paul Cooke, 'Literature and the Question of East German Cultural Identity since the Wende', in Grix and Cooke (eds.), *East German Distinctiveness in a Unified Germany*, 165; Hacker et al. (eds.), *Dritte Generation Ost*, 2012, 11.
54. Anne-Marie B. interview, June 2012.
55. McElvoy, *The Saddled Cow*, 234.
56. DTA 1071/1, Anonymous diary, 1988–1989, p. 94; Robert S. interview, December 2011; Hanna K. interview, December 2011.
57. Dyke, *Dresden*, 51; Fulbrook, *Dissonant Lives*, 358; Ide, *Geteilte Träume*, 43.
58. Cf. Robert S. interview, December 2011; Petra Bläss interview, June 2012; Peggy M. interview, January 2013; Jarausch (ed.), *After Unity*, 19.
59. Thomas J. interview, June 2012.
60. DTA 1350/131, Anonymous diary, entry from 3 October 1990.
61. Oltermann, 'Divided Germany Appears as Year of War and Wall Anniversaries Begin'.

Bibliography

Abrams, Lynn, *Oral History Theory* (Oxford, 2010).

Allinson, Mark, *Politics and Popular Opinion in East Germany 1945–1968* (Manchester, 2000).

Alter, Reinhard, and Monteath, Peter (eds.), *Rewriting the German Past: History and Identity in the New Germany* (Atlantic Highlands, NJ, 1997).

Ansorg, Leonore, and Huertgen, Renate, 'The Myth of Female Emancipation: Contradictions in Women's Lives', in Jarausch (ed.), *Dictatorship as Experience*, 163–76.

Applebaum, Anne, *Iron Curtain: The Crushing of Eastern Europe, 1944–1956* (London, 2012).

Arbeitsgemeinschaft Jugend und Bildung e.V. (ed.), *Wir in Ost und West—Jugend, Alltag, Freizeit* (Wiesbaden, 1986).

Becker, Arnold, *Jugendweihe: Ein unüberwindbarer Graben zwischen Ost und West?* (Frankfurt am Main, 1999).

Benedict, Nina, *Böse Briefe über Deutschland* (Schkeuditz, 1993).

Benz, Ute and Wolfgang, *Deutschland, deine Kinder: Zur Prägung von Feindbildern in Ost und West* (Munich, 2001).

Berdahl, Daphne, *Where the World Ended: Re-Unification and Identity in the German Borderland* (Berkeley and Los Angeles, 1999).

Betts, Paul, *Within Walls: Private Life in the German Democratic Republic* (Oxford, 2010).

Birthler, Marianne, 'Epilogue, The End of Dictatorship and Its Aftermath: Personal Reflections of the Federal Commissioner for the Records of the State Security Agency of the German Democratic Republic', in Caldwell and Shandley (eds.), *German Unification: Expectations and Outcomes*, 173–82.

Bunckenburg, Linda, and Muecke, Susan, 'Jugend im Aufbruch. Wendejugendliche erinnern sich an ihren Herbst 1989', in Hacker et al. (eds.), *Dritte Generation Ost*, 39–46.

Caldwell, Peter C., and Shandley, Robert R. (eds.), *German Unification: Expectations and Outcomes* (London, 2011).

Cate, Curtis, *The Ides of August: The Berlin Wall Crisis, 1961* (London, 1978).

Charlton, Thomas, Myers, Lois, and Sharpless, Rebecca (eds.), *Handbook of Oral History* (Walnut Creek, Calif., 2006).

Childs, David, *The Fall of the GDR: Germany's Road to Unity* (Edinburgh, 2001).

Cieslak, Juliane, and Hannaske, Paula, 'Vergangenheit heute: Einblicke in die Arbeit einer ostdeutschen Biografiegruppe', in Hacker et al. (eds.), *Dritte Generation Ost*, 47–57.

Cook, Paul, *Representing East Germany: From Colonization to Nostalgia* (Oxford, 2005).

Cordell, Karl, 'The Church: Coming to Terms with Change', in Kolinsky (ed.), *Between Hope and Fear*, 123–34.

Davey, Thomas, *A Generation Divided: German Children and the Berlin Wall* (Durham, NC, 1987).

Dennis, Mike, 'The East German Family: Change and Continuity', in Flockton and Kolinsky (eds.), *Recasting East Germany*, 83–100.

Deutsche Shell (ed.), *Jugend 2002: Zwischen pragmatischem Idealismus und robustem Materialismus, 14. Shell Jugendstudie* (Frankfurt am Main, 2002).

Diewald, Martin, Goedicke, Anne, and Mayer, Karl Ulrich, *After the Fall of the Wall: Life Courses in the Transformation of East Germany* (Stanford, Calif., 2006).

Dyke, Elizabeth A. Ten, *Dresden: Paradoxes of Memory in History* (New York, 2001).

Eghigian, Greg, 'Homo Munitus: The East German Observed', in Pence and Betts (eds.), *Socialist Modern*, 37–70.

Erler, Peter, and Knabe, Hubertus, *The Prohibited District: The Stasi Restricted Area Berlin Hohenschönhausen* (Berlin, 2008).

Fahlke, Eberhard (ed.), *Die Katze Erinnerung: Uwe Johnson—Eine Chronik in Briefen und Bildern* (Berlin, 1994).

Fenemore, Mark, *Sex, Thugs and Rock 'n' Roll: Teenage Rebels in Cold-War East Germany* (London, 2007).

Filmer, Werner, and Schwann, Heribert (eds.), *Alltag im anderen Deutschland* (Düsseldorf, 1985).

Flockton, Chris, and Kolinsky, Eva (eds.), *Recasting East Germany: Social Transformation after the GDR* (London, 1999).

Forrester, Sibelan, Zaborowska, Magdalena J., and Gapova, Elena (eds.), *Over the Wall/After the Fall: Post-Communist Cultures Through an East-West Gaze* (Bloomington, Ind., 2004).

Förster, Peter, '"Es war nicht alles falsch, was wir früher über den Kapitalismus gelernt haben": Empirische Ergebnisse einer Längsschnittstudie zum Weg junger Ostdeutscher vom DDR-Bürger zum Bundesbürger', *Deutschland Archiv*, 34/2 (2001), 197–218.

Franck, Julia, 'Die Überwindung der Grenze liegt im Erzählen', in Franck (ed.), *Grenzübergänge*, 9–22.

Franck, Julia (ed.), *Grenzübergänge: Autoren aus Ost und West erinnern sich* (Frankfurt am Main, 2009).

Friedrich, Walter, Förster, Peter, and Starke, Kurt (eds.), *Das Zentralinstitut für Jugendforschung Leipzig 1966–1990: Geschichte, Methoden, Erkenntnisse* (Berlin, 1999).

Fulbrook, Mary, *Anatomy of a Dictatorship: Inside the GDR, 1949–1989* (Oxford, 1995).

Fulbrook, Mary, 'Reckoning with the Past: Heroes, Victims, and Villains in the History of the German Democratic Republic', in Alter and Monteath (eds.), *Rewriting the German Past*, 175–96.

Fulbrook, Mary, *History of Germany 1918–2000: Divided Nation* (Oxford, 2002).

Fulbrook, Mary, *The People's State: East German Society from Hitler to Honecker* (New Haven, 2005).

Fulbrook, Mary, *Dissonant Lives: Generations and Violence through the German Dictatorships* (Oxford, 2011).

Funder, Anna, *Stasiland: Stories from Behind the Berlin Wall* (London, 2003).

Furian, Gilbert (ed.), *Mehl aus Mielkes Mühlen: Politische Häftlinge und ihre Verfolger* (Berlin, 2008).

Furian, Gilbert, and Becker, Nikolaus, *'Auch im Osten trägt man Westen': Punks in der DDR—und was aus ihnen geworden ist* (Berlin, 2000).

Galenza, Roland, and Hauvemeister, Heinz (eds.), *Wir wollen immer artig sein...Punk, New Wave, HipHop, Independent: Szene in der DDR 1980–1990* (Berlin, 1999).

Garton Ash, Timothy, *In Europe's Name: Germany and the Divided Continent* (New York, 1993).

Gässner, Gert-Joachim, and Wallace, Ian (eds.), *The German Revolution of 1989: Causes and Consequences* (Oxford, 1993).

Gaus, Günter, *Wo Deutschland liegt: Eine Ortsbestimmung* (Hamburg, 1983).

Gehler, Michael, *Three Germanies: West Germany, East Germany and the Berlin Republic* (London, 2011).

Gerstenberger, Katharina, and Braziel, Jana Evans (eds.), *After the Berlin Wall: Germany and Beyond* (London, 2011).

Ghodsee, Kristen, *Lost in Transition: Ethnographies of Everyday Life after Communism* (Durham, NC, 2011).

Gieseke, Jens, 'Ulbricht's Secret Police: The Ministry of State Security', in Patrick Major (ed.), *The Workers' and Peasants' State: Communism and Society in East German under Ulbricht* (Manchester, 2002), 41–58.

Gieth, Hans-Jürgen van der, *Leben und Alltag im geteilten Deutschland* (Kempen, 2001).

Glaeser, Andreas, *Divided in Unity: Identity, Germany and the Berlin Police* (Chicago, 2000).

Glaeser, Andreas, 'Why Germany Remains Divided', in Todd Herzog and Sander L. Gilman (eds.), *A New Germany in a New Europe* (New York, 2001), 173–93.

Glees, Anthony, 'Social Transformation Studies and Human Rights Abuses in East Germany after 1945', in Flockton and Kolinsky (eds.), *Recasting East Germany*, 165–91.

Görnitz, Anja, in Hacker et al. (eds.), *Dritte Generation Ost*, 23–6.

Grele, Ronald, *Envelopes of Sound: The Art of Oral History* (New York, 1991).

Grieder, Peter, 'The Leadership of the Socialist Unity Party of Germany', in Patrick Major (ed.), *The Workers' and Peasants' State: Communism and Society in East German under Ulbricht* (Manchester, 2002), 22–40.

Grieder, Peter, '"To Learn from the Soviet Union is to Learn How to Win": The East German Revolution, 1989–1990', in McDermott and Stibbe (eds.), *Revolution and Resistance in Eastern Europe*, 157–74.

Gries, Rainer, '"Hurrah, I'm Still Alive!" East German Products Demonstrating East German Identities', in Forrester et al. (eds.), *Over the Wall/After the Fall*, 181–99.

Grix, Jonathan, *The Role of the Masses in the Collapse of the GDR* (London, 2000).

Grix, Jonathan, and Cooke, Paul (eds.), *East German Distinctiveness in a Unified Germany* (Birmingham, 2002).

Hacker, Michael, Maiwald, Stephanie, Staemmler, Johannes, Enders, Judith, Lettrari, Adriana, Pietzcker, Hagen, Schober, Henrik, and Schulze,

Mandy (eds.), *Dritte Generation Ost: Wer wir sind, was wir wollen* (Berlin, 2012).

Harsch, Donna, *Revenge of the Domestic: Women, the Family and Communism in the German Democratic Republic* (Princeton, 2007).

Heins, Cornelia, *The Wall Falls: An Oral History of the Reunification of the Two Germanies* (London, 1994).

Held, Björn, 'Bei der tiefen Stimme der "Gloriosa"', in Filmer and Schwann (eds.), *Alltag im anderen Deutschland*, 115–23.

Hempel, Isabel, 'Zukunft ist kein Schicksalsschlag: Frauen machen Neue Länder', in Hacker et al. (eds.), *Dritte Generation Ost*, 170–7.

Hensel, Jana, *After the Wall: Confessions from an East German Childhood and the Life that Came Next*, trans. Jefferson Chase (New York, 2004).

Hertle, Hans-Hermann, Jarausch, Konrad, and Kleßmann, Christoph, *Mauerbau und Mauerfall: Ursachen-Verlauf-Auswirkungen* (Berlin, 2002).

Herzog, Dagmar, 'East Germany's Sexual Evolution', in Pence and Betts (eds.), *Socialist Modern*, 71–95.

Hilton, Christopher, *The Wall: The People's Story* (Stroud, 2001).

Hoffman, Ruth, *Stasi-Kinder: Aufwachsen im Überwachungsstaat* (Berlin, 2012).

Ide, Robert, *Geteilte Träume: Meine Eltern, die Wende und ich* (Munich, 2009).

Jahn, Roland, 'Wissen, wie es war', in Hacker et al. (eds.), *Dritte Generation Ost*, 73–5.

James, Harold, and Stone, Marla (eds.), *When the Wall Came Down: Reactions to German Unification* (New York, 1992).

Jarausch, Konrad, *The Rush to German Unity: Reconfiguring German Identities* (Oxford, 1994).

Jarausch, Konrad (ed.), *Dictatorship as Experience: Towards a Socio-Cultural History of the GDR* (Oxford, 1999).

Jarausch, Konrad, Seeba, Hinrich C., and Conradt, David P., 'The Presence of the Past', in Jarausch (ed.), *After Unity*, 25–60.

Jarausch, Konrad H. (ed.), *After Unity* (Berghahn, 1997).

Kahl, Alice, 'Housing and the Quality of Urban Living' in Kolinsky (ed.), *Between Hope and Fear*, 135–54.

Kaliski, Bartosz, 'Solidarity, 1980–1981: The Second Vistula Miracle?', in McDermott and Stibbe (eds.), *Revolution and Resistance in Eastern Europe*, 119–38.

Klessmann, Christoph, *Kinder der Opposition: Berichte aus Pfarrhäusern in der DDR* (Gütersloh, 1993).

Knabe, Frithjof H., 'Unemployment: Developments and Experiences', in Kolinsky (ed.), *Between Hope and Fear*, 71–86.

Knabe, Hubertus, *Umweltkonflikte im Sozialismus: Möglichkeiten und Grenzen gesellschaftlicher Problemartikulation in sozialistischen Systemen: Eine vergleichende Analyse der Umweltdiskussion in der DDR und Ungarn* (Cologne, 1994).

Koch, Hagen, and Lapp, Peter Joachim, *Die Garde des Erich Mielke—Der militärisch-operative Arm des MfS—Das Berliner Wachregiment 'Feliks Dzierzynski'* (Aachen, 2008).

Köhler, Romy, and Herrmann-Sinai, Susanne, 'Denken in Grenzen' in Hacker et al. (eds.), *Dritte Generation Ost*, 178–90.

Kolinsky, Eva (ed.), *Between Hope and Fear: Everyday Life in Post-Unification East Germany* (Keele, 1995).

Kowalczyk, Angela, *Negativ und Dekaden: Ostberliner Punk Erinnerungen* (Berlin, 2003).

Kubicek, Paul, 'The Diminishing Relevance of Ostalgie 20 Years after Re-unification', in Gerstenberger and Braziel (eds.), *After the Berlin Wall*, 85–104.

Langenhan, Dagmar, and Ross, Sabine, 'The Socialist Glass Ceiling: Limits to Female Careers', in Jarausch (ed.), *Dictatorship as Experience*, 177–91.

Leggewie, Claus, 'The "Generation of 1989": A New Political Generation?', in Alter and Monteath (eds.), *Rewriting the German Past*, 103–14.

Letrari, Adriana, 'Potenziale der Dritten Generation Ostdeutschland: Nicht entweder oder, sondern sowohl als auch', in Hacker et al. (eds.), *Dritte Generation Ost*, 202–11.

Lewis, Derek, 'The GDR: Wende and Legacy', in Lewis and McKenzie (eds.), *The New Germany*.

Lewis, Derek, and McKenzie, John R. P. (eds.), *The New Germany: Social, Political and Cultural Challenges of Unification* (Exeter, 1995).

Lindenberger, Thomas (ed.), *Herrschaft und Eigen-Sinn in der Diktatur: Studien zur Gesellschaftsgeschichte der DDR* (Cologne, 1999).

Loth, Wilfried, *Stalin's Unwanted Child: The Soviet Union, the German Question, and the Founding of the GDR* (Basingstoke, 1998).

Lüdtke, Alf (ed.), *The History of Everyday Life: Reconstructing Historical Experiences and Ways of Life*, trans. William Templer (Princeton, 1995).

Lummis, Trevor, *Listening to History: The Authenticity of Oral Evidence* (London, 1987).

Maaz, Hans-Joachim, *Behind the Wall: The Inner Life of Communist Germany* (New York, 1995).

McAdams, A. James, *Judging the Past in Unified Germany* (Cambridge, 2001).

McDermott, Kevin, and Stibbe, Matthew (eds.), *Revolution and Resistance in Eastern Europe: Challenges to Communist Rule* (Oxford, 2006).

McDougall, Alan, *Youth Politics in East Germany: The Free German Youth Movement, 1946–1968* (Oxford, 2004).

McElvoy, Anne, *The Saddled Cow: East Germany's Life and Legacy* (London, 1992).

McKay, Joanna, 'East German Identity in the GDR', in Grix and Cooke (eds.), *East German Distinctiveness in a Unified Germany*, 15–30.

McLellan, Josie, *Love in the Time of Communism: Intimacy and Sexuality in the GDR* (Cambridge, 2011).

Madarasz, Jeannette Z., *Conflict and Compromise in East Germany, 1971–1989* (Basingstoke, 2003).

Mählert, Ulrich, and Stephan, Gerd Rüdiger, *Blaue Hemden—Rote Fahnen: Die Geschichte der Freien Deutschen Jugend* (Opladen, 1996).

Maier, Charles S., *Dissolution: The Crisis of Communism and the End of East Germany* (Princeton, 1997).

Merritt, Richard L., and Merritt, Anna J., *Living with the Wall: West Berlin, 1961–1985* (Durham, NC, 1985).

Miller, Barbara, *Narratives of Guilt and Compliance in Unified Germany: Stasi Informers and Their Impact on Society* (London, 1999).

Mitter, Armin, and Wolle, Stefan, *Untergang auf Raten: Unbekannte Kapitel der DDR-Geschichte* (Munich, 1993).

Moses, John, and Munro, Gregory, 'The Role of the Churches in the Collapse of the GDR', in Alter and Monteath, *Rewriting the German Past*, 222–52.

Oezdamar, Emine Sevgi, 'Lieber Besson', in Franck (ed.), *Grenzübergänge*, 128–40.

Palmowski, Jan, *Inventing a Socialist Nation: Heimat and the Politics of Everyday Life in the GDR, 1945–1990* (Cambridge, 2009).

Parkes, Stuart, *Understanding Contemporary Germany* (London, 1997).

Passerini, Luisa (ed.), *Memory and Totalitarianism* (Oxford, 1992).

Pence, Katherine, and Betts, Paul (eds.), *Socialist Modern: East German Everyday Culture and Politics* (Ann Arbor, 2008).

Perks, Robert, *Oral History: Talking about the Past* (2nd edn., London, 1995).

Perks, Robert, and Thomson, Alistair (eds.), *The Oral History Reader* (2nd edn., London, 2006).

Philipsen, Dirk, *We Were the People: Voices From East Germany's Revolutionary Autumn of 1989* (London, 1993).

Pittaway, Mark, *Eastern Europe 1939–2000* (New York, 2004).

Plock, Ernest D., *East German–West German Relations and the Fall of the GDR* (Oxford, 1993).

Preuss, Ulrich K., 'Political Institutions and German Unification', in Caldwell and Shandley (eds.), *German Unification*, 137–52.

Pridham, Geoffrey, *The Democratization of Eastern Europe* (London, 1994).

Pritchard, Gareth, *The Making of the GDR, 1945–1953* (Manchester, 2000).

Rehlinger, Ludwig A., *Freikauf: Die Geschäfte der DDR mit politisch Verfolgten 1963–1989* (Berlin, 1991).

Richthofen, Esther von, *Bringing Culture to the Masses: Control, Compromise and Participation in the GDR* (New York, 2009).

Ritchie, Donald, *Doing Oral History: A Practical Guide* (New York, 2003).

Ritter, Gerhard A., *The Price of German Unity: Reunification and the Crisis of the Welfare State* (Oxford, 2011).

Rodden, John, *Repainting the Little Red Schoolhouse: A History of East German Education, 1945–1995* (Oxford, 2002).

Ross, Corey, *The East German Dictatorship: Problems and Perspectives in the Interpretation of the GDR* (London, 2002).

Ross, Corey, 'Protecting the Accomplishments of Socialism? The Remilitarization of Life in the German Democratic Republic', in Patrick Major (ed.), *The Workers' and Peasants' State: Communism and Society in East German under Ulbricht* (Manchester, 2002), 78–94.

Rubin, David (ed.), *Remembering our Past: Studies in Autobiographical Memory* (Cambridge, 1995).

Rusch, Claudia, *Meine Freie Deutsche Jugend* (Frankfurt am Main, 2003).

Sandford, John, 'The Peace Movement and the Church', in Gässner and Wallace (eds.), *The German Revolution of 1989*, 124–43.

Saunders, Anna, *Honecker's Children: Youth and Patriotism in East(ern) Germany, 1979–2002* (Manchester, 2007).

Scharf, Thomas, 'Older People: Coping with the Challenges of Everyday Life' in Kolinsky (ed.), *Between Hope and Fear*, 201–25.

Schöpflin, George, *Politics in Eastern Europe* (Oxford, 1993).

Schreiter, Anne, 'Bin ich ostdeutsch? Vom Umgang mit den kleinen Unterschieden', in Hacker et al. (eds.), *Dritte Generation Ost*, 78–80.

Schweizer, Peter (ed.), *The Fall of the Berlin Wall: Reassessing the Causes and Consequences of the End of the Cold War* (Stanford, Calif., 2000).

Seibel, Wolfgang, 'The Quest for Freedom and Stability: Political Choices and the Economic Transformation of East Germany, 1989–1991', in Caldwell and Shandley (eds.), *German Unification*, 99–120.

Seifter, Pavel, 'Foreword', in McDermott and Stibbe (eds.), *Revolution and Resistance in Eastern Europe*, pp. xiii–xiv.

Sheffer, Edith, *Burned Bridge: How East and West Germans Made the Iron Curtain* (Oxford, 2011).

Stämmler, Johannes, 'Ich entdecke den Osten neu: Ein Interview mit dem Chefredakteur der SUPERillu, Robert Schneider', in Hacker et al. (eds.), *Dritte Generation Ost*, 161–9.

Stämmler, Johannes, 'Wir, die stumme Generation Ost', in Hacker et al. (eds.), *Dritte Generation Ost*, 212–15.

Starke, Uta, 'Young People: Lifestyles, Expectations and Value Orientations since the Wende', in Kolinsky (ed.), *Between Hope and Fear*, 155–75.

Stevenson, Patrick, and Theobald, John (eds.), *Relocating Germanness: Discursive Disunity in Unified Germany* (Basingstoke, 2000).

Stitziel, Judd, 'Shopping, Sewing, Networking, Complaining: Consumer Culture and the Relationship between State and Society in the GDR', in Pence and Betts (eds.), *Socialist Modern*, 253–86.

Swain, Geoffrey, and Swain, Nigel, *Eastern Europe since 1945* (Basingstoke, 2009).

Taylor, Frederick, *The Berlin Wall: 13 August 1961–9 November 1989* (London, 2009).

Taylor Allen, Ann, 'Too Emancipated?: Women in the Soviet Union and Eastern Europe, 1945–1989', in Taylor Allen (ed.), *Women in Twentieth-Century Europe* (Basingstoke, 2008), 97–114.

Thiedemann, Elviera, *Es kame in langer lichter Herbst: Tagebuch der Wendezeit 1989/90* (Berlin, 2000), 46–7.

Thomaneck, Jürgen A. K., 'From Euphoria to Reality: Social Problems of Post-Unification', in Lewis and McKenzie (eds.), *The New Germany*, 7–30.

Thompson, Paul, *The Voice of the Past* (3rd edn., Oxford, 2000).

Veith, Ines, *Die Frau vom Checkpoint Charlie* (Munich, 2006).

Veith, Ines, *Leben und Alltag ... der DDR-Flüchtlinge* (Kempen, 2010).

Warchold, Katja, ' "So etwas ist in meiner DDR nich vorgekommen": Erinnerungen an ein Aufwachsen in der DDR und im vereinten Deutschland', in Hacker et al. (eds.), *Dritte Generation Ost*, 58–72.

Weber, Hermann, 'Rewriting the History of the German Democratic Republic: The Work of the Commission of Inquiry', in Alter and Monteath (eds.), *Rewriting the German Past*, 197–207.

Weber, Jürgen, *Germany 1945–1990: A Parallel History* (New York, 2004).

Wessendorf, Jana, and Wessendorf, Anne, 'Wendekinder:. Zwei Schwestern im Gespräch', in Hacker et al. (eds.), 81–92.

Wilkinson Johnson, Molly, *Training Socialist Citizens: Sports and the State in East Germany* (Brill, 2008).

Windmöller, Eva, and Höpker, Thomas, *Leben in der DDR* (Hamburg, 1980).

Wolle, Stefan, *Die heile Welt der Diktatur: Alltag und Herrschaft in der DDR 1971–1989* (Berlin, 2001).

Zilch, Dorle, *Millionen unter der blauen Fahne* (Rostock, 1994).

Zimmermann, Hartmut (eds.), *DDR Handbuch* (3rd edn., Cologne, 1985), 2 vols.

Magazine Articles

'Alle wollen an die Ostsee reisen', *Der Tagesspiegel*, 23 May 1963.

'Bin ich ostdeutsch? Vom Umgang mit den kleinen Unterschieden', *SUPERillu*, 30 (2012), 13.

'Bless Our Pax Americana', by Charles Krauthammer, *Washington Post*, 22 March 1991.

'Der Ossi: Ausländer im eigenen Land', by Rebecca Pates and Andreas Debski, *Märkisches Allgemeine*, 13 December 2012.

'Divided Germany Appears as Year of War and Wall Anniversaries Begin', by Philip Oltermann, *The Guardian*, 2 January 2014.

'Es geht um mehr als Bäumepflanzen: Interview mit einer Schweriner Umweltinitiative', *Kirche im Sozialismus*, 5–6 (1980).

'Geboren in der DDR, aufgewachsen in der BRD', by Nikola Richter, *Der Tagesspiegel*, 6 July 2011.

'Germany Still Divided 18 Years after the Fall of the Wall', *Der Spiegel*, 11 Sept. 2007.

'Homesick for a Dictatorship: Majority of Eastern Germans feel life better under Communism', by Julia Bonstein, *Spiegelonline*, 7 March 2009.

'Painful Memories of an East German Gulag: I thought I was in a Nazi Movie', Mario Roellig's story as told by David Crossland, *Spiegelonline*, 5 June 2009.

'Spiegel Spezial, Vereint aber Fremd', *Der Spiegel*, 1 (1991), 32–48.

'Wenn DDR-Bürger Urlaub machen' [When GDR Citizens Go on Vacation], by Wille Bremkes, *Frankfurter Rundschau*, 30 August 1980.

'Wir, die stumme Generation: Was haben unsere Eltern in der DDR gemacht? Es wird Zeit, dass wir sie danach fragen', by Johannes Stämmler, *Die Zeit online*, 18 August 2011.

Films

Am Ende Kommen Touristen (2007).

Das Leben der Anderen (2006).

Goodbye, Lenin! (2003).

Index